Achieving your Professional Doctorate

Mike
Mackenzie

Candidature
sept 13

Achieving your Professional Doctorate

Nancy-Jane Lee

Open University Press

Open University Press
McGraw-Hill Education
McGraw-Hill House
Shoppenhangers Road
Maidenhead
Berkshire
England
SL6 2QL

email: enquiries@openup.co.uk
world wide web: www.openup.co.uk

and Two Penn Plaza, New York, NY 10121-2289, USA

First published 2009

A catalogue record of this book is available from the British Library

ISBN-13: 978-0-335-22721-1 (pb)   978-0-335-22722-8 (hb)
ISBN-10: 0-335-22721-X (pb)   0-335-22722-8 (hb)

Library of Congress Cataloging-in-Publication Data
CIP data applied for

Typeset by RefineCatch Limited, Bungay, Suffolk
Printed in the UK by Bell and Bain Ltd, Glasgow

Fictitious names of companies, products, people, characters and/or
data that may be used herein (in case studies or in examples) are not
intended to represent any real individual, company, product or event.

The McGraw·Hill Companies

Contents

Figures

Tables

Acknowledgements

I am indebted to the people who have encouraged me to write this book, and especially to those who have contributed with their ideas and expertise.

I wish to acknowledge the professional doctorate students I have encountered since 2004, who have inspired me with their zeal to develop innovative professional practice. Professions in the current context do not always receive a positive press; sensational news is much more appealing than recognition of those professional stalwarts who practise against the odds.

In particular I wish to thank Singhanat Nomnian, Leslie Robinson, Ruth Strudwick, Janet Suckley and Claire Chatterton for sharing their doctoral experiences here and their reflections on professional doctorates and wider doctoral issues.

Colleagues Dr Carolyn Taylor and Dr Steven Hicks have used their expertise with reflexivity to develop an accomplished and meticulous discussion in Chapter 3. Mr Ray Stansfield used his knowledge of leadership theories and concepts to underpin Chapter 5, while Dr Carol Haigh used her expertise as Postgraduate Admissions Tutor to develop themes related to postdoctoral developments in Chapter 8. I would also like to acknowledge the feedback from Professor Peter Hogg in relation to Chapter 7 and for permission to use his work. Dr Ela Beaumont also needs thanks for permission to use her report writing checklist, again in Chapter 7.

Special thanks are reserved for my daughter Claire, who has had to navigate her way to the computer through swathes of papers, notes and drafts. I hope I have given you some inspiration for the future and shown what a determined woman can achieve. Special thanks too for Geoff who has patiently provided endless cups of tea and has never complained about my attachment to the computer at weekends.

Finally I would like to acknowledge the attentions of Mum, also called Nancy. She has brought my lunch, walked the dog and generally kept our household in brisk and pristine order during the writing process. You started all this; your bedtime stories prompted a lifetime of curiosity and enthusiasm about books and learning. Who would have thought it would turn into this?

N. J. Lee

Introduction

This book is designed for current/prospective professional doctorate students. If you are reading it then you have made the decision to embark on an exciting educational journey, and you are thinking about the implications of such a decision.

Overall responsibility for achieving your professional doctorate rests with you: your personal enthusiasm and professional zeal to utilize research in practice. However, you cannot undertake this process on your own. It is incredibly complex and will draw on your professional knowledge and skills, in addition to the development of research knowledge and expertise.

This book outlines some of the strategies to help you successfully achieve a professional doctorate. It helps you to reflect and consider the research knowledge and subject matter required for success, in addition to some of the underpinning personal and professional skills that may help you. You already have some of these skills by virtue of your role as an experienced professional practitioner. However, this book is also designed to help you question your skills, to appraise them and to develop new ones for the future.

Contents

The book has developed out of my experience as a professional doctorate programme leader, and is based on discussions with professional doctorate students about the challenges and opportunities facing them. Chapter 1 will illuminate the professional doctorate context and it will explore some of the factors which may have influenced your decision to undertake this kind of study. Doctoral study is reviewed historically.

Chapters 2 and 3 are concerned with 'a personal toolkit' to help you achieve your professional doctorate. In Chapter 2 issues such as originality and critical thinking will be explored. These are widely used to differentiate doctoral study from other programmes of study. There will be consideration of issues such as time management, managing references and information, developing a writing style and how to develop peer support with other students. Chapter 3 by Dr Carolyn Taylor and Dr Stephen Hicks will comprehensively examine issues in relation to writing and reflexivity.

Chapter 4 is related to research supervision issues. While many professional doctorate students have excellent knowledge of their professional area, and the kind of research undertaken there, they may be comparatively under prepared for their academic and professional relationships with the supervisors who can guide them through the doctoral process. This chapter aims to help you make the most of your research supervision, developing strategies to enhance communication and ultimately make the study experience as lively and stimulating as possible.

Chapter 5 reflects on your 'professional toolkit' and considers issues in relation to leading research in practice. Professional doctorate students are extremely competent in relation to their professional role, responsibilities and leadership requirements. However, for the majority of students the professional doctorate is their first experience of undertaking research themselves and generating knowledge and skills for the professional context. In this chapter Mr Ray Stansfield has used his knowledge of leadership theories and concepts to encourage you to question and analyse your leadership styles, considering how best to lead research in practice.

In contrast to the practical issues explored in Chapters 1 to 5, Chapter 6 will explore issues relating to the nature of professional knowledge and practice and the changing status and role of professions in societies. This will be complemented by discussion of ethical principles in relation to your research in the professional practice setting.

Finally, Chapters 7 and 8 are concerned with issues relating to dissemination of your knowledge and expertise, with professional colleagues and others. Having undertaken your professional doctorate studies, you want to present your work in the best possible light in your final thesis, or portfolio, and to be prepared for lively debate. Chapters 7 and 8 consider ways of sharing your knowledge with others, in relation to writing and other forms of presentation. Dr Carol Haigh in Chapter 8 explores life postdoctorate. As she says, such study is not a means to an end; it is the beginning of your postdoctoral professional career, and should open up further opportunities for research and development, for you to really influence and contribute to professional practice.

Layout

There are student activities throughout the book for you to explore yourself and to discuss with your student colleagues and other professionals. These are accompanied by practical tips and commentaries from professional doctorate and other doctoral students. Aims are given at the beginning of each chapter, and a summary of key points at the end of the chapters will help you navigate the book easily.

1

Appraising professional doctorates: what, who and why?

Aims of the chapter

- To introduce the professional doctorate and discuss its characteristics and history
- To critically appraise the politico-economical, social, educational and personal factors that may influence professional doctorate studies
- To identify the contextual factors influencing your professional role and research interests using a self-assessment exercise

Introduction

What is a professional doctorate? Who would study one and why? These questions will be considered in Chapter 1 through definition and discussion of the professional doctorate and exploration of the contemporary factors influencing professional doctorate provision. Evidence from the United Kingdom (UK), Australia and the United States (US) will be considered initially, to analyse the changing context of doctoral study and the nature of professional doctorates therein. Such review and discussion is considered important: to help you better determine if a professional doctorate meets your career needs and aspirations; to consider the implications of professional doctorate study; and to help you begin planning your professional doctorate journey.

Inevitably critics will argue that actual/potential professional doctorate students will have already identified what doctoral study entails and will understand professional doctorate requirements. However, doctoral study in the wider context is adapting, and professional doctorates have themselves prompted considerable discussion in the academic community and elsewhere regarding their characteristics and purpose. It is important you have an awareness of the doctoral debate, that you make an informed contribution and are able to consider your own ideological position and professional needs. For this purpose a range of literature will be explored in this chapter, representing some of the wider commentary and analysis surrounding doctoral studies and the nature of professional doctorates (Kemp 2004; Scott et al. 2004; Powell and Long 2005; Lunt 2006; Park 2007).

This chapter will define and explore the professional doctorate before comparing and contrasting its historical context and contemporary factors influencing development. The processes and outcomes of professional doctorates will then be considered, prior to discussion of professional doctorate student characteristics and the wider factors that may influence the decision to undertake a professional doctorate. The chapter will conclude with the Circle Exercise. This is a self-assessment exercise to help you, the student, identify the factors that may impact on your professional development and ensuing research interests.

Professional doctorates are available in an increasingly wide range of subjects, for example: education, engineering, health and social care, business, marketing, art and design, musical arts and clinical psychology. Bourner et al. (2001) describe the 1990s as 'the decade in which the professional doctorate came to England': such programmes being found in three-quarters of the 'old' universities and a third of the 'new' universities; (i.e., those established in 1992 from the former polytechnic system). Powell and Long (2005) identified 51 different professional doctorate awards in the UK, compared to 12 in the Bourner et al. study. Such growth in provision mirrors similar developments in Australia. For example in Australia professional doctorates have developed in the context of debate in the late 1980s and early 1990s, concerning the scope of the PhD and its resonance with government policies and wider global and economic issues (Green 2005).

Within the above discussion there has been some critique and questioning of the PhD as a suitable preparation for the transferable wider skills required in the contemporary workplace. Such skills have been compared and contrasted with the in-depth specialist subject knowledge and expertise said to emerge from the PhD. While professional doctorates are a comparatively recent addition to the doctoral repertoire in the UK and Australia, they have a more established history in North America. A doctorate in education was developed in 1924 at Colombia University and an earlier doctorate in education was developed in Canada in 1894. Doctorates in nursing were developed in the

1960s in the United States some considerable time before they appeared in the United Kingdom and elsewhere (Galvin and Carr 2003).

What is a professional doctorate?

An all encompassing definition is difficult given the range of professional doctorate awards and individual subject characteristics. However, professional practice, the development and/or application of expertise directly in the practice setting and practitioner research are central to professional doctorate activities. It should be acknowledged that this situation is not exclusive to the professional doctorate. Equally a PhD student could develop and apply research in the same manner, although this is not a key characteristic of the PhD as it is within the professional doctorate.

Professional doctorates are associated with the acquisition of knowledge and research skills, to further advance or enhance professional practice. Tennant (2004) describes professional doctorates as linking doctoral education with work related challenges and questions. He suggests this situation moves beyond the application of knowledge in practice, to the generation of knowledge from within the practice milieu itself. The relationship with practice, in particular professional practice, is developed further in the definition offered by the United Kingdom Council for Graduate Education (UKCGE) (2002: 62): 'a professional doctorate is a programme of advanced study which, whilst satisfying the University criteria for the award of a doctorate, is designed to meet the specific needs of a professional group external to the University, and which develops the capability of individuals to work within a professional context'. Powell and Long (2005: 8) describe the professional doctorate as: 'An award at a doctoral level where the field of study is a professional discipline and which is distinguished from the PhD by a title that refers to that profession'. To illuminate professional doctorate characteristics further Hoddell (2000) identified three key features:

1 A named subject area within the title of the award, for example education, engineering
2 Operation in a professional subject area as opposed to an academic subject
3 Inclusion of taught elements
(The final point is open to debate, as many PhD programmes also include taught elements to meet research training requirements.)

While the literature underpinning Chapter 1 generally supports the definitions above, there is some questioning of the emerging divide between the PhD and professional doctorate, perceived or real. For example Gregory (1995) compares and contrasts the characteristics of professional doctorates and PhDs and questions the need for differentiation. Instead he suggests that the overall purpose and processes of doctoral study should be made transparent rather than discussion focusing on the relative merits of a particular programme or doctoral pathway. For example, he asks if doctoral study should be concerned with the student's wider personal and professional development in addition to the acquisition of research based knowledge. This concern with the wider acquisition of skills such as communication and problem solving has been expressed by employers.

The concepts of 'professional scholar' and 'scholarly professional' are used by Gregory to question and explore the perceived differences between the PhD and the education doctorate, EdD, and consider the overall purpose of doctoral study. Traditionally one implicit purpose of the PhD has been suggested as being preparation or training for an academic and research career, though this situation is said to be challenged by the emergence of professional doctorates (Thorne and Francis 2001). Why the professional doctorate is evolving and its relationship to the PhD will be considered again later in Chapter 1 through analysis of politico-economic, social and educational factors influencing doctorate provision.

As suggested previously, doctoral study has typically been associated with the PhD, considered by many to be the *sine qua non* of academic expertise (Gemme 2005). However, binary distinction between the PhD and the professional doctorate does not fully illustrate the range of doctoral studies available. There are alternative doctoral approaches besides the PhD, with considerable variation in scope and purpose depending on the subject discipline. Scott et al. (2004) identify five forms of doctoral degree awarded in the UK alone:

1 The PhD
2 A practice based doctorate for creative and performing arts
3 The professional doctorate
4 The New Route PhD
5 A PhD achieved through the development of a portfolio of publications

The New Route PhD in the UK has been developed by a group of universities to meet the wider needs of the international student population, and has a significant proportion of taught components (UKCGE 2002).

Elsewhere Winter et al. (2000) appear to imply a professional doctorate type programme, when they explore practice based doctorates as undertaken by professional practitioners such as teachers and health professionals. Marion et al. (2003) by contrast refer to the practice doctorate as combining higher level clinical skill, leadership, research and professional knowledge to enhance changing health care practice in the US. First, professional degrees are studied in the US as preparation for practising law or veterinary medicine, for example, allowing the use of 'doctor' as a professional title (Lunt 2006).

The term 'taught doctorate' may also be used interchangeably with that of 'professional doctorate'; however, a taught doctorate may imply a modular element but not necessarily related to professional practice. In addition a doctorate of science (DSc) may be awarded to outstanding academics, particularly in the UK in recognition of their distinguished contribution to research.

Understanding the nature and purpose of the doctoral award is an important consideration when embarking on any doctoral study and when planning future career pathways. In an attempt to illuminate doctoral provision on a European level the European Universities Association (EUA) undertook a project to compare and contrast the characteristics, requirements and practices relating to doctoral provision in Europe. Within the EUA project, however, it emerged that the professional doctorate as preparation for an advanced level of professional practice was not widely acknowledged.

The EUA (2005) distinguished between the individual study programme and the structured study programme as routes for doctoral study. The former may be associated with the PhD approach: supervisor and student working in an apprenticeship type model. The latter refers to the use of taught and research elements within the doctoral programme – although this combination does not automatically imply a professional doctorate. Lunt (2006) further clarifies that professional doctorates are not widely known in Europe outside of the UK and Ireland. She does describe the industrial PhD used in Scandinavia whereby an adapted PhD approach may be used to explore work related issues.

It can be seen that there are now wide ranging doctoral awards and sometimes the doctoral awards and categories are used interchangeably in the literature. For example it can be seen that professional doctorates may also be referred to as taught doctorates or practice based doctorates. Powell and Long (2005) suggest that distinctions between doctoral routes and awards are confusing and along with Gregory (1995) question why such distinctions have evolved in the first place.

However, while varied terminology and philosophical standpoints are represented in the academic discussion of professional doctorate provision, the common factor in the professional doctorate's context is recognition of the key relationship between professional practice, the focus of study and the practitioner–researcher role. These components are complex in their own right; integration, development and application of research in and for the professional setting requires a particular expertise and determination.

The variety of doctoral studies, particularly professional doctorates, has the potential to reach wider professional student audiences; challenge accepted forms of knowledge acquisition; and explore new areas of research. Equally it could lead to confusion. Some would suggest that the growing number of doctoral titles and awards has the potential to weaken the status of the PhD (Donaghy 1996). While the PhD's position has appeared relatively strong and clear until recent times, it could be argued that it has also adapted historically depending on subject trends, societal need and demand. The following section will briefly outline the history of doctoral study and the juxtaposition of the PhD and professional doctorates through that history.

The history of doctoral study and professional doctorates

Bologna University is considered to be one of the oldest universities in the world, as students migrated there in the middle ages to study law and, later, arts, medicine and theology. Haskins (1957) describes university development as originating with the students' need to be organized into a single group: as protection from exploitation by unscrupulous landlords and to be assured of good lectures, particularly at Bologna. Within that protection professors were required not to be absent without permission and not to proceed with a lecture if fewer than five students were present. Furthermore, professors were required to obtain a licence to teach, a *licentia docendi*. From this tradition the higher degrees of master's and doctorate are said to have emerged. They were originally evidence of the professors' knowledge and skills to be used within student teaching.

Noble (1994) attributes the first doctoral degree to the University of Paris in the twelfth century. The subjects associated with doctoral study at that time are also interesting as Bourner et al. (2001) suggest that for six centuries doctorate programmes for theology, law and medicine were used as preparation for professional practice, and were not dissimilar to contemporary professional doctorates. In essence the modern professional doctorate could be a renaissance of the higher level study originally associated with preparation for professional practice. In 1792 Haydn was awarded an honorary doctorate of music degree by Oxford University, in recognition of his contribution to music (O'Mullane 2005).

The PhD by contrast has later origins at Humboldt University, Berlin, in the nineteenth century. Its introduction was accompanied by a belief that academics had more teaching expertise to offer if they also had direct experience of the processes involved in research inquiry and were able to transmit those experiences to students. The process of research or inquiry itself was considered important and was relevant in many contexts at that time, particularly with increasing industrialization (Shaffer 1990).

Until the nineteenth century universities' main focus had been teaching. At the time of PhD development in the nineteenth century, however, an increasing need and demand for scientific methods and systematic research skills was fuelled by the demands of industrialization. Relatively speaking the PhD itself has emerged out of educational and research trends, particularly related to industrialization. As such it is fairly new in the historical continuum of doctoral studies. The first doctorate of philosophy was awarded by Oxford University in 1920. At about the same time, universities in the US were adapting doctoral awards to include a taught element (Bourner et al. 2001).

What does a professional doctorate involve?

Embarking on a professional doctorate is an exciting challenge. The study journey should stimulate intellectual, personal and professional development in addition to the creation of knowledge and expertise that will better inform and underpin professional practice. As can be seen from discussion thus far in Chapter 1 professional doctorate study is concerned with questioning, analysing, developing or applying new practice knowledge in the student's professional practice setting. The student drives the process of research and inquiry which could inform the micro level of the student's day to day professional context, or professional practice at the macro level of policy, strategy, future direction or practice. Creativity and originality are integral to doctoral study regardless of the doctoral route (Gregory 1995). However, Gregory also acknowledges that creativity is a challenge when doctoral students are possibly engaged in their first major piece of research. The concept of originality will be explored further in Chapter 2. In the meantime the processes and outcomes of professional doctorates will be explored below.

Processes

It can be seen from the professional doctorate definitions earlier in the chapter that a key element is the investigation of a professional practice issue and the generation of new knowledge and expertise, using research strategies developed and applied by the professional practitioner themselves, while practising in that setting. Integration and application within the professional practice setting requires advanced expertise; effective leadership of research in practice; the effective management of change; and skilful communication with key stakeholders. In addition to the challenges of research and professional application professional doctorate students are perhaps shifting or testing the boundaries of doctoral convention. As Green (2005) relates in consideration of professional doctorate development in Australia, the programmes have a short history, further stating that there are 'tests of hazard' along their pathway. In essence the process and focus of study may differ from the PhD, though the outcomes are considered the same in terms of the level of knowledge and expertise developed and their intellectual rigour.

One difference between the PhD and professional doctorate process is that students on the latter tend to progress and study together as a cohort, group or intake, rather than by registering for an individual learning experience, as is the case for the PhD. The peer collaboration and collegiate nature of professional doctorate study therefore opens up possibilities for student support networks and the sharing of knowledge and expertise (Hoddell 2000). Many PhD programmes also encourage a student community; however, registering and working with a student group throughout the whole of the study process is still much more likely with a professional doctorate. The processes of professional doctorate study will also include the exploration and critical analysis of wider related professional issues: leadership, financial management, marketing, educational theory or advanced professional skills, depending on the professional subject studied.

Facilitation processes for professional doctorates are more likely to involve the use of action learning groups, small group discussion, workshops, residential workshops and master classes. Given technological advances and the drive towards flexible modes of study professional doctorates may also capitalize on blended learning. This combines face to face facilitation with the use of a virtual learning environment. Many universities have developed or are developing virtual doctoral schools and distance learning approaches for doctoral study. Actual attendance at a university campus may be minimal, with stipulated attendance during the study process for key assessment processes and milestones of doctoral study. This further enhances flexibility and student choice in how and where to study. Knowing your study preferences and what could best be adapted with your professional practice and personal life are key elements to consider when choosing a doctorate programme.

The focus on professional doctorate study with a like-minded student group or cohort regardless of whether contact is virtual or face to face enhances opportunities for students to share ideas and explore critical issues, receiving constructive feedback from peers and programme facilitators. Group discussion provides an excellent way of clarifying thoughts and ideas while in the long term preparing for wider professional discussion and critique of research ideas through conference presentations, academic papers and ultimately the viva. Professional doctorates offer potential for collaborative approaches to learning, sharing resources and expertise, developing critical thinking and rehearsing for key milestones in doctoral study, along with wider professional activities. Table 1.1 summarizes the processes of professional doctorate study as identified from the literature.

Outcomes

When exploring the outcomes of professional doctorates as opposed to other doctoral programmes, such as the PhD, it would appear that there is no distinction between the type of doctorate and the outcome or level of study (Lunt 2006). The Framework for Higher Education Qualifications in England, Wales

Table 1.1 The processes of professional doctorate study

Process	Source
Intake or cohort of professional doctorate students who study together.	Hoddell (2000)
Combination of taught and research elements. Although many PhDs incorporate research modules, professional doctorate facilitated elements are also likely to focus on professionally related issues, e.g. leadership and finance, in addition to research issues.	Green (2005)
Focus on professional practice issues through the development and application of knowledge and expertise for practice.	UKCGE (2002) Powell and Long (2005)
Practitioner–researchers from the professional setting undertake professional doctorates and research related professional practice issues. Knowledge generation for practice, developed from practice.	Tennant (2004)
The process of professional development emphasized with the professional subject in the title of the final doctoral award, e.g. education and engineering.	Powell and Long (2005)

and Northern Ireland, developed by the Quality Assurance Agency (QAA) (2001) describes the level of achievement denoted along the continuum of studies from certificate to doctoral level. It can be seen that doctorates in their widest context are concerned with the creation of new knowledge and/or understanding through original research:

The framework for higher education qualifications: doctoral descriptors

Doctorates are awarded to students who have demonstrated:

i. The creation and interpretation of new knowledge, through original research, or other advanced scholarship, of a quality to satisfy peer review, extend the forefront of the discipline, and merit publication.

ii. A systematic acquisition and understanding of a substantial body of knowledge which is at the forefront of an academic discipline or area of professional practice.

iii. The general ability to conceptualise, design and implement a project for the generation of new knowledge, applications or understanding at the forefront of the discipline, and to adjust the project design in the light of unforeseen problems.

iv. A detailed understanding of applicable techniques for research and advanced academic enquiry.

Typically holders of the qualification will be able to:

a. Make informed judgements on complex issues in specialist fields, often in the absence of complete data, and be able to communicate their ideas and conclusions clearly and effectively to specialist and non-specialist audiences;
b. Continue to undertake pure and/or applied research and development at an advanced level, contributing substantially to the development of new techniques, ideas, or approaches; and will have
c. The qualities and transferable skills necessary for employment requiring the exercise of personal responsibility and largely autonomous initiative in complex and unpredictable situations, in professional or equivalent environments.

(QAA 2001)

It can be seen from the above that the distinguishing characteristic of doctoral study is the ability to develop original knowledge for a subject discipline or, in the case of the professional doctorate, a professional discipline. Originality is underpinned by the ensuing assessment, planning and implementation of a suitable research design to investigate the research topic.

The processes and outcomes of professional doctorate study will be revisited in Chapter 2 when there will be detailed discussion of the criteria of original knowledge and critical thinking for doctoral study. In addition student expectations of professional doctorate study and the personal toolkit that may be required will be explored. Personal strategies such as working with others and managing time and resources will also be considered.

Who would study a professional doctorate?

Given the characteristics of professional doctorates it is not surprising that their uptake is primarily by professional practitioners. Powell and Long (2005) also comment that professional doctorate provision in the UK is geared towards the public sector professions. In most subject areas, for example business, education or health and social care, professional doctorate students are typically, but not always, senior professionals who have already accrued considerable professional expertise. For example, in relation to nursing in the United Kingdom, McKenna and Cutcliffe (2001) suggest the average age of the doctoral student is 35 years, compared with 25 years in other subject areas. Furthermore the authors state that doctoral study is usually undertaken after several years spent in nursing practice, whereas in other subjects students usually undertake full-time doctoral study following a first degree. Perhaps as a result of the need to combine professional practice with research, most professional doctorates are part-time, though full-time programmes do exist too.

Bourner et al. (2001) compare and contrast the entry and experience requirements for PhD and professional doctorate study in England. For example a professional doctorate student generally requires evidence of significant professional experience, along with a master's degree in a related discipline, though in some cases a good first degree or bachelor's degree is accepted. The authors found in contrast that the PhD student is usually required to have a good first degree in a related subject discipline, but no other experience of the subject is necessary as the PhD student is viewed as an apprentice researcher – unlike an experienced professional practitioner.

While the above may be a common scenario it is not the only scenario. In some subjects the professional doctorate may be considered a baseline entry requirement for professional practice. For example in the UK the engineering doctorate, EngD or DEng, has developed from the need to have a career route for young engineers into industry, combining subject knowledge with wider professional and practice related skills such as problem solving (UKCGE 2002). Bourner et al. (2001) state that the first engineering doctorate was introduced at Warwick University in 1992. Students on such programmes may have the backing of an industrial sponsor and undertake research that is relevant to their sponsor's work area. In relation to clinical psychology, the doctorate in clinical psychology (DClinPsy) is a requirement for professional clinical practice. Such programmes are accredited by the British Psychological Society and incorporate the supervision of professional practice.

Why study a professional doctorate?

Doctoral study has perhaps been stereotyped as an esoteric activity undertaken by academics in the isolating ivory towers of academia, in some ways protected from and almost superior to the realities of the external world. Subjects for doctoral study similarly could have been viewed as theoretical and not directly concerned with the real world. However, Gemme (2005) questions this view, explaining that many PhD students seek employment in industry or commerce, particularly when the PhD has practice placements or strong links with those areas. In contrast the doctoral survey by Golde and Dore (2001) found that many doctoral students wanted an academic career following their studies.

Despite the stereotypes the doctoral landscape is changing, possibly due to politico-economic, social and educational factors. This is not the first time in the doctorate's history that this has occurred. The emergence of the PhD in the nineteenth century as described earlier in this chapter was linked with socio-economic need and demand related to industrialization. Contemporary justification for professional doctorates is also made in the context of the knowledge economy (Tennant 2004; Green 2005). This has been described as the relationship between economic development and the effective use of knowledge, skills and innovation as opposed to reliance on physical resources and capital (Brinkley 2006). For example economic growth and increasing technological innovation are said to be dependent on and subsequently fuelled by the need for an increasingly educated and skilled workforce (EUA 2005). The purpose of knowledge in contemporary society is said to be changing as a result of the knowledge economy. Green (2005) suggests that the professional doctorate is seen as a means of contributing to the knowledge economy through its connections with workplaces and universities. This is predicated on the belief that economic success is related to the skills inherent in the workforce along with research capacity.

In keeping with this belief the Department of Education, Science and Training (DEST) in Australia recommends stronger links between professional doctorate programmes and industrial or professional sponsors. It suggests that industry and commerce should be considered active owners and deliverers of programmes, having a key role to play, as opposed to being the passive recipients of doctoral students (DEST 2005). While some argue that such recommendations are beneficial, enabling programme development that corresponds to need, others are more cautious stating that the role of the university as an independent knowledge source is being challenged (Tennant 2004). Chapter 6 will further explore the relationship between knowledge, professional practice and wider socio-economic factors through examination of professional practice and professional knowledge.

Evans (1997) also identifies economic and industrial drivers as central to the way universities organize and manage their educational portfolio. For example he states that universities have adapted their educational provision and modes of delivery to meet the needs and demands of professionals who would previously not have experienced or indeed have been expected to undertake a higher degree. In essence Evans (1997) states that the massification of higher education has increased the need for university places among school leavers, while professionals are similarly seeking postgraduate qualifications in increasing numbers.

To illustrate the relationship between professional doctorates and politico economic factors Ellis and Lee (2005) explore factors such as health modernization, the blurring of professional boundaries and the increasing demand for health care in fuelling the growth in health related doctorates. Other factors identified are the quest for evidence based health practice along with the integration of professional education, particularly in nursing, within the higher education sectors.

Discussion to date has been based on the premise that knowledge for economic growth along with politico-economic and global factors has influenced doctoral provision. Arguably it has opened up the scope of professional doctorates to a changing student audience, for a changing purpose: the professional generation and application of subject knowledge. Indeed Neumann (2005) identified the need to provide doctoral studies for the newly emerging professions as a factor influencing professional doctorate development in Australia. The self-assessment exercise at the end of this chapter will enable you to reflect upon these and other issues in relation to your professional context and research interests.

Given the discussion to date, professional doctorates could be viewed as a positive development offering opportunities to student professionals who would not otherwise have sought doctoral study. On the other hand, it could also be suggested that they are a reaction to the pressures of international market forces and the knowledge economy. Evans et al. (2005) have undertaken a study of the PhD in Australia and argue that its position is actually strengthening with increasing student numbers and professional fields of study. Rather than developing professional doctorates as an alternative to the PhD the authors recommend that resources be used to strengthen and maintain the PhD, given its established currency.

In addition to the political and economic context for professional doctorates there has also been debate regarding educational issues and the purpose of doctoral study. For example some have explored the rationale for doctoral study, questioning whether it is preparation for an academic career or a career in another professional arena (Thorne and Francis 2001). Gregory (1995) considers the differences between the PhD and the educational doctorate EdD, suggesting that the PhD's focus on detailed knowledge and expertise in a narrow aspect of one subject area does not perhaps meet employers' demands for broader transferable skills. Furthermore there has been concern about the time taken to complete a PhD and attrition rates have been estimated at 40 percent in the case of some social science doctorates (Winfield 1987).

While McWilliam and Singh (2002) report that doctoral completion times and attrition rates are causes for concern in Australia, there is no evidence as yet that this is any different within professional doctorate programmes. Meanwhile in America doctoral dissatisfaction has been reported, with student concerns relating to the specialized nature of doctoral study versus preparation for other employment skills (Golde and Dore 2001). Neumann (2005) suggests professional doctorates were also viewed by the education establishment as an opportunity to enhance and widen academic recruitment at a time when the size of the academic workforce was due to decline.

McVicar et al. (2006) report that professional doctorate study is a positive option for employers, as students can demonstrate the following skills on completion:

- Development of research skills
- Development of organizational skills
- Improvements in skills such as management and leadership
- Improvements in the organization's performance or outputs

These skills are especially desirable as they are developed and generated within the organizational or professional context, for use in that context. In summary the student's research development has the potential to make a direct contribution to the organizational or professional context through the acquisition and application of higher level transferable skills such as research expertise, advanced communication and leadership, critical thinking and problem solving.

In addition Kemp (2004) states that the PhD has been a 'privileged' programme in terms of government funding: university focused and university driven, meeting the needs of universities and academics as opposed to external stakeholders. The professional doctorate is further described by Kemp as a sign of change in doctoral provision. This possibly reflects wider changes as universities are increasingly required to strengthen their relationships with industries and other partners external to the university. In England, for example, the role of the doctorate, its range and its provision in the widest sense is being explored and questioned, particularly in the context of economic development and need, combined with academic development and the challenges of transparency across Europe and beyond (Park 2007).

While this section has focused on the factors influencing professional doctorate development at the macro level, namely policy and politics, there are other factors at the micro level of personal student experience which may influence students' choice of doctoral programme. Leonard et al. (2006) comment that research and other evidence relating to student reasons and motivations for doctoral study is scarce, as is information about how students subsequently apply their doctoral learning in their future careers. There are, however, some emerging studies relating to professional doctorate students and their motivations.

For example Wellington and Sikes (2006) identified personal and professional reasons as providing strong motivation for students to undertake an education doctorate. Their student survey found that the quest for educational knowledge and theory to underpin professional practice was one reason for study. On a more personal level students in their survey saw the professional doctorate as the culmination of their career and personal achievements, enhancing their self-esteem, confidence and personal identity. The authors also found that students had practical rather than personal reasons for such study. For example the structure of the programme, with modules, workshops and group discussion enabled some students to better combine doctoral study with their professional working lives.

The structured approach inherent in many professional doctorate programmes, along with the opportunities to link research developments within the practice setting was also perceived as valuable in a student study by Neumann (2005). This involved semi-structured interviews with 134 students and academics associated with doctoral studies.

While self-esteem and achievement featured strongly in the Wellington and Sikes (2006) study, students also reported that the professional doctorate had enhanced their professional life, enabling wider career development, and the acquisition of more effective knowledge and expertise with which to undertake their work. Some students cited the professional doctorate as a key factor in helping them to achieve promotion. For others it had helped them become more reflective and thoughtful about their practice and how they approached professional challenges. The latter point identified by Wellington and Sikes (2006) also has resonance with findings by Scott et al. (2004), where students emphasized professional attitude, values and beliefs, and professional confidence as being enhanced by professional doctorate study, rather than focusing on the more tangible aspects such as knowledge and practical skills.

Scott et al. (2004) also identified extrinsic and intrinsic factors that influenced professional doctorate study. For example extrinsic factors influencing students' decision to pursue a professional doctorate related to career development, exposure to wider professional experiences; and opportunities for research. These reasons may be characterized by what Scott et al. (2004) describe as 'professional initiation': influencing students at the outset of their professional careers, particularly if financial sponsorship was available from the students' employers. Engineering doctorate students' experiences are used by the authors to illustrate professional initiation type extrinsic factors influencing study. The second extrinsic factor identified by the authors related to professional continuation. In this context professional doctorate students were well established in their professional careers and wished to widen their career options and make an informed contribution to professional practice in their area of expertise.

Scott et al. (2004) also identified intrinsic motivation for doctoral students in terms of rewards perceived as self-efficacy, personal achievement and the development of personal goals and interests. With intrinsic motivation students were more likely to consider professional doctorate study as providing opportunity for a personal journey of change and development. These students were likely to be at the pinnacle of their professional career, being well established in senior, strategic positions. In addition to personal reward, professional doctorates may be viewed as bestowing professional credibility. Scott et al. (2004) also argue that while knowledge acquisition is no longer the sole responsibility of universities, given advances in technology enhancing access to information and learning, universities still have the right to award status or gravitas through their qualifications.

The following extract will illustrate some of the reasons discussed for undertaking a professional doctorate through the example of a doctorate student called Kenny, who undertook an EdD in TESOL and applied linguistics. Kenny's background and decision to enrol on his EdD are given below:

> I decided to enrol on an EdD programme rather than the PhD one because I wanted to gain specific research training in TESOL (Teaching English as a Second Language) and Applied Linguistics, to help me form my research

interests to undertake my thesis. I was initially unsure whether an EdD would be recognised like the PhD because scholars and other people still found the PhD more rigorous and research-oriented whereas the EdD was rather less valued as such. I have, however, realized that they are the same and different. These two degrees are the same in the sense that they aim to equip learners with relevant research skills. The difference is EdD graduates can particularly aim to work in education related fields, as teachers, lecturers or principals, whereas a PhD graduate can become a researcher in a wider social context . . . an EdD was quite suitable for me with an MA in TEFL (Teaching English as a Foreign Language), as I did not have an intensive research background . . . I also presented my assignments at national and international conferences and later had them published. I began to realise that an EdD was widely recognized.

Professional self-assessment exercise

So far this chapter has explored professional doctorate characteristics and requirements and it has considered the politico-economic, social and educational factors that may influence their current development in the context of educational debate concerning doctoral provision and purpose. The following exercise aims to help you reflect and apply the issues explored in this chapter in your specific professional context and in your developing research ideas. Reflection is important at the decision making and planning stage of your study. First, it helps you to gain insight into the wider issues affecting professional practice beyond your immediate professional specialisation. Second, it helps you explore how these factors may affect your studies overall and influence your chosen research topic. If you have more than one idea for research or if you are not sure how to focus on a particular aim or question then the self-assessment exercise can usefully help you consider a range of issues.

Student activity 1.1 **The circle exercise: factors influencing professional research ideas**

1   Work through the circles identifying factors which may impact directly or indirectly on your current professional practice and choice of research topic. Examples may include:

   • Professional or statutory policies
   • Professional literature
   • Reports, organizational trends or policies
   • Other evidence

2   Use the circle 'Beyond your domain' to consider the wider literature related to your research ideas, which are as yet outside your conventional professional and subject boundaries.
3   Keep a record of your ideas as you will need these to undertake more development work in Chapter 2.

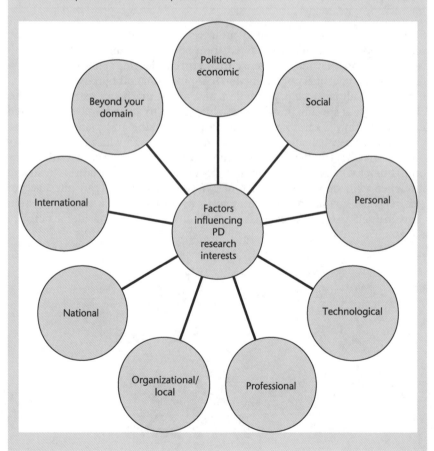

Conclusion

Beginning the professional doctorate journey is an exciting but daunting prospect. Many students have been, or will be, experiencing these feelings. The preceding exercise can help you clarify ideas, and subsequent reading, writing and reflecting will also help you make a start. If you feel overwhelmed by your research ideas or have several ideas and cannot focus then take comfort, as Kenny says:

'At present, I feel that I have gained more confidence about my study and attempt to complete it as soon as possible. I always tell myself that this EdD experience is like an exercise for me to learn mistakes from doing research and to learn that there is no perfect piece of research . . . I learnt that the word "focus" is very important for research students because we can become overwhelmed by large literature reviews and we do not know exactly where "relevance" is supposed to end'.

The information in this chapter represents a snapshot of the contemporary debate concerning professional doctorates. The overall aims of the chapter were to explore the professional doctorate and to analyse its key character-istics, processes and outcomes. It can be seen that doctorates in the widest sense have adapted significantly through history, with professional doctorates being related to the needs of professional groups who wish to develop research based knowledge and skills for professional practice. There is synergy in approach among developed countries, notably in the US, Australia and the UK, where professional doctorates have had considerable impact. Presenting the information in this chapter is considered important as a backdrop to base-line critical reflection and self-assessment of your own personal and profes-sional context.

Some would argue that professional doctorate development is related to the growing needs and demands of the knowledge economy: globalization, innovation and advanced skills development. Professional doctorates have been appraised along with their context. While the name of the professional doctorate awards, programme structure and processes may vary according to subject discipline or their academic location, they share a common principle. This relates to the professional doctorate as concerned with the student's prac-tice context, to further develop and enhance that practice or to have greater knowledge and understanding of its implications. Related research studies could be associated with the micro level of the student's practice context itself, or the macro level of policies or related roles and responsibilities. While this situation is not unique to the professional doctorate, as arguably other types of doctoral provision could equally achieve this, it is central to the professional doctorate.

Summary of key points

- Professional doctorates facilitate the investigation and development of knowledge and other expertise to enhance the student's professional practice
- Arguably they have formed the basis of professional studies since medieval times, the PhD evolving since the Industrial Revolution
- Renewed interest in professional doctorate programmes could be related to the emerging needs of the knowledge economy and globalization
- Doctoral level descriptors do not appear to differentiate between the academic levels of study required for the professional doctorate and the PhD. Originality and creativity are required regardless of the doctoral route
- Professional doctorate students are perhaps more likely to have accrued a significant amount of professional experience prior to their doctoral studies, and work at senior or strategic levels in their professional settings. Some students by contrast undertake professional doctorates at the outset of their careers as a means to fast track career development opportunities

2

Developing a personal toolkit for professional doctorate study

---

Aims of the chapter

- To discus actual and potential expectations of professional doctorate study
- To consider the principles of originality and critical thinking and review them in the context of professional doctorate study
- To consider the wider personal factors that may influence professional doctorate studies and develop strategies to enhance the study experience

---

Introduction

What are your expectations of professional doctorate study? How well do you understand its requirements? What would you like to gain from the professional doctorate and how are you going to achieve this? Exploring your expectations and developing a personal toolkit for study is essential when planning your professional doctorate.

This would appear to be common sense in order to successfully balance and integrate professional doctorate study with your professional and personal life.

However, in the quest to reach the desired outcome, the doctorate, and also to enhance professional practice through research development and/or application, it is possible to overlook the personal toolkit required. This is especially so when contemporary practice is in a constant state of change for many professionals, possibly due to some of the factors identified in Chapter 1. There may be pressure to respond rapidly and in some instances reactively rather than proactively.

In addition the thrill of being accepted on a professional doctorate programme combined with encouragement from family and work colleagues may prompt you to 'get started'. However, embarking on the journey without planning for arrival at the destination has the potential for you to feel overwhelmed later and for you to lose focus and motivation when challenges inevitably arise. Also the stakes are high for professional doctorate students. In many cases they are returning to education following a sustained period in professional practice, where they have acquired significant knowledge and expertise in addition to professional status and presence. Re-adjusting to the role of doctoral student can be difficult, regardless of doctoral route, when there are competing professional and personal priorities.

The aim of this chapter is to help you consider the factors which may influence your professional doctorate studies and reflect on how your skills can be enhanced for achievement. Issues related to research and professional supervision are vitally important and will be addressed in Chapter 4. Meanwhile within this chapter the concept of a 'personal toolkit' has been used to explore the following themes:

- Identifying your personal expectations and personal development planning
- Considering the requirements for originality and critical thinking in professional doctorate research
- Developing peer support: communities of practice
- Developing writing strategies: reflection and reflexivity
- Managing time, information and resources effectively

The development of effective personal study strategies will help you in the following ways. First, it will enhance your intellectual independence and confidence during the professional doctorate process. Second, effective study strategies will also help you to focus on a substantial piece of work, using personal development planning to arrange the work into manageable segments while identifying the resources required. It will also help you develop strategies to better integrate research with your professional practice through the exploration of issues such as leading research in professional practice.

While there will inevitably be adaptation during the study process, prior planning will enable exploration of a variety of research issues which may impact on your practice, even those considered and not pursued. For example if you are asked to justify and explain methodological approaches at viva you may be required to discuss strategies you considered and subsequently ruled out. In addition you may be required to discuss significant events from professional practice, and the impact of your research in practice. Being able to critically reflect on these areas in detail and demonstrate how your ideas have been adapted and developed is an important part of the professional doctorate process. It indicates you have thought carefully about your research and have explored a wide variety of options critically rather than working from a limited perspective. Finally, planning for the professional doctorate process will help you clarify your expectations and study needs, strengthening relationships with your supervisor and professional colleagues, so that you can be better prepared and focused for your work with them.

Identifying your personal expectations and personal development planning

Golde and Dore (2001) found that doctoral students did not always fully appreciate what the study process involved, and did not always know at the outset how to manage and organize the process of learning and research. Indeed the authors suggested that the processes underpinning doctoral study should be made more explicit, with realistic expectations identified by the academic staff supporting and supervising doctoral students. In order to help you identify expectations and possible requirements of professional doctorate programmes, the following section draws on student reflections in relation to the knowledge and skills, processes and resources to enhance successful study.

Identifying your expectations

Three possibilities relating to student expectations will be considered here:

1 Integration of the practitioner–researcher role with an established professional identity
2 Expectations regarding the level and volume of work
3 Expectations regarding personal development planning

Integration of the practitioner–researcher role with an established professional identity

Some aspects of the practitioner–researcher role relate to self-identity and professional role, and how these may overtly or covertly influence our interactions with others. Combining the roles of student and professional can be a challenge. While all students sensibly consider the scope and volume of work and how it is to be achieved, the associated challenges are worthy of exploration.

There are many expectations to reflect upon in relation to role, professional identity, to some extent personal identity and the work of the practitioner–researcher. The first issue relates to the emotional agility of the student. For example Delamont et al. (2000) describe doctoral study in terms of faith: the ability to maintain optimism, stay the course and deal with the unexpected challenge that will arise during the research process. Put simply, this relates to the student's personal zest, enthusiasm for their professional subject and the emotional drive to maintain a sustained period of study and concomitant professional practice development. It requires the ability to adapt to the unforeseen, and to feel comfortable with a degree of uncertainty.

This may or may not be a characteristic of professional practice, depending on the area of practice. For example there may be more scope for adaptation and individuality in relation to creative art and design, or the crafting of a musical composition. In other areas of practice, for example social work, there may be little or no scope for adaptation, when practice is influenced by predetermined policies, in relation to child protection for example, where there must be clear communication and factual accuracy and certainty. Integrating the established norm of professional certainty with the doctoral requirement to view professional practice from a critical perspective is potentially challenging to the self, the professional role and the researcher role. However, such a critical stance will help to further develop practice and its theoretical basis.

Second, being a doctoral student is possibly similar to returning to a novice role, in this case the novice practitioner–researcher. That statement is not meant to imply doctoral students will be treated as juniors, simply that there are adjustments required on the part of the students and their academic colleagues who are working with them. Evans (1997, 1998) raises questions about professional students' expectations and attitudes when commencing their professional doctorate studies. He suggests that these can potentially underpin the study experience. Imagine that you are a senior strategist in your organization, leading decision making and directing others around you – potentially you could bring those characteristics to study. In essence if you are used to telling others what to do and they respond to your direction, how are you in turn going to adjust to receiving advice, questions and challenges regarding your own practice – particularly if this is not something you are accustomed to or comfortable with? How are you going to adjust from being perceived as competent expert professional to being seen as a 'novice' researcher?

Knowing that the professional doctorate is likely to require critical reflection and analysis of your professional practice and how you internalize your professional role is important. If the doctoral programme does not at some point make you deeply question your role, the knowledge and skill you use and your professional practice and identity, then it is not interrogating your practice at a level commensurate with a professional doctorate. Feeling defensive is possibly a normal response in this situation; however, there does need to be a balanced willingness to view the world of practice through a different pair of eyes, to see things differently, and to read and think extensively beyond your usual repertoire of professional literature, values and beliefs. Ruth's account below illustrates some of the potential:

Ruth's account

'The two years of the taught programme have been a voyage of discovery where I have learnt a lot about myself and others, as Chesney (2000: 68) says "clearing the view to myself" [sic] has served to help me understand others:

I have learnt about research methodologies and how to relate these to my specific research question.
I have learnt how I learn, what subjects interest me and I have learnt about my writing style.
I am much more measured in my responses to issues, questions and discussions. I think I am more able to see others' point of view.
I am much more interested in how people act and interact together.
I have developed my critical thinking skills, and feel better equipped to read and listen to the work of others and question their approach.
I have benefited from working in interprofessional groups at this level as I have been much more able to see the perspectives of other health and social care professionals and how they work.
I have explored the reasons for my career pathway thus far as part of the critical professional biography module and I feel more secure about where I am and where I intend to go in my career.'

It is important to gain a sense of the support that will be available during the 'voyage of discovery'. For example exploring professional practice and the implications of developing research to underpin practice is going to be problematic, if not disappointing, in the absence of a thriving and supportive learning environment. Informal meetings with the course leader, postgraduate tutor or members of the course team can help to gain a sense of the facilitation style and culture the programme operates in. Likewise it is important to discuss expectations in your professional context with colleagues.

The students in the doctoral survey undertaken by Golde and Dore (2001) advised students to search around and assess the learning environment and support available before making any commitment to study within a particular institution. The readiness with which the course leader or postgraduate tutor respond to email queries and invite you for informal discussion, the provision of orientation or induction opportunities and opportunities to meet and network with a full range of doctoral students are indicative of underlying philosophies relating to student support and facilitation.

Likewise the administrative support available is an extremely important factor. If you are a part-time student it is likely you will be studying off site, away from the immediate academic environment, for significant periods of time. Increasingly it is possible that your professional doctorate studies are delivered using a virtual learning environment or other distance learning strategies. If that is the case then it is important to know that good administrative support is available should there be technical problems or difficulties with other aspects of the learning experience. Evans (1997) argues strongly that the support and follow-up administration is of equal importance to the supervisory relationship for doctoral students. By the same token, however, sensible expectations of your support needs are required and it is important to discuss these at the outset of your studies with your supervisors, peers and other members of the programme team.

While supervision will be explored in detail in Chapter 4, it is worth mentioning here that one way of developing open and honest communication and transparency of expectations in the supervision process is through the development of a learning agreement/contract. In many higher education institutions this may already be an intrinsic part of the supervision process. If it is not then as part of introductions within the supervision team it is good practice to explore mutual expectations, roles and responsibilities. Similarly, discussion of group expectations, roles and responsibilities are important if this is likely to be a key aspect of professional doctorate studies. This theme will be explored later in the chapter in relation to communities of practice.

This section to date has aimed to promote thinking about your expectations of professional doctorate study and the emotional adjustment that may be required. However, it is not only the students who need to consider these issues. Hopefully academic staff are equally receptive to such challenges and are able to adapt in response to the needs of experienced professional students. Bowerman (2000: 125) describes her initial experience of doctoral study before transfer to another action learning based doctoral programme:

> Returning to university . . . after almost a quarter of a century in the workplace was a shock. Because I had changed I was expecting the university to have changed; to acknowledge that I was now an adult with full earning power and a lot of experience in organisational transformation. The university, however, seemed to have changed little from the days when I had completed my Master's Degree in my 20s . . . The road to the PhD was littered with hurdles that were not about me and my abilities or interests, they were all about what others had pre determined to be important, without any input from me . . . The university was still catering for me as though I was 20. I had moved on. They had not.
>
> (Bowerman 2000: 125)

Expectations regarding the level and volume of work

> I asked my supervisor what the doctorate (PhD) would look like, what
> was it meant to contain? The answer was less than helpful, 'I don't
> know, it's hard to explain but I know it when I see it.'
>
> (Ali)

Doctoral expectations can be shrouded in mystery to the outsider. Perceptions
of study in an ivory tower like environment almost protected from the
demands of the real world still persist. However, no one expects you to hit the
ground running. You are not expected to immediately produce work that provides radical insights and stretches the boundaries of professional knowledge
and/or practice. While there may be an expectation you are receptive to critical
reflection on your practice as described earlier, and you are familiar with the
overall requirements of academic study in terms of good writing, referencing
and study skills, you may not know immediately what to expect in terms of
doctoral level and style. Your style of writing and argument will develop as you
practise them through the doctoral experience. The issues central to doctoral
study, for example originality and critical thinking, will be explored in the
next section of this chapter.

The initial processes are about settling in to a study routine, getting to
know the course and the staff, beginning to sort out your research ideas and
how they will relate to your professional practice, reading widely about your
research aim, and thinking about the knowledge and skills required to take
your research ideas further. Phillips and Pugh (2000) suggest that students
at the outset of their doctoral studies have ambitious research ideas that
require further focus and clarification in relation to a particular area or
theme.

The overall aim is to develop a realistic, manageable, though exciting and
stimulating focus for study, combined with the application of appropriate
research methods for professional practice. Very few students implement the
exact research proposal used as part of their application process. PhD students
similarly use the preliminary stages of their studies to read, explore and question more widely, and refine their research ideas.

Crotty (2003) emphasizes the importance of developing a clear research aim
and focus prior to consideration of methodologies. For example having an
interest in action research, wanting to 'do' action research, or wanting to 'do'
something about adult literacy is not the same as developing a clear research
question or focus related to your professional practice and then considering
the appropriate methodological strategies to explore them further. Students
commonly proceed to a research question or aim rather too quickly and without considering the options carefully. Remember it is not unusual to spend
considerable time examining the literature thoroughly and laying down the
foundations for your research in the professional practice setting: communicating fully with key people about your preliminary ideas, seeking feedback,

thinking about how the literature relates to your area of interest and your practice context.

It is important at this point to explore the notion that research always proceeds in a linear, orderly manner: ranging from development of a research question; literature review; selection of research methodologies; data collection and analysis; discussion of findings and study limitations; and conclusion. While research texts and journals present information in this mutually recognizable fashion the reality is likely to be different and there are almost certainly going to be adaptations and adjustments as new learning develops.

The term 'iterative' is used to describe a process of thinking and planning where ideas are worked through to consider and reconsider the options available before they are approved or discarded. As such iterative thinking does not proceed from A to B; rather thinking loops backwards and forwards considering and trying various options. Iterative processes have evolved from computer sciences where the term is used to describe instructions which can be repeated several times. In software development the iterative process may be applied where an application is developed in stages, with models or diagrams being used to identify what has been tried, approved or disproved. Similarly, the term iterative is used in mathematics to denote numerical analysis, for example Newton's method (Wikipedia 2007).

Expectations regarding personal development planning

This is another comment from Ruth, and outlines her expectations of professional doctorate study:

> I see the professional doctorate as providing me with the research and writing skills to continue with research and carve out a niche for myself. I also see the professional doctorate as a journey of self-development which will enhance my teaching and supervision of students.

There are two possibilities within the above. First, Ruth is identifying the longer term impact of study on her professional career; to enhance research capability and associated writing skills; the enhancement of her own teaching and supervision strategies. Second, there are more immediate process implications about how that will be achieved; through a journey of self-development. Articulating ideas and expectations about professional doctorate study are an important start for personal development planning. In essence considering the professional destination requires some route planning. The personal development exercise opposite is designed to help you further develop your preliminary ideas as identified in the Circle Exercise in Chapter 1.

Personal development planning is now a requirement of all Higher Education programmes, as described in the Code of Practice for the Assurance of Quality and Standards in Higher Education (QAA 2004). In 2001 Universities UK, The Standing Conference of Principals and The QAA considered personal development planning as, 'A structured and supported process undertaken by an individual to reflect upon their own learning, performance and/or achievement and to plan for their personal, educational and career development' (Ward and Baume 2002).

Personal development planning could be considered on an individual and group basis, developing immediate, short-term and long-term goals. Goal setting helps to organize personal and professional developmental issues into manageable segments and helps to prevent the overall prospect of doctoral study from being overwhelming or daunting. Goals have a threefold purpose:

1 They can help you move your research ideas along, consider the options and formulate a clear research aim or question along with the methods to underpin investigation and developments that are pertinent to your professional goals
2 They can help you identify the resources and wider strategies to achieve your professional doctorate. These should include key people in your professional context who may have a significant impact on your studies; key organizational policies or professional characteristics which will impact on your research themes; relevant literature; research skills training; other professional training; wider personal and professional issues such as leadership and the management of change
3 They can help you think about realistic timescales for achievement, helping to keep your study requirements manageable and achievable

To assist with personal development planning the UK Graduate Programme provides resources and tips on the planning process (www.grad.ac.uk):

Student activity 2.1

1   Return to the circle exercise (Student activity 1.1) completed at the end of Chapter 1. Review the factors identified in each circle and prioritize which will impact on you personally and which are directly related to researching your professional practice:

  • immediately
  • in the medium term
  • in the long term

2   Now consider:
  • Which personal/professional factors may help/hinder your research achievements?
  • How can you address them?
  • Who can help you?

- What knowledge and skills do you need?
- What additional personal and professional development/training is required?
- When will this be achieved?
- Are your goals realistic and achievable, given time and professional responsibilities?
- What are the outcomes for your practitioner–research ideas?

3   Share your analysis with student peers, supervisors and professional colleagues, and make adaptations based on their feedback: wider discussion will enhance the process of clarification through mutual questioning and the exchange of ideas and resources. It is most important to keep a note of the processes and the ideas generated in a notebook or research journal

Considering the requirements for originality and critical thinking in professional doctorate research

Originality

Having considered possible student expectations of professional doctorate study, this section attempts to explore the notion of originality and critical thinking. Most people would associate originality with cutting edge theory, produced with prodigious genius and academic panache. While the scientific works of Einstein or Curie provide historical examples of research originality, the works of Stephen Hawking offer a contemporary illustration. Beethoven and Mozart exemplify musical artistry, originality and genius. However, very few of us are fortunate enough to have such outstanding capability.

The essence of originality is bespoke, unique and individual. However, Cryer (2000) also argues that work which defies convention in the context of doctoral research may be viewed with caution in academic circles. Similarly, Delamont et al. (2000) suggest that the doctoral student's work is not likely to be concerned with a major change in theory, knowledge or skill within a particular discipline. Ironically the notion of originality within the accepted boundaries of a subject or discipline may be a hidden criterion of doctoral assessment. Kuhn (1996) discussed the notions of paradigms: prevailing theoretical norms in particular disciplines, recognized and accepted – however changeable over a period of time, when ideas and assumptions underpinning a subject are challenged and subsequently shifted. It is not likely that a student's doctorate is going to result in paradigm shift, unless they are a genius.

Given the centrality of originality in doctoral study, comparatively few student texts explore the concept in detail. Cryer (2000) is original in this sense with an entire chapter devoted to the subject. There are wider examples, however, of how originality may emerge based on case studies or biographies. Wallas (1926) suggested four stages to the preparation of original ideas:

1 Preparation. Complete immersion in the concept and the application of thought: discussion with others and reading, for example
2 Incubation. Described as rest or distraction: putting the idea or concept to one side
3 Illumination. Described as insight, understanding and a breakthrough with further development of ideas, clarification and inspiration
4 Verification. Further revision of ideas: questioning, interrogating, critical scrutiny

In the above outline there is some resonance with intellectual challenge: grappling with a problem followed by a 'Eureka' moment. Hudson (1973) describes the activities of the German poet, Rilke, who famously penned ten elegies and 55 sonnets over a 20-day period. In total 1200 lines of verse were developed, remaining by all accounts largely unedited. This prolific output is said to have been inspired by the death of a young woman and a picture of Orpheus viewed by the poet through a shop window.

If doctoral originality is not the ground-breaking development of theory or of the kind of inspiration identified above, what is it and how can it be recognized? Cryer (2000: 196) offers excellent examples of how originality could be discerned within a doctoral study:

- A new or improved research tool or technique
- A new or improved model or perspective
- An in-depth study
- An exploration of a topic, area or field
- A critical analysis
- A portfolio of work based on research
- A fact or conclusion, or a collection of facts or conclusions
- Something else

Emerging themes from Delamont et al. (2000) demonstrate that research supervisors considered doctoral originality to be represented by an exciting piece of work, which has strong critical analysis and thinking combined with meticulous presentation and appropriate methodological choice. In addition rigorous academic argument extending beyond current knowledge or literature into new areas of learning and discussion should be evident.

Professional doctorate research can demonstrate originality in several different ways. First, it could involve the application of existing knowledge or expertise in a new professional practice setting, or the adaptation of existing knowledge to develop new models or frameworks of practice. For example 'problem based learning' has been established as a concept of medical education for some time, originating first in Case Western University and then

McMaster University (Feletti 1993). Contemporary education research has focused on its application in the new settings of health and social care, for example (Haith-Cooper 2000). Elsewhere facilitation processes for problem based learning have been examined (Haith-Cooper 2002). These examples have all considered the central concept of problem based learning; however, the originality lies in the interpretation, application and analysis of that concept.

Second, originality may be demonstrable through the development of new knowledge or skill germane to a local area of professional practice. In relation to health service research, for example, there may be the development of locally based solutions to national issues (such as user involvement, caring for carers, teenage pregnancy and contraception), the development of new professional roles or the blending of professional roles. Emerging knowledge does not necessarily have to be generalizable to other settings as in the positivistic tradition of research and the development of theory. Professional doctorate studies may be concerned with the 'particular' rather than the 'universal'. Studies may involve taking some aspect of practice that is known and already used elsewhere and embedding this within another practice context. Returning to Ruth's voyage of discovery reviewed in the earlier stage of this chapter, originality of knowledge may develop from reflection on the student's professional experience and learning. This may be an important element of action research studies or other methods where critical reflection on self and role underpin research strategies.

Critical thinking

The word critical has negative connotations of criticism or dissatisfaction. To be critical of someone or their ideas suggests disapproval, that some element is lacking or not to the standard or expectation required. Use of the word critical resonates with something we dislike or disapprove of, as it may clash with our knowledge and inherent values and belief systems.

In the context of professional doctorate or indeed other doctoral study, 'critical' is used to describe higher level intellectual thinking, reasoning and analysis imbued with reflection. Being critical in the professional doctorate context allows for consideration of a wide range of ideas or concepts: hence critical thinking. In essence the ability to construct an independent argument or analysis, question a viewpoint or appraise evidence or related research knowledge underpins doctoral study. Furthermore the ability to extend critical thinking beyond academic endeavours and into professional practice and practitioner research issues is highly regarded and essential. There is an expectation that critical thinking will be used to question, analyse, reflect and develop alternative frameworks, concepts, knowledge or professional practices and perspectives. This section will now outline the principles of critical thinking and their utility within professional doctorate study.

Critical thinking has been defined as: 'The art of analysing and evaluating thinking with a view to improving it' (Paul and Elder 2006: 4). Paul and Elder are key proponents of critical thinking and their definition suggests that the ability to take thoughts apart and consider them from a wide range of viewpoints is important. For example the essence of critical thinking lies in the ability to ask challenging questions, to compare and contrast, to critique sources of evidence, to challenge implicit and explicit assumptions, rather than acceptance of an argument or evidence at a superficial level.

In the UK a popular TV show, *Question Time*, illustrates the principles of critical thinking. A panel comprising politicians, literati, celebrities and others is invited to respond to topical questions presented by the audience. These are commonly based on political or news events reported in the media. Each person on the panel presents their perspective or analysis of the question, which is challenged, contrasted or further discussed by other members of the panel and through audience participation. In that way, rather than each question having one answer a variety of answers or considerations are suggested and from varied perspectives.

Critical thinking is considered important within doctoral level study and within professional practice itself, where decisions and actions are complex and may be underpinned by a variety of factors. Hupp (2006), however, questions why some students do not challenge the information they are given and he reflects on why this apparent lack of critical thinking is evident. He argues that critical thinking is essential in any subject given the rate of expansion of scientific knowledge and the amount of information and evidence available. While the concept of 'evidence' is used to denote empirically based health care, other subjects and professional knowledge have also grown at an exponential rate and also require thought and analysis. In his reflections Hupp argues that critical thinking is not so much an intellectual skill as a state of mind or a particular attitude.

Glaser (1941: 5) in a seminal work defines critical thinking thus, 'Critical thinking calls for a persistent effort to examine any belief or supposed form of knowledge in the light of evidence that supports it and the further conclusions to which it tends'. Thomson (2002) associates contemporary interest in critical thinking with thinkers such as John Dewey, Richard Paul, Michael Scriven and Robert Ennis. In addition to Glaser, Ennis has developed influential writing to illuminate the characteristics of critical thinking. In particular Thayer-Bacon (2000) describes critical thinking studies as re-emerging in America in the 1960s against a backdrop of concern about the threat of communism, the Cold War and the perceived threat to democracy. The debate presciently centred on how others could be encouraged to engage in critical thinking in relation to policy and politics and the ability to consider truth and justice.

However, critical thinking has a much longer history, being attributed originally to the ancient Greek philosopher and scholar, Socrates. He liked to discuss his ideas publicly and also to challenge the Greek public about their views and opinions on key matters of the time. He did not do this through formal teaching, instead he posed questions to individuals as he walked around the public spaces of Athens. While he used his questions to challenge and encourage people to consider their assumptions, his views were not popular with influential members of the Athens community, as he typically challenged accepted ideas and the status quo. Eventually he was found guilty of corrupting the young and promoting sedition with his questions. Famously he was put to death by drinking hemlock. One of his most famous students was Plato (Boswell and Kemp 2001). The notion of Socratic questioning may be used to illustrate the development of critical thinking through the exploration, challenge and questioning of assumptions.

In order to examine information and beliefs, consider alternatives and raise critical questions, Hughes (2000) argues that three strategies are required. These are:

1 Interpretive
2 Verification
3 Reasoning

Interpretive strategies

Interpretive strategies relate to the ability to understand or find meaning within an argument or debate posed. In application to professional doctorate study this could relate to critical analysis of the professional practice context; critical analysis of accompanying knowledge and expertise; and critical review of strengths and weaknesses and the actions of the stakeholders therein.

Verification strategies

Verification strategies relate to the ability to find truth and meaning within the argument or ideas put forward. In the context of professional doctorate study this could include consideration of the quality of information provided. This information may be empirically or research based or it may be based on the practitioner's experience and reflection.

Reasoning strategies

The final element of critical thinking identified by Hughes (2000) relates to reasoning and the ability to think through a variety of options; compare and contrast; consider strengths and weaknesses; and make decisions about the information and ideas presented. All of the above strategies should be applied in professional doctorate study: when considering the original research interest; and developing ideas and understanding to refine a research aim or question, considering how the situation could be investigated and weighing up the implications for professional practice.

Brookfield (1987) suggested that critical thinkers are aware of the assumptions held by others and by themselves as regards thinking and acting. They also reflect and analyse the situation or location in which ideas are developed and discussed. Furthermore critical thinkers are said to have a degree of scepticism, and are suspicious of simple answers and claims to universal truth. Instead they are receptive to alternative ways of viewing, thinking and behaving in the world.

The references used above provide a good foundation to the principles of critical thinking. They consider reasoning, the ability to think and to consider assumptions and inferences relating to concepts such as truth and knowledge. Cotterill (2005) also offers an excellent practical text with exercises and case studies relating to critical thinking. Facione and Facione (1994) have developed the *Holistic Critical Thinking Scoring Rubric*. This will enable you to self-assess your critical thinking skills and provide comprehensive insights into critical thinking.

At the culmination of your professional doctorate you will be required to demonstrate critical thought, not only in the process of your learning and subsequent research, but in its outcome and subsequent relationship with and for professional practice. Demonstrating your critical thinking skills will be evidenced in your final thesis or equivalent, such as a professional portfolio, and in your ability to articulate and debate questions, should you have a viva. In addition to these academic criteria, critical thinking should be embedded in the strategies used to further develop and understand professional practice. The following questions are examples that may be used to generate critical thinking about professional practice:

- What have I achieved in professional practice?
- How and why?
- Who/what helped or hindered?
- What evidence is there regarding professional knowledge and skill and my research study?
- How was this evidence generated?
- What are the theoretical perspectives underpinning the evidence?
- What kinds of strategies were used to collect evidence?
- What is the nature of that evidence?
- Are there other sources of evidence?
- What have I learnt?
- What do I need to do next and why?
- Could things be done any differently?

Developing peer support: communities of practice

Chapter 1 suggested that professional doctorate students are more likely to study within a group or cohort. This offers the potential for a variety of activities which promote peer support and provide a consistent focal point during the study experience. This should help minimize what Neumann (2005: 178) describes as the 'lone researcher syndrome' of the PhD.

There are several skills required from professional doctorate students that perhaps emphasize or reinforce the need for effective group support and mutual learning. For example while meeting the criteria of doctoral study in terms of originality, creativity and the advancement of knowledge through research, students are also developing and applying their research in their professional practice. In essence they are advancing professional knowledge using research strategies while also integrating this knowledge with professional practice. This characteristic distinguishes the professional doctorate from other modes of doctoral study, as explored in Chapter 1.

Group cohesion and support offer the opportunity to critically reflect on the experiences generated during the professional doctorate process and to rehearse for some of the issues and challenges to be faced when engaged in practitioner type research. For example a later chapter will explore the issues of leading research in professional practice. In addition students can use groups to develop the academic skills commensurate with doctoral study. For example there are opportunities to further develop academic writing style, which may be completely different to the formal report writing required in some professions. Furthermore groups can be used to prepare for key milestones in doctoral study: interim assessment or review and preparation for viva. Increasingly there is an expectation that students will disseminate their research work through conference presentations and publications. Again groups could be used as a learning opportunity in relation to these requirements.

While all of these issues focus on particular professional doctorate outcomes, such as knowledge and skill, there are wider process benefits of group membership, such as mutual encouragement and reciprocity of learning.

Communities of practice could be used as a conceptual framework to underpin group activities for professional doctorate students. These comprise groups of people who have a shared interest and a common need to learn about their practice, their role in practice and how that practice can be strengthened and developed. The guiding principle for learning is through a group approach to developing and exploring common issues, rather than the pursuit of learning on an individual basis (Smith 2003).

A community of practice is defined as, 'A set of relations among persons, activity, and world, over time and in relation with other tangential and overlapping communities of practice' (Lave and Wenger 1991: 98). In the context of professional doctorate study the community of practice is the student community who seek to develop their practice through the effective implementation of research strategies and the enhancement of professional skills, such as leadership, change management and reflection. The definition above also implies that communities of practice overlap. For example while students may work as a group or cohort within one community of practice as it were, there is an overlap with other communities of practice, for example:

- The students' workplace and colleagues
- Professional organizations
- Research or professional networks
- The wider doctoral student population in the university

Wenger (1998) identifies three characteristics for a community of practice:

1 *The domain*: this is described as the common purpose or aim shared within the group
2 *The community*: members of which share common practice needs and have discussions to support each other and facilitate practice. The community is based on relationships that foster learning and development. This characteristic distinguishes the community from an interest group, which may have a shared interest but does not necessarily use this to advance or change practice
3 *The practice*: the work and practice that is common to community members who collect resources and/or develop and apply these resources and practitioner experiences

If the three components are applied to professional doctorate students then Wenger's initial concept, the domain, relates to the students' research purpose in terms of knowledge and skills gained to advance professional practice through research. It should include process as a focus within the domain, given that the journey towards a professional doctorate is of equal importance to knowledge outcomes. Within the domain the shared element is practitioner–research: the enhancement of practice expertise and change in practice through study.

The second element, the community, could be the cohort or group of students working through the process of professional doctorate study together. The remit within the community is to communicate together to share resources, advance learning and facilitate support for members' development. Within this community there is a strong element of reciprocity. For example in conventional study scenarios the student may take responsibility for their own learning, gather their own information and make their own notes. This may happen in a community of practice; however, there is also mutual obligation or reciprocity in relation to the learning of others.

Put simply, when time is a precious commodity and if things appear to be going well during the professional doctorate study process, it may be tempting to miss some group sessions or opt out of them completely. However, you have an obligation to help others with their study processes, as they may have helped you previously. Thus the process of study and research development takes on a reciprocal rather than individualistic stance.

The final element from a community of practice (Lave and Wenger 1991) relates to practice itself. There may be consideration of developing a particular aspect of practice, for example education, or of changing or evaluating the practice milieu. The commonality within the community of practice for a professional doctorate programme is how best to engage with practice and work towards goals to improve practice knowledge and expertise. Within a cohort or group studying for a professional doctorate there is huge potential to share resources, which may be based on practical experiences, reading or people and professional networks that could influence practice.

Lave and Wenger (1991) also identify and discuss legitimate peripheral participation. They consider this to be the process that enables new members of the community of practice to interact with other experienced community members and then engage with increasing expertise and confidence in the activities of the community. In the context of professional doctorates this kind of participation could relate to the expertise within the small cohort or group of students, and it could equally relate to participation with other professional doctoral groups and the wider doctoral community in the university or, externally, including research supervisors. Equally it could apply to a professional community, a professional group of practitioners such as clinical psychologists or counsellors for example, and participation in practice using a higher level of skill and expertise.

The following is Paul's account from a community of practice:

Paul's account

'I had done a Masters previously; that was different somehow, something I "did" in University, separate from the workplace. The doctorate was different as I was developing knowledge and testing new approaches in practice. On the doctorate our group worked in the health services but had different professional backgrounds. At that time I did not know about communities of practice though on reflection now that is how we functioned.

Initially we needed to get to know each other and develop our ability to work as a group. We did this by sharing our respective research interests and common themes emerged about practice: evidence based practice and change, for example. Initially we did not have a focus on our research aim or how we were to proceed, which methods were suitable. Through discussion and critical questioning, part of which involved exploring our beliefs about practice, our ideas were clarified. We also had to access and critique the relevant literature, and discuss our ideas with colleagues in practice.

This was challenging: group members really asking us why we had chosen our subject and research methods. This could have been perceived as criticism, it really made us reflect and justify our approaches to enhance practice. In our professional areas there was some potential for resistance to our research ideas and we used our group to explore how best to negotiate in practice, identify key people who could help the research process and who understood our workplace.

Another way we helped each other was through problem solving. We came up against hurdles when researching practice, for example encouraging people to participate, ethical issues, data analysis, generally how to proceed and we shared resources and experiences. It wasn't that anyone in particular had the right answers we were able to reflect and discuss our experiences. It wasn't cosy or chatty; sometimes there was a real difference of opinion in the group. We used the group to pool our resources. These resources could be articles, textbooks, good websites, other people with specific expertise and our own experiences. We brought information back to the group from conference attendance or from our respective professional organisations.

Going through the doctoral process in a group helped to push us along and hold our enthusiasm.'

Student activity 2.2

Undertake the following discussion in the group or cohort you are studying with on your professional doctorate programme. If a group is not clearly identifiable then think who such a group could include and suggest collaboration. If there are group facilitators involve them in the discussion along with your research supervisors and professional colleagues where possible. Use the following questions as prompts:

- Who are the members of your community of practice?
- What other professional networks/communities do members belong to?
- What other resources are available to enhance professional practice and to advance learning (for example group members, the wider university and other professional groups)?
- How would you like your community of practice to operate? For example what are the boundaries for communication and discussion? What are the parameters or ground rules? What activity/behaviour is acceptable? What about confidentiality?
- What are the roles and responsibilities of the group members?
- How will you develop and challenge critical questioning and constructive discussion in the community of practice?
- How will you evaluate learning as a community of practice?

Discussion of the above can take place face to face, within a virtual learning environment or by email. Keep notes of the discussion and review on a regular basis.

Developing writing strategies: reflection and reflexivity

To date it has been suggested that professional doctorates are as much about the process of learning – your research journey and subsequent professional development – as they are about knowledge outcomes. Developing writing strategies to embrace reflection and reflexivity are an influential part of the professional doctorate process. Reflection on professional practice is advocated as a means of learning about practice, exploring practice through the application of structured or critical thinking to consider a particular professional event, or professional theme. Schon (1983) is considered to be a seminal work in relation to reflection; however, there are also numerous other texts written for specific professional audiences.

While reflection is perhaps considered an element of focus on professional practice, there is some overlap with the notion of reflexivity. This is used in research to conceptualize, analyse and make transparent to others the researcher's relationship with the research. This could include discussion of their interaction in a particular setting, their ideas and thoughts before, during and after the research, or discussion of particular challenges they have encountered during the research process (Holloway 2005). The following quote illuminates the issue of reflexivity: 'There is no one-way street between the researcher and the object of study; rather the two affect each other mutually and continually in the course of the research process' (Alvesson and Skoldberg 2000: 39).

Such transparency of thought and decision making helps to make the research authentic and credible for others to follow. On a deeper level it also contributes to interpretation of the research activities and findings; how the research developed; how themes were identified; and actions taken. While the processes of reflexivity and reflection are associated predominantly with qualitative research it is equally a valuable mechanism in terms of quantitative methods, enabling exploration of the options considered and discussion and justification of the actions taken, from the generation of research ideas to the implementation of the final research project.

In order to further develop reflexivity and critical reflection on the experience of being a practitioner–researcher, writing things down using a journal or notebook is invaluable. On a practical note it is simply not possible to remember all your ideas and discussions during the whole process of doctoral study. In addition, from the author's personal experience of doctoral study and supervising students, it is tempting to focus too early on the final thesis write-up, thinking of work in terms of thesis chapters and outcome. Adopting this pragmatic approach has the potential to limit critical analysis, as students focus on the final destination rather than considering and exploring a range of options. This in turn can create anxiety. For example if the words do not flow in a cohesive manner, it may feel as if 'nothing is being done'. Before long the self-inflicted pressure of writing and doing something may cause mental barriers, which in turn feed further anxiety and despondency.

Using a journal or notebook to capture ideas is an important aspect of doctoral study. It can be used to identify emerging thoughts in relation to research ideas; to record impressions of the literature; to capture significant events from professional practice; to illuminate data collection and analysis; and to explore discussions and study limitations and wider thoughts and feelings about learning and the process of research. All of these areas are important aspects that can be used selectively when writing up the final thesis. Over a sustained period of study it will be impossible to remember all the thoughts and ideas generated, comments from peers and colleagues, and ideas relating to an analysis.

Moon (2004) offers a practical text with different strategies for reflective writing. For example writing for creativity, professional development, self-identity, widening experience and personal support are explored in the text, along with other activities to promote learning and also to develop a personal style of writing. Elsewhere the act of writing has been described as a vehicle for developing, clarifying and refining original ideas: 'I spent a lot of time on writing, but usually while the work was still going on . . . I find in general only when one tries to write it up, then do I find the gaps' (Hans Krebs in Wallace and Gruber 1989: 63).

While the journal will focus on your process of learning the following are examples of sources of learning:

- Personal reflection when you are alone or having some quiet time. Don't think you have to be involved in 'doing' all the time; quiet contemplation and reflection is very powerful
- Notes from supervision meetings; peer group tutorials and discussions; communities of practice
- Notes from your literature searching, which databases were accessed and when; inclusion and exclusion criteria for the literature reviewed
- Ideas emerging from the literature; how the literature is influencing your ideas and development of research; implications for professional practice
- Discussion with professional colleagues in the practice setting
- Significant events in the professional practice setting relevant to your research development and implementation
- Eureka moments: some students have commented that their best ideas come in the early hours of the morning. Keep a notebook at the bedside just in case, as you won't remember as clearly in the morning

Reflection and reflexivity will be detailed in the following chapter by Taylor and Hicks, along with wider analysis and application of critical reading, critical appraisal and critical thinking.

Managing time, information and resources effectively

One of the most frequently asked questions is, 'How much time do I need to set aside for professional doctorate study?' Estimating study requirements is difficult, although an average of seven to 12 hours' independent study per week could be used as a guideline. This is in addition to the time requirements to attend to modular components or other taught or facilitated elements in the programme, and/or engage in virtual learning. It may be that more time is needed at the beginning of the professional doctorate to adjust to the study experience. There are likely to be peaks and troughs in the use of weekly study time depending on key milestones in the programme; assignment submission; preparation for research review; or relevant research work in the practice setting. Rather than thinking of setting aside so much time per week, it may be more helpful to build up study time into more significant chunks, giving more opportunity to explore issues in depth.

One technique derived from project planning is the development of a Gantt chart. This enables the identification and mapping of key tasks associated with a project in a sequential fashion against the time span required to achieve the tasks. Key stages of a study or project can be clearly identified and the time they require. More information can be found at www.ganttchart.com and www.mindtools.com. Other alternatives are to simply use a wall calendar or year planner and use coloured pens to denote study and development activities.

It is not only personal study that requires time flexibility, arranging appointments to speak to other professionals, fieldwork in the professional practice setting, attending relevant skills training and addressing ethical requirements all take time. While the chapter to date has focused on doing, there is also the need for private thinking and reflection to really develop analytical skills and consider the professional doctorate in terms of your own development.

While everyone has read the books and can dispense advice regarding time management, applying the principles is much more difficult. Rigid timetables and study plans do not take account of the overall life, work and study balance, or simply how we are feeling on a particular day. In addition while planning is essential, over-planning can disrupt the spontaneity and joy of study and project development – when breakthrough and understanding of a key issue emerges unexpectedly.

The term time management can carry implicit messages of control and discipline. It can also imply a life with every minute marshalled and accounted for: a joyless existence filled by work and study. That is certainly one way of achieving your professional doctorate; however, by the time you have completed your doctorate, your personal life will be non-existent as friends and family will have given up on you. If your time management lapses do not beat yourself up; a break from study usually means more insight and development in the longer term.

Given that many professional doctorate students are engaged in full-time employment and part-time study then time is a precious commodity. Study and learning preferences need to be applied practically within the context of daily living and all that this entails. While it is essential to think about how the extra time will be found for professional doctorate study it is important to be realistic. One way of being clear about time is to be focused about what to do with the time allotted, no matter how short the time may be. Use of a Gantt chart, as described previously, or a similar mechanism will help you map out specific tasks and assess the time required.

We return to Paul:

I used to go into the study, generally tidy up my papers, switch on the computer and look at what I was reading/writing last time. By the time I had done this and picked up the pieces of my thinking from last time as it were, I would have to stop.

Now I focus prior to any study time and think about the immediate things that I would like to achieve, even if this is as small as writing another paragraph, or making a list – this is how I work. Keeping that focus has made me more disciplined. It has also helped me use time effectively. For example I can use short periods of time to organize references and notes, prioritizing longer periods of time for in-depth study and reflection . . .

I apply the same principles in professional practice as the doctorate is not separate from that. It is part of my working life. When I am working I think of one thing that I need to do that week, that day, to progress my research. This might be a meeting with my professional adviser; identifying participants for my study and speaking to them or something . . . having a specific aim, no matter how small has helped me.

Managing information

The availability of Internet resources, online journals and e-books has significantly changed how and where people study. It has also radically changed access to knowledge. University information services departments offer enormous scope and expertise in relation to the management of the information and the literature you will need for your professional doctorate. Library departments have experienced staff, accustomed to the relevant subject discipline databases, with considerable experience of searching strategies and the use of e-books and e-journals. Your employer or professional networks and organizations may also offer similar services.

Receiving advanced training in literature searching and the identification and use of key databases is important given the scope and range of information now available. It is now possible to receive e-updates relating to journals, books and conferences. In the area of education, for example, see www.tandf.co.uk/eupdates and www.educationarena.com. In addition to training and support from your university information services department your supervisors and professional colleagues should be able to advise you on key networks and updates. Identifying and utilizing these resources is an essential part of your personal development planning strategies to support your professional doctorate studies.

Given the plethora of information now available there are also examples of reference management software that can be used to store references; import them into your academic work; and adapt your references to provide a full reference list in your thesis, or tailored to journal style when you publish your work. Endnote and Reference Manager are examples (see www.endnote.com). As part of the postgraduate training programme in your university you should be able to access free training to use these resources, in addition to the purchase of software at competitive rates.

You will also require a system to store other information: records of supervisor meetings; group discussions with your professional doctorate cohort or study group; copies of assignments or coursework you submit in the early stages of professional doctorate study; your personal journal as explored earlier; early drafts of work as you progress your research; paper copies of references or reports; and so on. Having a dedicated laptop, notebook or equivalent is essential – with a good back-up system should you need to restore damaged information. When you register for your studies you may find that the university provides a personal folder within the university network. This is invaluable to back up and store your academic work as a contingency.

Secure and safe back up is especially important if others are to use your computer: from bitter personal experience teenagers in particular may download information from spurious sources thus risking viruses and other problems. At the outset of study it would be helpful to obtain technical advice and have your computer systems assessed regarding specification, security and safety with the relevant software. This may seem lavish given the expenditure on programme fees, research books, attendance at conferences and other training required. However, time spent at the outset is money well spent in terms of prevention.

In addition to accessing the considerable amount of literature now available digitally and storing your doctoral work effectively, there are also strategies to help you manage the information generated during the research process. For example there are software packages to assist data management, analysis and interpretation (e.g., SPSS for quantitative research and NVivo to assist with the analysis of qualitative data (see http://training.spss.co.uk and www.qsrinternational.com). Your university will offer training in the use of such packages and may have licences to enable you to purchase software at a reduced rate. It is worthwhile to look around and make the most of the training and support on offer in the university.

Universities offer a wide range of training programmes for all doctoral students, from seeking ethical approval to working with your supervisor, developing an academic writing style and specific research training. Making use of these will definitely help you manage your information and your precious resources, particularly time, much more effectively. It is also an effective way of meeting other doctoral students and sharing ideas. Seeking feedback from other doctoral students and your supervisor is an important way of evaluating the resources available.

Conclusion

This chapter has aimed to explore your personal expectations at the outset of professional doctorate study and introduce some strategies for inclusion in your personal toolkit for professional doctorate study. It is considered essential to think about and plan for the process of professional doctorate study, thinking about networks, groups and other resources that will be helpful, along with the development of writing style and other doctoral study skills. There is an inherent risk in thinking only about the end product – achieving the doctorate – without reference to the process and planning. While it may feel as if these issues are simply common sense, overlooking the preparatory stages can lead to challenges later.

Throughout the chapter there has been emphasis on collegiate and collaborative approaches to study: the development of communities of practice, for example. While you alone are responsible for the writing of your thesis and the planning and implementation of your research in professional practice, this does not mean you have to attempt the whole process alone. Sharing resources, discussing your ideas with others, and seeking support and guidance are an essential part of the process, and reflect the kind of teamwork and communication required directly in the professional practice setting if the research process is to be effective.

In the spirit of collaboration some insights into managing time and balancing work, academic and personal life are offered from Ruth, Ali, Paul and Louise in this chapter. Ruth and Louise have given their 'Top ten tips' for professional doctorate study processes below:

Ruth's top ten tips

1 Write lists and tick things off when they are completed, this gives you something to aim for and a sense of achievement
2 Set aside time to write
3 Keep a notebook with you to jot notes in about your research ideas

4 Get into the habit of reading around the subject and take a book with you to read, you will be amazed at how many opportunities you have to read!

5 Make time to spend with your partner, family and friends

6 If possible negotiate time with your employer to spend on your doctorate each week

7 Start a bibliographic matrix where you can record useful references and a summary of the main points of the book/article

8 Find a critical friend in your workplace who is willing to read your work for you and will give you honest feedback

9 Meet your supervisor early on in the process

10 Make sure that you take time out to relax

Louise's top ten tips

I am in the third year of a part-time Doctorate of Education programme, the first being the taught element which comprised three research theory and methods modules each being assessed by a 10,000 word assignment. I loved this first year; the subjects were fascinating, especially research theory and philosophy but most importantly, the peer support that exists in a classroom environment was invaluable. How interesting that my research thesis is underpinned by the concept of learning as a function of social interaction, when in fact, conducting the research thesis may be the loneliest piece of work any student can undertake!

My top tips therefore relate to engagement with other people during your studies:

1 Make sure you have the right supervisor. This is an important relationship and if you feel it is not working for any reason it is your responsibility to do something about it. I did and I'm much happier

2 Find a confidante who is geographically close and who has the time and inclination to listen to your ideas

3 Find others who are in 'the same boat' and try to form an action learning group

4 Contact the authors if you have resonance with their work and arrange to meet them and share your ideas; it's amazing how many of them say yes. I have had some extremely thought-provoking discussions doing this

5 Be critical with the feedback you get. Other people's ideas and perspectives are important to consider but ultimately this is your work and you have to arrive at your own conclusions. I imagine that if you aren't clear in your own mind about what you have come to know and believe then this will be difficult to defend at viva

6 Don't be flattered by other people. I was congratulated by my supervisor for the progress I was making. I spent the next six months thinking I could relax and consequently did very little! Set your own time plan and stick to it

7 Book time in your work diary for your doctoral study and make sure you don't give in to pressure from work colleagues to re-schedule time. They will learn it is a priority for you and come to respect study time as you do (even if they don't like it)

8 Ditto regarding family and friends

9 Keep a personal diary. Maintaining a personal dialogue can be just as cathartic as talking to others, as long as it remains on the page

10 Come to appreciate that as there are multiple perspectives to living, thinking and organising one's life, someone else's top ten tips may be completely irrelevant for you!

Summary of key points

- Discussing personal expectations with student peers and facilitators/ supervisors helps adjustment to the practitioner–researcher role
- Personal development planning is an excellent way of identifying the skills and resources required for doctoral study, in addition to mapping out a research plan
- Originality and critical thinking underpin doctoral study, exploring these in relation to your subject or professional discipline is essential
- Developing the notion of communities of practice (Lave and Wenger 1991) can enrich the knowledge and skills gained from study, in addition to reducing loneliness and isolation during the study experience
- There are a variety of software packages and reference alerting services that can help you manage your information resources more effectively. Find out more from the university information services department or your relevant professional organization

Useful websites

- www.grad.ac.uk Provides resources on personal development planning, supervision tips, local and national training and support networks, post-doctoral career planning
- www.ewenger.com Provides resources relating to communities of practice
- www.criticalthinking.org Provides excellent resources to facilitate critical thinking

Please note that the websites listed in this book were correct at the time of going to press. If you have any problems accessing the sites you should be able to locate the information using a search engine.

3

The practitioner–researcher: a critical and reflexive approach to professional practice

Dr Carolyn Taylor and Dr Stephen Hicks

Aims of the chapter

- To strengthen your critical reading skills for professional doctorate study and research
- To consider the implications of reflexivity in practitioner research
- To enable the skills to develop a research proposal for professional doctorate research
- To critically reflect on methodological, data collection, generation and analysis issues in practitioner research

Introduction

The professional doctorate combines a practice and a research focus. This provides an exciting challenge because 'real world' issues and practice relevance are placed at the centre of your enquiry. At the same time it can be a little daunting because you are making the transition from practitioner to practitioner–researcher. This involves demonstrating your own competence in research, and your potential to assist others with their research and promote research within your organization. Engaging in practitioner–research demands different knowledge and skills from those associated with your 'day job' (although many of the skills you already possess will prove very useful in research activities). In this chapter we want to explore this concept of 'practitioner–researcher' thus helping you to make sense of these new challenges. In particular we will explore three areas that are vital to the successful completion of your doctorate:

- Reading for professional practice and research
- Reflexivity in practitioner research
- Developing your own research project

Reading for professional practice and research

Undertaking a research study and locating it within the work of the wider research community is fundamental to the professional doctorate. It will involve you in explaining the relevance of your topic and approach, and how and why it adds to existing knowledge – appraising the research process and considering how you might have done things differently. In this regard it is helpful to think of your own research as forming a dialogue or conversation with others working in the field. Presenting research inevitably involves 'taking sides', in the sense that you will be explaining why you have chosen your topic and particular methods of enquiry as opposed to other topics and approaches. You will inevitably be aligning yourself with certain traditions and distancing yourself from other research paradigms. This necessitates an engagement with a range of literatures, for example those dealing with the same topic and those relating to other topics, but relevant in terms of theoretical approach or methodology. Reading, then, is a core activity within the research process. That being the case, it's a good idea to start by undertaking an assessment of your current reading. There are no right or wrong answers here. It's simply important to recognize where you are starting from.

Student activity 3.1 **Reading: a self-appraisal**

1 What have you read in the previous seven days (or in your most recent working week) relating to your professional practice?
2 How much time did you spend on this reading?
3 Does reading form part of your core work time or does it have to be fitted in as an extra activity?
4 How do you regard reading for professional practice: as a chore or as an interesting and pleasurable activity (rating yourself on a scale of 1 to 10, where 1 = chore and 10 = extremely interesting and pleasurable)?
5 To what extent do you plan and organize your work reading or does it just happen fairly haphazardly?
6 In your opinion how important is reading for performing your current job well (rating this from 1 to 10, where 1 = irrelevant and 10 = essential)?
7 What are the barriers to reading?

There are several points to be made here. First, it would not be at all unusual if you answered 'No' to the first and 'Yes' to the second part of question 3. In many professional jobs and workplaces reading is an 'add on' rather than a core activity. Indeed there are significant tensions between the evidence based practice agenda (to which we will return in due course) and the increasing demands made on professionals to work quickly and efficiently in the context of high volumes of work. This means that you may have found limited opportunities for reading, and what you have achieved may well have occurred outside your designated working hours and been undertaken in a rather ad hoc fashion in response to a specific work situation. Often it is encountering something out of the ordinary in our everyday work that prompts us to turn to the literature.

Second, it's interesting to consider *what* you read. As busy professionals you may be more likely to read trade journals and abbreviated research reports in an effort to assimilate information in an easily digestible form. Access to the Internet may now be influencing the scope of your reading, but this can itself be both a blessing and a curse. The Internet offers information on just about everything, often in short documents, but the choice can seem overwhelming and assessing the quality of material can be a real issue. Third, where did you place yourself in relation to question 4? Is reading for professional practice a chore or a delight for you? The fact that you are reading this book suggests that you are disposed to engaging in advanced study and one might expect a relatively high score. However, undertaking a professional doctorate does not necessarily mean that you really enjoy reading for work. There could be many different reasons for this. It could be a legacy of previous educational experiences. It could relate to the level of pressure you are currently under. It could also be the case that reading for professional practice seems rather dull compared with other forms of reading, such as fiction or biography. Technical and professional writing does not necessarily provide a riveting read! It needs to be recognized that sometimes reading for the doctorate will seem onerous, but getting into the habit of regular reading and engaging with difficult material is essential. It should also be said that reading can be enjoyable and stimulating – challenging ideas or ways of doing things that you have come to take for granted over the years.

A further issue to note is that reading tends to be a rather private activity. We often know little about other people's reading habits or how, when and what they read. We may sometimes discuss what we have read / are reading but we are less likely to talk about the *how* of reading, and what helps and hinders us in the process. One exception to this is William Horder, a social work practitioner/ manager turned academic. Horder (2004) explores the difficulties in reading for professional practice drawing on his own practice experiences and referring back to diaries kept over a number of years. He notes the scepticism towards intellectualized practices that can be found in (certain areas of) professional practice. In fact he points out that practitioners may not even read case files and policy manuals let alone research material, citing the findings of the public inquiry into the death of Victoria Climbié from abuse and neglect (Laming 2003). Horder asserts the importance of reading while acknowledging that practitioners can find it problematic. However, he avoids getting into 'practitioner blaming' mode. Instead he argues that learning from experience is what is emphasized in professional practice; practical action is often more highly valued than formal, propositional knowledge in getting the job done. Reflecting on his career in social work Horder refers to the oral culture that has tended to prevail:

Oral communications were used by preference as sources of knowledge and ideas. Books were not widely used. Knowledge was handed on by experienced staff, as in traditional cultures. High value was placed on solidarity within workplaces, especially when threatened with organizational change. The apprenticeship model encouraged learning from supervisors rather than reading. The way work was organized encouraged a culture of talk.

(Horder 2004: 306)

While oral culture is undoubtedly important in professional practice, as a professional doctorate student you will of necessity have to immerse yourself in a culture of reading. We want to emphasize that by this we mean a critical engagement with reading, not simply reading to acquire nuggets of information. In the rest of this section we explore this in more detail.

Jewell and Freeman (1995) suggest three different levels of reading:

- *Browsing* – to select interesting, useful or stimulating material from readily available sources, e.g. the weekly and monthly 'trade' journals that circulate in workplaces

- *Reading for information* – to gain answers to specific questions, e.g. about the effectiveness of a particular intervention method or drug treatment
- *Reading for research* – the reader is seeking to obtain 'a comprehensive view of the existing state of knowledge, ignorance and uncertainty in a defined area'

(1995: 8)

Browsing clearly serves an important function but it can easily remain 'a passive routine of uncritical reading with little retention' (Jewell and Freeman 1995: 8). Similarly *reading for information* may be done in a rather sketchy fashion and sources may be chosen because they conform to our expectations or state what we want to hear, ignoring disconfirming evidence and more nuanced findings. Jewell and Freeman (1995) argue that browsing and reading for information demand a degree of intellectual rigour, but this need is considerably amplified when *reading for research*. In reading for research, which lies at the heart of the professional doctorate, a more systematic approach is required, in which a careful search is made for relevant source material and a critical, questioning approach is adopted in relation to this material. Reading of this kind also helps us to interrogate a topic and to question taken-for-granted assumptions.

There is insufficient space here to go through all the stages of collecting and analysing source material. Fortunately there are now many helpful guides to conducting formal literature searches (see for example Hart 2001; Greenhalgh 2006) and literature reviews (Hart 1998). Here we will focus on the process of critical reading. Searching carefully and systematically to find out the scope of what is written that is relevant to your topic is clearly vital, but once material has been obtained it is essential not simply to slip into browsing or reading-for-information mode.

Critical reading

It is important to bring to your reading a form of 'respectful scepticism'. By respectful we mean treating authors politely, in a 'do as you would be done by' way. Work should not be dismissed out of hand or treated with contempt. But neither should we err too far in the other direction; we should not simply accept everything that is written at face value or be so much in awe of published work that we could not possibly question it. A questioning and sceptical stance is needed in order to test out the robustness of arguments; how they fit with our own current thinking; and how they advance, even challenge, our previous knowledge and understanding. In their discussion of critical reading Mike Wallace and Alison Wray (2006: 5) illustrate this by means of an invented example of an assertion based on research: 'In the reading test, the five children who were taught to read using phonics performed better overall than the five children taught by the whole word method. This shows that the phonics method is a better choice for schools.' Wallace and Wray (2006) suggest that this statement raises a significant number of questions about the adequacy and sufficiency of the evidence, the validity of the claim in favour of phonics, the generalizability of the findings and the manner in which the research was conducted:

- Is a study of just ten children sufficient to draw such a strong conclusion?
- What does 'performed better overall' signify?
- Were the differences between the two groups sufficiently great for us to be satisfied that they would occur again in a re-run of the experiment with different subjects?
- How were the two teaching programmes administered, and might there have been 'leakage' of the whole word teaching into the phonics teaching and vice versa?
- What was the reading test actually testing, and might it have been unintentionally biased to favour the children taught phonics?
- What care was taken to check how parental involvement at home might have influenced what and how the children learned?
- Were the two sets of children matched for intelligence, age, gender, or other factors?
- Is it reasonable to infer from such a small study that what works well in a small experimental group will work well in all school environments?
- How does [the author] envisage phonics being used in school? Would there still be a place for the whole word method?

(Wallace and Wray 2006: 5–6)

The example cited here is perhaps easy to critique in this way given the shakiness of the evidence in favour of the assertion. However, it serves to illustrate the sort of scepticism that should underpin reading for research. This kind of detailed questioning should also be supplemented by attention to the wider debates about the usefulness of phonics. The issue of how best to raise standards in relation to reading among primary school pupils is not simply a technical matter but also has political dimensions which would need to be explored in a doctoral dissertation. In these endeavours it is useful to approach the literature in a purposeful and organized way with specific questions in mind, since a clear focus is essential.

Questions for critical reading

Why am I reading this?

This is where you establish your own agenda in reading particular texts. Within the professional doctorate you will be largely responsible for giving direction to your reading. It's important to read purposefully and systematically (although the occasional serendipitous find may help to leaven your argument and is not to be ignored). Ask yourself, 'What is the purpose of my reading this? Is it to locate information/findings, to consider the research approach, to understand an argument, to assess the theoretical stance?' and so on (Evans and King 2006).

What are the authors trying to do in this writing?

This involves establishing clearly what the authors' aims are, which could be to report on research; to review others' work; to advance a particular argument or theory; and so forth. This helps you to establish the difference between the authors' agenda and your own. Without this, you can lose sight of your own agenda as you get drawn into other people's.

What are the authors saying that is relevant to what I want to find out?

This involves, first, clarifying the main points within a text and, second, connecting them to your own interests and concerns. This latter point is extremely important – there will be times when authors are saying things that are interesting but tangential to your studies. Keeping a grip on what is properly relevant to your research is extremely important, as time is such a precious resource. A delicate balance needs to be struck between, on the one hand, rejecting things that could have proved useful and, on the other hand, becoming so concerned with reading everything about a topic that you turn reading for research into information overload. Being awash with facts that no longer make any real sense is a danger to be avoided.

How convincing is what the authors are saying?

Next, it is useful to assess the robustness of the authors' argument and evaluate the quality of the data or evidence. Are the claims being made warranted by the evidence? What are the values and assumptions that underpin them? Are the claims consistent with those made by other authors? What precisely about this work convinces you of its coherence and credibility?

In conclusion, what can I make of this?

This is the 'So what?' question, which involves assessing the importance you attach to a particular text given your chosen topic. Is this work central and deserving of in-depth discussion or is it something that will warrant a brief mention (e.g., as a caveat to a widely held and well supported view) in your writing? Is it a view with which you agree or one that you will challenge? In short, how does this text advance your thinking about the topic in question? (These questions have been adapted from Wallace and Wray 2006: 32–4.)

Conducting your reading in this way encourages you to assess the significance of a range of source material to your own research and to give more weight to some sources than others. This will have the benefit of ensuring that you avoid a 'laundry list' approach to your reviews of literature for the dissertation and other assignments. In other words, one that makes no distinctions among the material cited and simply paraphrases arguments in the following manner: 'Smith found . . .', 'Jones concluded . . .', 'Anderson stated . . .' and so on (Rudestam and Newton 2007: 62). If you treated the literature in this way you would simply be acting as a passive transmitter of information, in effect assigning to the reader the task of sifting the evidence and assessing its relevance. We are suggesting a much more active process of reading and shaping your research enquiries, where you take command of the material and shape it to form part of your argument (Evans and King 2006).

Student activity 3.2 Critical reading: key messages

1   Make regular time for and plan your reading – a professional doctorate demands an organized approach!
2   Identify 'must read', 'could read' and 'icing on the cake' material – remember that classic texts are vital, but your literature must be up to date
3   Start making a list of references from the start, adding to it as you go along – this can save a lot of pain in the long run! Chapter 2 introduced some software that can help you
4   Learn the art of making brief notes that distil the essence of what you read – and file them systematically
5   Read critically and questioningly – be sceptical, play devil's advocate with propositions and arguments
6   Discuss your reading with your tutor group and supervisor
7   When it's hard going (as it will be sometimes) use your research diary (see later in 'Being a reflexive practitioner–researcher') to work through issues and then share this with others
8   Find things to read that excite and stimulate you – especially those that make you look at your topic and/or your method in a fresh and different way

---

Being a reflexive practitioner–researcher

Undertaking a professional doctorate differs in its approach, in some respects, from the kinds of funded research you may get involved in afterwards. In the latter there tends to be a tightly defined brief and the focus is primarily on the outcome and the findings. Methods may be described rather than debated, and process issues tend to be secondary. In contrast there is a key emphasis on *process* in the professional doctorate. Essentially you have to establish your research credentials by satisfying the awarding institution that you have reached a particular level of expertise in research in your area of practice. In order to do this you have, as it were, to 'show your workings out' as well as setting out 'the answer' you have arrived at. It isn't enough to simply achieve a good outcome, and in the case of some interesting findings you have to demonstrate that you are able to set up and implement a clearly thought out and ethical research plan. In addition you have to show that you have gone through a process of self-appraisal that has exposed the research process to sustained reflection and analysis. In sum, a focus on *how* and *why* you did things is as important as what data you generated.

In this section we will explore these issues. We suggest that the current emphasis on evidence based practice tends to privilege the *what* at the expense of the *how* and *why*. It can also take a rather narrow view of 'evidence', which again can be unhelpful for doctoral study and the sorts of questions you might want to ask. We suggest that even where quantitative methods are being deployed, there is much to be learned from the way that qualitative researchers approach their studies and their way of dealing with, and writing about, issues relating to the research process and issues of reflexivity. It can help you to move beyond thinking simply in terms of techniques, technicalities and results to addressing the fundamental issues that emerge during your journey towards joining the community of practitioner–researchers.

Evidence based practice

A strong emphasis on evidence based practice (EBP) has emerged in the past decade or more in the UK and North America. There are many definitions of EBP but this is perhaps the most widely used: 'The conscientious, explicit and judicious use of current best evidence in making decisions about the care of individual patients [or service users], based on skills which allow the [practitioner] to evaluate both personal experience and external evidence in a systemic and objective manner' (Sackett et al. 1997: 71).

The rationale for EBP lies in a critique of previous and/or existing practice. It is argued that without a firm evidence base practitioners continue to use interventions that have been proved to be ineffective or indeed harmful; similarly practitioners are said to be slow to recognize and introduce new techniques and treatments, despite knowledge of their proven effectiveness being widely available; and practice, based on 'old knowledge', habit, custom and intuition, lacks standardization, varying considerably within and across different providers, and leading to a 'postcode lottery' of provision. In short there is a considerable gap between knowledge produced by research and its use in practice (Trinder 2000: 3–4). To overcome these problems a process has been developed for applying proven research knowledge systematically to practice problems to drive up standards:

The seven explicit steps of EBP

1 Patient/service user presents problem
2 Practitioner identifies gap in knowledge
3 Formulation of structured, answerable question regarding care/treatment (e.g., regarding diagnosis, prognosis, effective interventions, methods of service delivery)
4 Search for information (best evidence) to answer question (from clinical examination, diagnostic laboratory, research evidence and other sources)
5 Critical appraisal of evidence regarding validity (closeness to truth) and usefulness (clinical applicability)
6 Application of evidence to practice with specified specific user/group of users
7 Evaluation of the outcome/process/performance
(Adapted from Reynolds 2000 and Sackett et al. 1997)

As a professional doctorate student it may well be that your aim is to contribute to the evidence base in your field as part of a broader endeavour to promote EBP. Your research may be designed to provide an answer to a specific clinical or practice question, tested in a rigorous way to provide valid and relevant knowledge in the staged approach outlined above. This is an entirely worthwhile project and the practical utility of your research is likely to have a major influence upon your choice of topic. However, there are important points that should be made here: first, we would want to caution against adopting a narrow conception of validity and utility; second, even if you decide to work within a quantitative paradigm for the purposes of the professional doctorate you will also need to comment on the research process and engage in a process of reflection and reflexivity that is aided enormously by adopting some of the methods and approaches of the qualitative researcher. Let's look at these issues in turn.

A hierarchy of evidence?

There are undoubtedly many positive aspects to EBP. No one would seriously argue in favour of the use of harmful treatments and against the use of new interventions of proven efficacy. Neither is it difficult to accept the contention that over time professional practice may settle into comfortable routines and become somewhat stale. Minds may become rather closed and new ideas may be resisted, regardless of their worth. Questioning the old and appraising the new seem essential to dynamic and engaged professional practice. However, the strong association with a quantitative paradigm and a narrow conceptualization of 'evidence' with the EBP movement, as demonstrated in the 'hierarchy of evidence' commonly found in EBP textbooks (see for example Pierson et al. 2006), is, in our view, considerably more problematic:

Table 3.1 'Hierarchy of evidence' commonly found in EBP textbooks

Hierarchy	Type of evidence
Type I	At least one good systematic review, including at least one randomized control trial (RCT)
Type II	At least one good RCT
Type III	At least one well-designed intervention study without randomization
Type IV	At least one well-designed observational study
Type V	Expert opinion, including the views of service users and carers

Source: Glasby and Beresford (2006: 271).

A hierarchy of evidence places greater value on certain forms of research activity. The (double-blind) RCT is placed at the pinnacle of research, while data derived from qualitative methods are placed near the bottom (or even excluded) on the grounds that they do not conform to the tenets of scientific research. We seek to challenge the hierarchy on two grounds: first, it is problematic to place research methods in a hierarchy in this way. We would argue, as would many others, that no research design should take precedence over all others (Murphy and Dingwall 2003; Bryman 2004). What matters is the nature of the proposed study and the best means to generate data.

The following example illustrates our argument. Dr Cassy Workman, an Australian GP working primarily with gay men with HIV and AIDS, found worrying levels of non-compliance with HAART (highly active, anti-retroviral therapy). Despite the proven efficacy of the regime, patients were failing to adhere to the rigid and intensive routine of taking medication – to the detriment of their health. Survey data suggested that concern about side effects was the statistically significant issue in relation to non-adherence. Unconvinced by this explanation, Workman conducted her own research, using in-depth interviews with patients. Her findings were rather different: first, a significant issue for patients concerned spontaneity and not wanting to be tied to a drug regime at the expense of unplanned opportunities for socializing. Second, the rigidity of the drug regime raised an issue for patients about confidentiality: they were concerned about work colleagues' reactions and the possibility of being stigmatized if their condition became known through taking medication at work. Armed with this new understanding, the GP began to work intensively with individual patients to address barriers to treatment and in doing so was able to raise adherence rates very significantly to approximately 90 percent (Workman 1998, cited in Brechin and Sidell 2000: 16).

Thus a qualitative study tells us a great deal about the successful implementation of a drug regime. An RCT can prove the drug's efficacy, but is silent on the issue of non-adherence and how to overcome it. Survey data may also be too generalized to explain and deal successfully with individual patients and the specificity of their lives. Moreover, we would argue strongly that qualitative methods should not simply be regarded as an adjunct to quantitative methods. There are occasions where qualitative methods are superior to quantitative ones and in our view it is preferable to move away from thinking hierarchically about methods to judging them by their usefulness and appropriateness in relation to the question(s) being asked (Taylor and White 2000). This does not mean ignoring matters of rigour, validity and reliability – these are relevant no matter what kind of methods are being used – but different criteria will need to be used for judging these depending on the choice of method (Silverman 2004).

The second, related, point to make is that the 'hierarchy of evidence' could have a pernicious effect on research undertaken for the professional doctorate. This is because it could encourage a view that the only worthwhile research is that which conforms to the hierarchy – only an RCT or experimental design will do; a qualitative study would be of lesser status. Again, we would want to challenge this. There have been rather unproductive arguments about the merits or otherwise of quantitative and qualitative methods which seem to have generated more heat than light. Our approach is to adopt a more inclusive stance on what constitutes 'evidence' (Taylor and White 2002; Glasby and Beresford 2006). Clearly those working with HIV/AIDS patients could learn much from the qualitative study described above. It might also have relevance to other areas of chronic illness. There are also many other examples of the contribution of qualitative studies to our understanding of professional practice and the views and perceptions of service users. David Silverman's study of HIV/AIDS counselling provides an interesting use of conversation analysis (for an exposition, see Wooffitt 2005). In studying the interactions between counsellors and patients Silverman is able to illuminate the process of engaging in difficult talk about a complex, emotive and value-laden subject. Counsellors showed considerable skills in conveying the messages of safe sex without alienating their patients by appearing overly didactic or directive (Silverman 1997). Using a similar methodology there are studies that illuminate various aspects of professional practice, for example clinical talk between doctors and patients (Morris and Chenail 1995); doctors giving 'bad' news to patients and families (Maynard 2003); 'backstage' case talk among haematologists (Atkinson 1995); and the cross-examination of witnesses in rape trials (Drew 1992). All of these aid our understanding of the ordinary, everyday routines of professional practice by focusing on the particularities of interaction and communication in institutional settings (see also Drew et al. 2001; Murphy and Dingwall 2003) – invaluable areas of study for practitioner–researchers.

In fact we would go further and suggest that an engagement with qualitative methods is essential to the professional doctorate, given that you will need to reflect not only on your current practice but also on the process of undertaking research and becoming a practitioner–researcher. This forms the basis of the discussion in the next section.

Learning from qualitative enquiry

The professional doctorate will place different demands on you as a writer. Those of you who engage in a piece of scientific research will be encouraged to adopt the more impersonal style that has come to be seen as the hallmark of scientific writing: for example it is customary to use the passive tense ('tissue was removed', 'cells were harvested' and so forth) and/or to focus on the researched rather than the researchers as exemplified in the following statement: 'Although severely obese adults experienced more wheeze and shortness of breath, this was not associated with a higher prevalence of atopy or AHR [airway hyperresponsiveness], suggesting that this group does not have a higher prevalence of asthma' (Peat et al. 2002: 194). In this form of writing the researchers' agency is hidden in order to emphasize their neutrality, the replicability of the method and the generalizibility of the data. You may decide to use this form of writing in your dissertation when discussing your findings. However, regardless of your methodology, you will also need to demonstrate your ability to reflect on your progress as a practitioner–researcher, as you advance through the professional doctorate programme. In this regard there is much to be learned from qualitative research where the relationship between research and researcher has been placed under close scrutiny. Positivist influenced quantitative studies have tended to emphasize the neutrality and objectivity of the scientific process, thus excluding the influence of personal and social factors on research.

In contrast qualitative research with its focus on human subjects and their experiences has needed to confront directly the issue of the researchers' relationship to their research subjects, and issues of voice and representation. As Amanda Coffey notes, 'the qualitative researcher or ethnographer are [sic] simultaneously involved in auto/biographical work of their own' (Coffey 2002: 314). Whatever kind of research you undertake for the professional doctorate it is precisely these processes that you will engage in so that you can demonstrate your understanding of the research process and your part in it. In what follows we explore some ways of engaging in these reflexive processes.

Practising reflexivity

First, let's briefly explore the rather slippery term 'reflexivity'. This is not straightforward because there are many different usages of the term and various typologies have been proposed (Lynch 2000; May 2000; Macbeth 2001). However, at the heart of reflexivity lies a concern with the issue of the status of research knowledge. In the quantitative paradigm objectivity is prized, personal bias and prejudice must be kept from the research process. Thus formal procedures undertaken in laboratory conditions are regarded as the acme of the natural science method. There 'pure' data can be obtained with much greater certainty by adherence to standardized methods and procedures. Within the social sciences there has been serious questioning of objectivity, both as a goal and as practical possibility. Instead 'the constitutive inseparability of knower and known' (Pels 2000: 2) is asserted. Researching human subjects raises inevitable questions about the impact of researchers' own values and beliefs on their choice of research subject; their conduct of research and engagement with research subjects; their interpretation of these subjects' actions and words; and the presentation of their research. Should qualitative findings be presented as objective facts or should their production in particular historical and cultural circumstances by specific individuals be recognized? In recent times qualitative inquiry has tended to the latter view and this has led to an emphasis on 'reflexive self-disclosure' (Pels 2000: 1) within research writing. Audible rather than silent authorship is thus advocated:

> Silent authorship comes to mark mature scholarship. The proper voice is no voice at all. Disciplines cast out the image of scientist as icon, as responsible source of definitive knowledge, in favour of scientist as oracle, as the transparent mechanism through which empirical 'facts' . . . express themselves . . . There is also merit to audible authorship . . . We go and see and sometimes join; we ask and listen, wonder and write, and tell our stories, not necessarily in that order. We believe that these simple acts of outward inquiry and inward reflection together with effort and creativity will give us something to say worth sharing.
>
> (Charmaz and Mitchell 1997: 194)

Thus voice has become a central concern and has led to what could be called a 'reflexive turn' with authors seeking to develop a more 'autobiographical and personalistic style' (Pels 2000). This acts to make visible both the authorial voice and what lies behind the particular description of the social world. Personal narratives and confessional tales of the research process have thus become commonplace (Coffey 2002) and incorporated into the disciplinary apprenticeship of students of the social sciences (Burman 2006). In his characterization of 'confessional tales' John Van Maanen (1988) suggests that: '[t]he confessional attempts to represent the fieldworker's participative presence in the studied scene, the fieldworker's rapport and sensitive contact with others in the world described, and something of the concrete cultural particulars that baffle the fieldworker while he learns to live in that setting' (Van Maanen 1988: 91).

There are, of course, clear parallels here with reflective practice as promoted within education, health and social care and other professions (Bulman and Schutz 2004; Bolton 2005). Despite the insights offered into the research process, this form of reflexivity with its emphasis on inward reflection has been criticized as becoming little more than 'self-fascinated observation' (May 1999: para. 3.14). Erica Burman (2006: 324) goes further, suggesting that 'the talk has become the walk: the researcher's reflection upon the action *is* the action'. In other words the focus is shifted from the research subject to the researcher, with potentially negative effects. In consequence, there have been attempts to refine and extend the concept of reflexivity beyond notions of rather narrow and potentially self-absorbed ruminations on research practice. In this vein, it is argued that academics and practitioners should go further to consider their practices of knowledge making, interrogating 'the process by which interpretation has been fabricated'. The definition of reflexivity is thus extended from simple reflection to encompass: 'analysis which interrogates the process by which interpretation has been fabricated [i.e., made]: reflexivity requires any effort to describe or represent to consider how that process of description was achieved, what claims to "presence" were made, what authority was used to claim knowledge' (Fox 1999: 220).

Examples of this kind of reflexivity are to be found in Taylor and White (2000) and Taylor (2006a, b) where talk and written texts are examined in detail. Engaging in these activities can help with examining the assumptions that underpin our practice and research, as well as opening up to scrutiny how practice problems and their solutions are constructed. In the next section we explore methods for incorporating reflexivity into your research in a constructively critical way so that you chart developments in the research process and challenge your thinking as you go along.

Becoming a reflexive practitioner–researcher

Developing reflexivity as a practitioner–researcher can be helped by keeping an up-to-date research journal. Buy yourself a cheap notebook and keep a diary of your thoughts, feelings, decisions, actions and reflections on your research project as it unfolds. This is useful because (a) it is very easy to forget how and why decisions were made, how or why things came about or how things went; (b) it will help you later to account for the research decisions that you made, whether they be about methodology or ethics or analysis and so on;

and (c) it will help you to develop a reflexive account of your research. For example over the course of a research project most people's view of their topic (and how it is conceptualized) will change quite significantly. A record of these thoughts and changes of mind will help you later when you come to account for your research journey. It will also help you with the various formal 'milestones' of the project: annual reviews, progress reports, 'upgrading' or assessment panels and the final viva. Examples of a research diary or journal can be found in Wield (2002: 39–40) and Silverman (2004).

A reflexive account of research is likely to:

- Give some attention to the researcher's own role or self in the production of knowledge
- Make your theoretical position on knowledge and on your topic explicit
- Account for methodological and ethical decision making as a *process*
- Examine your own role in the production of data
- Where possible, provide 'retrievable' data (i.e., full data extracts) so that the reader may examine these. This might include interview transcripts; reproductions of documents; experimental data tables; records of observations; photographs or video/dvd recordings; and so on
- Account for the analytical decisions made
- Reflect upon the limitations of the research and of your conclusions
- Show that other interpretations – including those of your respondents or readers – may be very different to your own

Liz Stanley and Sue Wise's work on feminist research has some points on how to develop a reflexive account (Stanley 2004; Wise and Stanley 2006). They argue that a feminist concern with 'analytical reflexivity' is more than just 'descriptive reflexivity'. This quotation uses the language of 'sociology', which may not be the discipline/approach that you would use, but the research processes discussed are the same:

> Descriptive reflexivity provides descriptions of an 'I'm white/black, I'm a woman/man; it was in a youth club/on a housing estate; they were nice/ horrible' kind. Such things can be quite interesting as a way of contextualising a piece of research and are useful for readers in 'placing' the researcher and their approach. But beyond this, it tells readers very little about the actual sociology involved. By contrast, analytical reflexivity involves how we respond as sociologists to the fact that understanding and theory are rooted in the experience of the sociologist qua investigator of (aspects of) social life . . . Analytical reflexivity is concerned with the act of knowing and the claim to possess 'knowledge about' things
>
> (Stanley 2004: 9)

For Stanley and Wise this means developing 'accountable knowledge', that is research that makes the intellectual or analytical processes open and available to readers, rather than just presenting the 'end *product*' (Stanley 2004: 10). Stanley and Wise recommend putting 'accountable knowledge' into practice by using 'retrievable data' (Stanley 2004: 10), that is presentation of extended data extracts as well as the researcher's analysis of this. The purpose of this is 'to provide key elements of evidence, argument, and interpretation in texts that readers can "argue back to", because they are provided with the detail to reach their own conclusions' (Wise and Stanley 2006: 448). Qualitative data can be presented in retrievable form by providing extracts of interview or focus group transcripts, documents, observation notes, photographs or other visual materials. Quantitative data can be reproduced in the form of experimental results, questionnaire answers and other visual materials. These may be included as appendices in a thesis.

In addition, Stanley and Wise suggest analytical reflexivity may be developed through accounting for the ethical and interpretive decisions made by the researcher. This means taking responsibility for our own interpretations of data and our own accounts of events, rather than 'hiding behind' suggestions that our research merely presents the views of our subjects or respondents:

> Analytical reflexivity entails writing an open research text that adduces evidence in retrievable form that is appropriate and sufficient for the argument being made, outlines all stages of the argument properly evidenced, in which each successive level is properly supported by those prior. It accounts for interpretations and conclusions by closely linking these to evidence and argument and provides sufficient detail regarding all of the above for readers to be able to make their own interpretations and so evaluate conclusions and claims
>
> (Wise and Stanley 2006: 449)[1]

Such ideas about accountable and reflexive research knowledge have been debated within feminist research theories for some time (see, for example, Stanley and Wise 1993, 2008; Letherby 2003; Stanley 2004; Wise and Stanley 2006). They also link to questions about the *person* or *self* at the centre of the research process; that is you, the researcher. For, as Donna Haraway noted, all knowledge is 'situated' and comes from a particular personal and political location (Haraway 1988). This means that, in addition to questions about reflexivity that we have been considering, it is worth thinking about auto/biographical and affective issues within your research.

Liz Stanley's work on auto/biography reminds us that any text concerned with lives, experiences, actions and so on is not 'factual' but rather 'artful': 'The facts, then, are a product of their time and place as well as of their author. They are also . . . a product of their readers. Reading is both active and a process' (Stanley 1992: 130–1). Any research account relates to a particular social and temporal location (Haraway 1988) but also, crucially, to the person(s) producing the account and to the interpretations arrived at by readers. The social context of research data – a crucial concern of sociology as a discipline – is therefore vital. Stanley's book reminds us to consider how research material has been selected and put together (including, of course, what has been left out); how the author has affected the text; and from what viewpoint the text has been authored. She argues for an 'anti-realist stance' on texts; that is one that recognizes *versions* of a life (or of events) and that tries to show the complexity and contradictions present in any everyday situation (Stanley 1992).[2]

Research affect is also important here. This encompasses your role as researcher in producing your text (Stanley and Wise 1993; Letherby 2003); how your work/research might affect others, whether that be through the actual data generation, through the use to which your research might be put (which you cannot control) or through your role as an educator, practitioner–researcher or research leader; how your text might affect others (and on this, see authors such as Behar 1996; Kiesinger 1998a, b; Ellis 2004, on writing more 'affective' research texts); and, crucially, how the research affects you.

Research involves 'emotion work': handling your own responses, those of others and the emotional labour of doing the research (Letherby 2003). The process of doing research will inevitably result in feelings of uncertainty and of questioning things. You may begin to question your professional role; your views on things in the workplace; your understanding of your research topic and/or discipline. You will also have to deal with emotions that the research provokes in you, and these may at times include anger, depression, upset, boredom as well as emotional highs.

Researchers have to deal with research subjects' emotions too: (a) they may talk about things that you do not feel are directly 'your business'; (b) they may become upset, angry and so on; (c) you may need to have further referral resources in place (in fact, most ethics committees will ask about how you are going to deal with people who become upset by your research); (d) you yourself may need to talk it through afterwards. Even in experiments or surveys, you may encounter distress, upset and other emotions.

Although these are everyday practical questions, they are also epistemological ones: the researcher's 'self' is central to the research; and the researched are also knowing/thinking subjects, not just research 'fodder' (Stanley and Wise 1993). The latter will have their own interpretations and opinions which will differ from yours, and they will be affected. This is not to overstate the case. Most research respondents will be quite happy to participate and will carry on with their daily lives after you have finished your research. However, you should also be prepared to deal with emotions or behaviours provoked by your work.

A reflexive research practice, then, is to be aware of these questions of affect rather than trying to remove such 'contaminations' through notions of objectivity. As Alvin Gouldner argued:

> . . . the notion of contaminated research presupposes the existence of uncontaminated research, and this is pure folly. All research is contaminated, for all research entails relationships that may influence both

sociologist [researcher] and subject. The aim of the reflexive sociologist [researcher] is not to remove his [sic] influence on others, but to know it

(Gouldner 1973: 77)

Developing reflexivity

Student activity 3.3

1 Write a brief account of how and why you chose your research topic: what influenced you? Were you influenced by other people, by what you have read, heard or seen? What about you as a person: how has this influenced your study? How have you influenced your conceptualization of your topic? Are there aspects of your identity, your politics, your ethics or your professional role that have influenced the study?
2 Repeat this exercise at a much later date: how have things changed and why?

Developing your research

Having considered the role of critical reading and reflexivity, we now move on to a discussion of the development of your research project. Studying for a professional doctorate requires the development of a well thought out and achievable project, but there are many aspects involved in thinking through and designing your research. This section will help you to consider these various aspects and to produce a coherent research proposal.

Choosing a topic

When thinking about and choosing the topic for your research project, it's always a good idea to write down, and talk through, two or three potential subjects. Ask yourself which of these topics you feel enthusiastic about – which interests you the most. Another way to do this is to ask someone else to listen to your description of your various potential projects. They will probably be able to tell you fairly easily the one that animates you the most. It's often a good idea to pursue the topic that most fires you up, because you will have to sustain this interest over a long period of time and through some very hard work (Rudestam and Newton 2007). However, guard against choosing a topic about which you feel very emotional or angry. This does not mean that you cannot pick a personal topic, but using a doctorate to try to solve an emotional issue or to 'grind an axe' may cause you more problems or may prevent you from being able to analyse the data carefully (Rudestam and Newton, 2007: 10–11).

All researchers tire of their project or topic at some point during their doctoral career, and so enthusiasm or genuine interest will really help to sustain you to the end. If you have been asked to research a topic by someone else (that is, to pursue someone else's agenda or problem), then ask yourself some honest questions about whether you will genuinely be able to maintain an interest in this topic over a lengthy period of time. The best doctoral projects usually spring from the personal and political concerns of the researcher. Les Back, for example, says, 'Trust your own interest . . . The indulgence of individual inquisitiveness is part of what is precious about doing sociological research' (Back 2007: 173). Lisa Tillmann-Healy's *Between Gay and Straight* (2001) is a study of friendships between gay and heterosexual people. The study arose serendipitously when Tillmann-Healy's boyfriend (later husband) joined a gay men's softball team (the league rules allowed for up to two straight players in an otherwise gay team). Her study consists of an ethnography of friendships amongst the gay softball team, of developing bonds between the team, herself and her partner, and between the gay men and other heterosexual people in their lives. A personal situation became the site of academic study (Tillmann-Healy 2001: 6–10), which is a feature of many research projects. (For more on this, see Stanley 1992; Behar 1996; Newton 2000; and Ellis 2004.)

Student activity 3.4 Choosing a research topic

Jot down two or three possible research topics. For each topic, describe or make notes on your answers to the following questions:

- Why do I think this topic is important and worth researching?
- Who would benefit from the research?
- Whose research agenda is this?
- What kinds of research questions would I be asking?
- Do I have the resources to conduct this project?
- In what setting and with what data sources (or with which people) would I do the research?
- Do I think this project is achievable in my given timescale?

Remember that deciding on a topic may take some time and will involve a process of elimination. You may have several ideas and need to work out the topic that interests you the most. However, at some point, you will need to alight on a definite project. The research student who keeps changing their mind will ring alarm bells, as prevarication can act as a block to, or way of avoiding, doing the research. If you are struggling with two or three topics, then forcing yourself to write a research proposal on each can be a good way to help you decide which is achievable, realistic and appealing (see section on

'Writing a research proposal' below). Try to make use of as many opportunities as you can to present your ideas to others: feedback on an intended project is always useful.

Having decided on a research topic, there are two further issues common to all research that must be considered: (a) how have you theorized your topic? and (b) are you trying to cover too much? First, the ways in which researchers conceptualize a topic needs careful thought. All of us will think about a topic in certain ways, and this will rest upon assumptions that need careful analysis. It is sometimes hard to notice the assumptions that we make, but we do need to consider how we have theorized a topic in the first place. This is sometimes a puzzle to novice researchers because they have assumed that a topic is 'obvious'. For example workplace stress is often researched within many professional fields, but the way in which 'stress' is conceptualized is important. Some research will:

- Assume that 'stress' exists as a property of people
- See 'stress' as a psychological state
- Assume that 'stress' is a measurable entity
- See 'stress' as a way to account for employee or workplace performance

However, this would not have taken into account that 'stress':

- Can be seen as a socially constructed idea (see Burr 2003 on 'social constructionism')
- Is a way of accounting for people's talk and actions (and indeed making judgements about them)
- Does not take account of structural and political issues in the workplace (such as lack of resources, poor quality of workplace facilities, power struggles and dynamics, over-work or poorly coordinated work, and so on)
- Is not a 'thing' that can be measured
- Is context dependent

The second issue to consider is that it is very common for researchers at the start of a project to attempt too much. Your project will and must shrink in size 'due to the necessity of maintaining a manageable project for one person' (Rudestam and Newton 2007: 21). This is inevitable but also important: you must refine your topic so that you have an achievable research aim that also allows you to say something interesting and different to that which is found in the existing research. Issues relating to originality were explored in Chapter 2. Trying to cover everything or 'change the world', however, is not possible in a doctorate – especially if you want to complete it.

Narrowing the focus of your project will give you a clearer set of research questions. David Silverman, too, guards against research that tries to cover 'everything but the kitchen sink'. He says, 'this "kitchen sink" approach is a recipe for disaster. Unless you have the resources for a big team of researchers, depth rather than breadth is what characterises a good research proposal. If you define your topic very widely, you will usually be unable to say anything at great depth about it' (Silverman 2005: 80). At doctoral level, in-depth analysis is what's needed. Harry Wolcott puts this succinctly: 'Do less, more thoroughly!' (Wolcott 2001: 128).

Theories and methods

> Justification of our choice and particular use of methodology and methods is something that reaches into the assumptions about reality that we bring to our work. To ask about these assumptions is to ask about our theoretical perspective.
>
> (Crotty 1998: 2)

You will eventually have to justify a methodology for your research project, which means an overall strategy or approach for generating and analysing your data. We might think of methodology as a combination of theory and method because it draws upon your theory about your topic and about what counts as knowledge about your topic, and because it specifies or suggests methods for the gathering of data. Stanley and Wise define methodology as

> a shorthand term for a theoretical or practical idea to be explored together with a set of tools which specify how it is to be investigated – including what is appropriate and also sufficient evidence for doing so and how this should be produced, what counts as good arguments about this evidence, and what conclusions can be justifiably drawn from this.
>
> (Stanley and Wise 2008: 221)

Methodology is not merely a technical matter, it has to do with what you think counts as knowledge about your topic and whose knowledge is seen to count.

Thus it is crucial for researchers to think about their research questions and about their own political and theoretical perspective on their topic before considering methodology. It's not always obvious or easy to work out what theoretical perspective sums up your approach, and it is worth remembering that: (a) it may take you some time (and considerable reading) to find a theoretical position that fits; and (b) this may combine aspects or elements from more than one approach (e.g., you might be attracted by aspects from feminist research theory, from discourse analysis and from social constructionism). It's a good idea to have a look at texts which provide an overview of philosophies of social research, such as Williams and May (1996) or Hughes and Sharrock (1998).

Choosing a methodology is a 'reality shaping' choice (Gubrium and Holstein

1997: 98) because it influences the way that researchers go about their work and the kinds of data that are produced. Ken Plummer (2001) reminds researchers, therefore, to think about their research project and questions in order to ensure that any chosen methodology is appropriate. The research questions he suggests are:

1 Substantive questions: what is your topic of enquiry? Just what is it that you want to know?
2 Methodological (or what Plummer calls 'social science') questions: what kind of knowledge do you want to produce? Are you after objective/measurable data or subjective/interpretive data?
3 Technical questions: how will you go about the research practically?
4 Ethical/political questions: what political justification is there for your study? What are the ethical implications?
5 Personal questions: what impact will the research have on you the researcher and on those you research?

(Plummer 2001: 120–1)

Plummer's questions are 'difficult', but they are necessary for any researcher. This is because the questions are challenging and they require you to answer points that you may be trying to avoid. Although pinning yourself down in this way is not necessarily a comfortable process, it is an important building block for *any* successful research project. Planning, preparing, thinking through and discussing your intended research is crucial and will have many benefits in the longer run. For example, you will be asked about these points in the final viva voce examination.[3] In addition you will need to ask yourself these kinds of questions (and probably struggle with them for a time) if you are to work out what theories/methods will be appropriate to your study and which fit with your own 'take' on the world.

Student activity 3.5

Spend a bit of time thinking through Plummer's five research questions in relation to your intended project. Jot down your thoughts/answers.

Having thought about these research questions, you should now consider those concerned with theory and method. Michael Crotty (1998: 5) has defined these, along with epistemology and methodology, as follows:

- *Epistemology*: a theory of knowledge or what we think counts as knowledge about a topic (e.g., social constructionism, objectivism, feminism)
- *Theoretical perspective*: the philosophical position that guides our research (e.g., feminism, post-structuralism, interpretivism, positivism)
- *Methodology*: an overall research design or approach that shapes choice

of methods (e.g., ethnography, discourse analysis, survey research, experiment)

- *Methods*: techniques, tools or procedures (e.g., questionnaire, observation, interview, analysis of texts)

Stanley and Wise have argued that these questions are central to all research because 'researchers' understandings are necessarily temporally, intellectually, politically and emotionally grounded, and are thus as contextually specific as those of "the researched" ' (Stanley and Wise 1990: 23). By now, it should be clear that these questions open up a far more complex (but also interesting) set of dilemmas than those raised when research is merely termed 'quantitative' or 'qualitative'. Each of these terms actually encompasses a huge range of different epistemological and methodological perspectives and – at doctoral level – it will be important to address your perspective as carefully as possible. Referring to your work as merely 'qualitative', for example, will be inadequate. Instead, you will need to work towards explaining your own epistemological and methodological position in some detail. Read as much as you can in this field of research theory and read as many methodological texts as you can. Researchers' ideas about method/ology change over the course of a project, and some aspects may not become clear until towards the end. It may take some time to alight on a chosen approach, but you should try to be as clear as you can about methods before going out and generating data.

However, there is no 'perfect' method/ology that will guide you clearly in the research field – research always throws up dilemmas and 'messy' problems that will have to be resolved on the ground. Indeed John Law reminds us that, in the complex and confusing world that research tries to analyse, we should be wary of the idea that 'method' will solve all problems:

> events and processes are not simply complex in the sense that they are technically difficult to grasp (though this is certainly often the case). Rather, they are also complex because they *necessarily exceed our capacity to know them* ... The world is not to be understood in general by adopting a methodological version of auditing. Regularities and standardisations are incredibly powerful tools but they set limits.
>
> (Law 2004: 6)

Writing a research proposal

Producing a formal proposal at an early stage in your research career is a key part of the planning, preparation, thinking through and discussion process that we mentioned earlier. In other words, a proposal will help you to clarify your intended project and identify any potential stumbling blocks. In addition you will have to write a proposal, in all likelihood, to get your intended project approved and for submission to an ethics committee. Remember that most researchers revise their research proposal a number of times in the early stages of their project; this is normal because our ideas about a piece of research evolve over time. But it is also necessary that you settle on a project and spend time working up a detailed proposal. Colleagues, funders and supervisors will be concerned about a researcher who keeps changing their mind about a project, or who is reluctant to or cannot produce a proposal. The process of working up a research proposal takes time and is not necessarily comfortable, but it is always helpful in the longer run as it enables us to clarify aims and purposes, and identify and iron out potential problems and unrealistic plans. It's also a good learning process for any further postdoctoral research since all projects require a well thought out proposal.

The proposal explains and justifies your research to others and allows for critical appraisal of your project. This is something that many researchers find difficult in the early stages of their project: they are unclear about aspects of the research; they have not thought the whole project through; and they are unused to explaining their research to others. However, this is a skill that you will have to develop because, ultimately, a doctorate is a 'defence' of your project, approach and analysis. Silverman suggests, therefore, that a proposal involves 'shifting away from your own concerns and thinking about the questions that the reader(s) of your research proposal will be asking' (Silverman 2000: 113). In order to do this, he argues that you should attempt to be persuasive (e.g., convince your reader(s) that the project is worth doing, make a case for a realistic and achievable project); make broader links with your field of practice (e.g., show how your research might contribute to professional change or development); and aim for clarity (e.g., make sure that your proposal can be understood by those who are not specialist in your chosen professional and/or methodological field; try to explain things clearly) (Silverman 2005: 141). The proposal is not just a chore, it's a map of the research terrain that will help to guide you through your project.

Proposal word lengths vary so check with your institution, but a good overall guide would be a maximum of eight sides of A4 paper:

A research proposal ought to include:

- *Title*: keep this concise and make sure it reflects the topic/content of your research
- *Abstract*: a brief summary of the entire research project (about 300 words only)
- *Introduction*: your topic and why it is timely or important. Make links to your field of professional practice
- *Aims and research question(s)*: what is the purpose of your research and what are you trying to find out? Research may be about testing, measuring,

counting, assessing, evaluating, exploring, explaining, reflecting upon, discovering, observing, asking, proving, informing and/or challenging: what are you trying to do?

- *Brief literature review*: an initial review of some of the relevant literature in your chosen field. What key themes arise in classic and current literature? What do you think is missing and how will your project fill a gap or contribute something new?
- *Methodology and methods*: explain your chosen research approach and then show what methods you will use and why these are appropriate to your research question(s). Show why other methodologies and methods have been considered but rejected
- *Sample or subject group*: where will your data come from: texts, people, an experiment? Explain your sample (if you intend to generalize) or your subject group/data source (e.g., what texts will you use and why, or which people will you talk to/observe and why). How will you gain access to your data or to people?
- *Data and analysis*: explain what kinds of data you will produce, how you intend to store them (in a confidential and ethical way) and how you propose to analyse the data. It's sometimes hard to say how you intend to analyse data when you are in the early stages of your project, but you must articulate some preliminary ideas
- *Ethical issues*: how will you ensure confidentiality/anonymity of subjects? How will you gain informed consent? How will you deal with any potential harm to your subjects? (e.g., if you are talking to people about a potentially upsetting subject, then you must discuss how you will ensure they can access further help or support if needed). What ethical dilemmas specific to your project are raised? How will you deal with these? On ethics, please refer to Chapter 6 of this book
- *Outputs/dissemination*: in addition to the thesis, what other outputs will be produced? (For example, will you produce any summaries for participants? Will you hold any events to communicate findings back to your participants, colleagues or funders?) Chapter 7 will explore these issues in more detail
- *Resources*: what resources will be needed to complete the project (e.g., do you require a digital recorder? What about postage costs for a survey?) and who will fund or provide these?
- *Timescales*: produce a realistic timetable that shows the time devoted to each stage/aspect of the research leading up to submission of your thesis. This is usually best done in chart form, using a Gantt chart, for example
- *References*: include references for any literature referred to in the proposal[4]

Student activity 3.6

Work through and make notes on your intended research project using the proposal structure outlined above

Conducting research: generating and analysing data

You should attempt to be as clear as possible about what your data are and how you are going to go about analysing them before you set out to collect them. If you are doing experimental, survey or field research of any sort, then you should always pilot and revise your research tool (whether that be a particular test, a questionnaire by post, observational methods or interviews, and so on):

- Check the kinds of questions you are asking: are they clear, relevant and useful?
- Check your own research skills: can you structure an interview well? Do your observational skills work? Do a 'dry run' of your experiment or test
- How are you going to record your data so that they are clear and useable? It's a good idea to check your fieldnotes and/or recording at the end of each day
- If you are using technical equipment (digital recorders or DVD) do you know exactly how to use this properly? Many researchers have told of carrying out a long and important interview, only to find that they have not recorded it because they made a mistake with the equipment

Pilot your tools by practising with a friend (or another doctoral researcher) and then carrying out an initial attempt with a research subject who is prepared to help you think about your own skills. Ask them to fill out your questionnaire, or carry out an interview with them (or whatever your research tool is) and then spend some time asking them about the process: were the questions clear? What about the structure? Were there things that they did not understand? Did they feel comfortable?

Many researchers talk about collecting or gathering data, but Mason says, 'it is more accurate to speak of *generating* rather than *collecting* data, precisely because [no] researcher can be a completely neutral collector of information about the social world' (Mason 2002: 36). This is an important point and it is therefore vital to be aware of how your own actions and interpretations as a researcher influence your data. Even documents or numbers, for example, will be interpreted by you, and you will have made decisions about what to ask, how to ask it, what to look at and what to disregard (i.e., what is and isn't relevant).

When generating data 'in the field', it is worth remembering the following points:

- Pace and timing
- Anticipating problems
- Being professional
- Emotions
- Not being put off by others

- Thinking while doing
- Recording data

Pace and timing

You will have to pace and sustain data collection. For example, if you are conducting a series of interviews, then think about how many is realistic in one day. Try to allow time for a breather between interviews and space them out across a few days if possible. Interviews are tiring and you will not perform as well if you are worn out. Postal or email questionnaires will have to be chased up, and you should not expect a high return rate (the average is about 30 percent). You will send out far more than you get back. Experiments often take considerable time and thought to set up, and may need to be repeated. Sometimes, experiments fail or they do not generate meaningful data. Observational methods are very tiring and may have to take place over a lengthy period of time.

Anticipating problems

In experimental and laboratory based research, equipment and test failure are to be expected (e.g., see accounts in Delamont et al. 2000). This is quite normal in scientific research, and will need to be discussed with your supervisors or team. There may also be technical problems with interviews, observations or surveys (such as equipment failure, cancellations, interruptions and so on). You may need to repeat aspects of the data generation in this case, and so your timetable thus may be delayed.

Being professional

Gaining the trust of participants and agencies/organizations is vital, so you can't afford to be ill prepared. You should attempt to be professional in your approach. If you are carrying out research with people, then set up appointments with participants, be on time, but be prepared to reschedule appointments if necessary. You will probably need to give a brief explanation of your research to participants, so be prepared for this. Remember they will want a brief overview of what you are doing, not an in-depth analysis. Participants may ask for a copy of the 'results' once you have finished the research. Try to be clear about what they would like and what you can realistically offer (e.g., a summary) – most people would like to see a brief summary of what you have found or have argued, but they don't want to read an entire professional doctorate thesis.

Emotions

You may have to deal with participants who become emotional or upset during interviews or observations. Think about how you will handle this and how you will refer them to further support if needed. Remember that being upset in an interview is not necessarily a bad thing: some participants appreciate the time to talk through difficult issues. You may also be upset or disturbed by some of what you hear, read or see. In addition to what people say to you, case records, other documents and photographs may be upsetting. Think about where you might get support from and talk things through with friends, colleagues and supervisors. Check in with your supervisor and other researchers during your data generation phase – it's good to chat about how it's going and about any potential problems.

Not being put off by others

Don't be put off by those in the field who might make it difficult for you and/ or make disparaging comments about 'research'. There may be people in your professional setting who will be suspicious of you; will feel defensive about their own practice; or will say that 'all research is a waste of time'. Some may even try to block your work. Maintain a focus on what you are doing, explain your work politely, avoid being defensive and don't get too drawn in to these kinds of arguments. If someone doesn't want to participate, see this as their choice. Compensate for this by using your support networks to keep your enthusiasm up. Chapter 5 provides further insights into leading research in professional practice.

Thinking while doing

You will have to 'think on your feet' during data generation: for example some interviewees will go off on tangents – while it is important to allow some of this (partly because sticking rigidly to a script is not that useful and may mean missing some very important but unanticipated areas), you will have to refocus participants onto your questions. You will have to listen very carefully, deal with your subjects' questions and respond to unanticipated data. You may come across data that is unexpected but very useful to you; however, this may necessitate negotiating ethical access to 'new' or unexpected data. You may develop stronger research relationships with some people ('key informants') – this is helpful, but remember to seek the views of others (including those who are quieter or in less 'powerful' positions). Howard S. Becker's book, *Tricks of the Trade: How to Think About Your Research While You're Doing It* (1998), is a good read.

Recording data

Make sure you record data thoroughly (including a 'research diary' of your impressions of people, places, issues and so on, as we discussed earlier in 'Being a reflexive practitioner–researcher'). Think about how you are going to transcribe interview or observational data. Consider the level of transcription that will be needed (e.g., discourse analysts transcribe in far more detail than others, see Wooffitt 2005) and whether you can use 'voice recognition' transcription software. Make sure that you store questionnaire or experimental results safely.

Data analysis

Analysis of your data can be an exciting and motivating phase of your research, as you begin to develop a sense of what your arguments will be and how your thesis is shaping up. However, it is important to remember that data do not 'speak for themselves'; you will have to make sense of the data and draw your own conclusions, and so you should remember that this phase is time-consuming.

You will need to allow yourself plenty of time for analysis, whether you are using statistical packages (such as SPSS – originally 'Statistical Package for the Social Sciences' – see www.spss.com); qualitative software analysis packages (such as NVivo); analysis of experimental results; discourse analysis of texts; or thematic analysis of written data. It's worth reading texts that deal with approaches to data analysis as some of these have lots of ideas that may help (see Miles and Huberman 1994; Wolcott 1994, 2001; Coffey and Atkinson 1996; Mason 2002; Cramer 2006; Silverman 2006; Osborne 2007). However, it is important to make sure that your analytic approach matches up with your overall methodology, for example a discourse analytic approach to research/ texts would not use a thematic analysis of written data because thematic analysis does not consider the ways in which language is used to make claims about the world.

The first step in data analysis is to organize your materials into some kind of order. For example, interviews should be transcribed and saved as separate (and labelled) files. If you are using any kind of computer analysis package, then you will have to enter your data, and this will also take quite some time. Experimental results, observational notes or documents for analysis will all have to be organized and sorted so that you can see all of the data you have before you.

The next step we might call 'getting to know' your data – this involves listening to, reading or looking at your data *over and over*, until you get a feel for what is there and for key themes or findings or for common ways of speaking or writing. At this stage, many researchers describe almost 'drowning' in a mass of data, feeling overwhelmed and being unsure as to what they are going to do with all this material. Although this is not a comfortable feeling, it is quite normal and you should try to stick with it while you get a sense of your data. Reading about others' research experiences may help you through this phase (see, for example, Roberts 1981; Burgess 1984; Van Maanen 1988; Stanley 1990; Shaw and Gould 2001; Darlington and Scott 2002). You should also keep regular contact with your supervisor when analysing data. Present analysis in progress and check out your ideas as they develop. Make use of formal opportunities (research seminars) to present your data analysis in progress, where these are available.

We do not have space to go into different forms of data analysis here, but this may involve statistical and other numerical tests, textual or narrative analysis, key theme or content analysis and so on (see readings listed above). You should try to be methodical in your approach and think about developing visual aids (e.g., charts, tables, diagrams, 'mind maps', sketches) as these can really help with the analysis of numerical, textual or visual data. Remember that the same data can be analysed in different ways, for example textual data such as documents or interview transcripts can be analysed using discourse analysis, by content analysis or by key theme analysis (see Prior 2003; Silverman 2006).

It is also vital to think about the differences between presentation of findings/data and analysis of these. A common error of many early researchers is to describe and present findings/data (which is necessary and important) as though that were analysis. Instead, at doctoral level, you must go on to interpret your data, explaining what they mean and giving your account for why this might be the case. Harry Wolcott's book, *Transforming Qualitative Data* (1994), is a good text on this because he distinguishes between (a) description, in which the 'story' of events or an approach or a situation is outlined; (b) analysis, in which data are examined and reported; and (c) interpretation, in which we make sense of or account for the data. On quantitative analysis, see Duncan Cramer's book (2006).

David Silverman's 'rules' for qualitative data analysis can usefully be applied to all research involving human subjects: he suggests that we avoid treating the respondent's point of view as an explanation, since this rests on the mistaken assumption that research is about capturing 'authentic' experiences. Silverman reminds us, instead, that interview data, for example, are situated (in a particular time, place and dialogue) and textual (that is, they make claims rather than 'tell things as they really are'). He also reminds us that all data are mediated by our reasoning or interpretation as much as by our participants, and so we should not treat data as 'simple statements of events' (Silverman 2006: 209). He also warns against relying on single element explanations for events and reminds us that 'the phenomenon always escapes' (Silverman 2006: 201). What he means by this is that treating a social phenomenon (such as 'stress', the example that we referred to earlier) as a thing that can be captured and measured is a problem (as we saw in our discussion of the limitations of evidence based practice). Instead, researchers ought to build up a picture of how, why and when 'stress' is made use of by people as a phenomenon.

As you begin to analyse and write about your data, you will quickly realize that you probably have too much. Most researchers find that some data ends up on the 'cutting room floor' because they simply do not have the space to write about or make use of all of it. You may well have to jettison some of your data, and so you should begin to focus down on key themes that you wish to analyse in depth. As you write and redraft analysis, you will begin to see that some sections are less important while others are vital. If you have trouble spotting these, then ask a friend or supervisor to identify 'tangential' and less important sections for you. Be prepared to let go of some of your data. This 'discarded' data may be used later for further analysis (such as in a journal article), but it is very unlikely that you will be able to use all data in your doctoral thesis. Ask yourself: what *must* go in, what *could* go in and what *shouldn't* go in?

Finally, it is helpful to remember that the writing process is part of analysis, since *explanations are often developed as analysis progresses*, and it is to the topic of writing research that we now turn.

Developing your writing

Unfortunately many researchers talk of the writing of their project as 'writing up' – as though this is something done only at the end of a project once the 'real work' of data collection and analysis has been completed. Try to write your project as you go along – you can work on literature review or methodology chapters fairly early in the process (like most chapters, they will probably be revised later), and it is important to get into the habit of writing regularly (Becker 1986). This is because writing about your research helps you to clarify and work out your ideas, and writing also involves analysis of data. As Laurel Richardson says, 'writing is not just a mopping-up activity at the end of a research project. Writing is also a way of "knowing" – a method of discovery and analysis' (Richardson 1998: 345).

Writing *is* analysis, and Richardson argues that researchers 'can write up the same material in different ways. The material is malleable. That is why we call it material. How we shape the material depends upon how far along we are in our research, and who we want to read it, and for what reasons' (Richardson 1990: 49).

An interesting example is Margery Wolf's book, *A Thrice-Told Tale* (1992), which analyses an incident from ethnographic fieldwork in Peihotien, a Taiwanese village. Wolf presents the same material in three different forms: a fictional account called 'The Hot Spell', her fieldnotes and an article, 'The woman who didn't become a shaman,' originally published in the journal, *American Ethnologist*. Wolf says that each text 'takes a different perspective, is written in a different style, and has different "outcomes," yet all three involve the same set of events' (1992: 7). She adds that the three texts represent 'quite different versions of what had happened' (1992: 2). Wolf's analysis is interesting because it shows how data may be used in very different ways, and that questions of expected form, style and audience influence the 'believability' of research accounts. In addition, her book raises questions about whose interpretation of events is seen to count and the power dynamics that are present in any research text.

Student activity 3.7

1   Think about different writing styles that you use:

- How does the style you use for a work report differ to that you might use in a research report or in a journal article?
- How would your style in a research diary (see 'Being a reflexive practitioner–researcher', earlier in the chapter) differ from the style used to write up your thesis?

2   Think about ways that you can avoid repeating a 'work report' style in your research. Watch out for other common pitfalls too: e.g., personal 'rants' about the workplace and/or about 'other professional groups' don't belong in a research thesis.

Some tips for writing your research

Making time and space to write

Think about where and when you write best – try to develop habits that encourage you to write and discourage distractions. However, do take regular breaks. Set yourself (and agree these with your supervisor) realistic deadlines.

Style and presentation issues

Check the style requirements (e.g., layout, referencing style and so on) and expected thesis word length for your institution, as these differ. Use these guidelines from the start – this will save lots of editing later. Develop your writing 'voice' through examining and reworking your own style, looking at styles of others in your field and through feedback from your supervisor(s). Think about the audience for your work (e.g., the thesis has an academic audience, while summaries or reports may be intended for practitioners). Further thoughts and questions about your writing are examined in Plummer (2001: 172–3). Other helpful texts include Becker (1986); Richardson (1990, 1998); Wolcott (2001); Ward (2002); Veroff in Rudestam and Newton (2007)

Organizing/structuring

Break down your intended thesis into anticipated chapters and/or sections with an estimate of word length for each. Focus on one section at a time and stick to the required word length as much as you can. Plan your chapters or sections before writing and once you have drafted a chapter, then seek advice and revise it later (Wolcott 2001). Many researchers start with a literature review, move on to methodology and then on to the data/analysis chapters, but others suggest beginning with the data. Do your conclusion and introduction *last* when you know what you have said elsewhere.

Seeking feedback

Submit drafts of work for comments and discussion by your supervisor(s) as you write them. Discuss with them how often and how much they are able to read for you. Your work will be a priority for you, but your supervisor(s) will be dealing with many other things too, and so instant feedback in unlikely and should not be expected. You need to negotiate feedback with your supervisors, make agreements about what can be read and also give them prior warning and enough time to read through your work.

Taking constructive criticism

You must expect to receive some criticism of your work – everyone has to rework and redraft chapters. The idea that ' "real writers" (or "professionals" or "smart people") get it right the first time' is wrong (Becker 1986: 46). Ask for constructive criticism and get feedback on what you need to do, preferably in writing if you can, or make notes in supervision sessions. It's easy to forget what has been suggested in a face-to-face situation, and supervisors get frustrated or concerned by research students who appear to ignore sensible advice. Becker includes some helpful tips on editing your own work (Becker 1986: 79–89).

Conclusion

In this chapter we have focused on the researcher aspects of the practitioner–researcher role, emphasizing the importance of reading carefully and critically, developing a reflexive approach and planning your research from its inception. It can be seen that organization and planning at every stage of the research in professional practice will pay dividends: in time, in clarity of your emerging ideas and in the articulation of your final thesis and viva. Strategies such as keeping a research diary or learning journal and making notes of key ideas, issues and problems will provide a rich source of information for your writing and for discussion with your supervisor, student peers and professional colleagues.

Finally, remember that research is a process. Sometimes it takes a while to work out where you are going and what you are doing. Various stages (e.g., designing a proposal, working out a methodology, doing data analysis, writing chapters) will require significant reading, initial drafts, rethinking and reworking. In addition there are the issues of leading research in professional practice – to be considered in Chapter 5. Sometimes this will feel uncomfortable as you work out what you are trying to say and do.

Summary of key points

- Choose a topic for your dissertation for which you can maintain enthusiasm; also choose something which is contained and fits with the dissertation word length
- Build your support networks so they are there when you need them
- Be prepared for times when the going gets a bit tough and then talk things through
- Above all, embrace the opportunity to expand your knowledge and skills. Your professional doctorate can make a really valuable contribution to your area of practice, so both you and your workplace can gain

---

Notes

1 Stanley and Wise demonstrate this in an article that presents documentary and photographic data and their analysis of that data (see Stanley and Wise 2006).
2 For texts on auto/biography and research, see Stanley 1992; Plummer 2001; Roberts 2002.
3 The 'viva' is held after you submit your thesis, and your examiners will formally interview you about the research and thesis (see Chapter 7).
4 For further guidance on writing a research proposal, see Wield et al. 2002; Kelly 2004; Silverman 2004: ch. 9; Rudestam and Newton 2007.

4

Making the most of research supervision

Aims of the chapter

- To outline the principles of research supervision
- To discuss professional doctorate supervision: strengths, weaknesses, opportunities and threats
- To enhance your professional doctorate supervision experiences through application of the above

---

Introduction

The relationship between student and supervisor underpins the research process and outcomes on any doctoral programme. Wisker (2005: 1) describes it as, 'rewarding, essential, potentially taken for granted and relatively under theorised'. Supervision is a lengthy professional relationship, drawing on: coaching, reflective practice, the facilitation of research and professional expertise on the part of the supervisor; and the motivation, adaptability and intellectual capacity of the student. Despite its centrality to doctoral study, however, supervision practices, the experiences of doctoral students and the interactions between students and supervisors are comparatively under-researched (Delamont et al. 2000).

For example communications and supervision activities between student and supervisor are described as private (Boucher and Smyth 2004). Such privacy contrasts with the public information relating to supervision policies and practices, such as institutional codes of practice and research regulations. In summary the 'what' of supervision appears to be clearly publicized, whereas 'how' supervision is applied in practice remains essentially hidden between student and supervisors.

This chapter aims to illuminate professional doctorate supervision principles to enable you, the student, to reflect and plan strategies that best meet your professional needs. Such planning will require discussion with your supervisor and professional supervisor, if one is available, along with your student peers. It will also require a good understanding of the institutional policies and research regulations pertaining to your professional doctorate studies.

Initially the chapter will outline general supervision principles prior to exploration of the actual and potential issues related to professional doctorate supervision. The professional relationship between student and supervisor, and the role of professional supervisors and practitioner research issues will be explored. Strengths, weaknesses, opportunities and threats will then be used as a framework to reflect on professional doctorate supervision. Finally, there will be exploration of strategies to enhance the supervision experience through reflection on two case studies of professional doctorate supervision.

The characteristics and scope of research supervision

The Wikipedia (2007) definition of supervision is; 'The act of watching over the work or tasks of another, who may lack full knowledge of the concept at hand'. Supervisory concepts are applied widely in the doctoral setting to describe the important working relationship between the supervisor and student. Gray and Roy (2005) equate some aspects of research supervision to mentoring, with notions of guiding and helping the doctoral student through the complex and challenging process of research. McKenna and Cutcliffe (2001) describe supervision as an expert skill requiring in-depth knowledge of the research subject; something usually only undertaken by experienced academics who have already successfully supervised other doctoral students.

As doctoral studies encompass a wide range of subjects and professional disciplines, there are clearly going to be varied styles and approaches to research supervision in order to meet student need and subject/professional requirements effectively. Delamont et al. (2000) explore supervision styles and strategies in their text, *The Doctoral Experience*. For example they explain that within a laboratory based discipline doctoral students may work and study alongside each other, as part of a larger research team, thus learning from and supporting each other. In contrast, within the social sciences, doctoral students may work independently on individual research projects, and may be more dependent on the relationship with the supervisor or a small supervisory team.

Supervision precepts and standards

The Quality Assurance Agency for Higher Education (QAA) has precepts or standards for all postgraduate research programmes, including professional doctorates. Precepts 11 to 14 focus on supervision requirements, while the others relate to standards for admissions to research degree programmes; the quality of the student learning environment; strategies for student progress and review of studies, appropriate institutional mechanisms for obtaining student feedback; and the conduct of student complaints and appeals.

The following is a summary of the supervision precepts. In the first instance the appointment of supervisors with suitable subject expertise and supervisory skills commensurate with the needs of students are emphasized, along with the need for supervisors to support, encourage and also monitor student progress effectively. There is a clear requirement for students to have access to at least one named supervisor during their doctoral studies, although the increasing use of supervisory teams is also discussed. The importance of having supervisors adequately trained for supervision and with the workload capacity for supervision is acknowledged. Furthermore the roles and responsibilities of students and supervisors should be clearly outlined in written guidelines and university policies (QAA 2004). The supervision precepts are summarized below in Figure 4.1, while the Code of Practice for the Assurance of Academic

Precept Eleven	Institutions will appoint supervisors who have the appropriate skills and subject knowledge to support, encourage and monitor research students effectively.
Precept Twelve	Each research student will have a minimum of one main supervisor. He or she will normally be part of a supervision team. There must always be one clearly identified point of contact for the student.
Precept Thirteen	Institutions will ensure that the responsibilities of all research student supervisors are clearly communicated to supervisors and students through written guidance.
Precept Fourteen	Institutions will ensure that the quality of supervision is not put at risk as a result of an excessive volume and range of responsibilities assigned to individual supervisors.

Figure 4.1 Supervision precepts

Source: QAA (2004).

Quality and Standards in Higher Education, section 1: Post Graduate Research Programmes is available in full from the QAA website (www.qaa.ac.uk).

That supervision processes are critical within the doctoral student experience is evident in the research study undertaken by Delamont et al. (2000). This sought to establish student and supervisor experiences during doctoral study using interviews and in-depth discussion. The limitations of these data collection methods were themselves critiqued by the authors on the basis that participants could potentially discuss what they *thought* they were developing in supervision: the espoused principles of supervision, as opposed to *actual* supervision practices. In essence there was potential for participants to discuss or disclose only what they thought the researchers wanted to hear. However, the direct observation of supervision practices was considered too intrusive.

Despite the challenges of data collection the authors found that difficulties or controversies within the supervision experience were not uncommon. One issue identified was the difficulty in establishing a rapport or working relationship between the doctoral student and supervisor. Supervisors in the study tended to base their practice of supervision on their own doctoral experiences. Generally these were perceived as negative and non-supportive, with supervisors subsequently wanting to facilitate a much more academic and stimulating experience for their own students (Delamont et al. 2000).

The above study uncovered several important themes. For example supervisors described a tension or conflict between enabling independence, originality and creativity in the students' development of research ideas, and the supervisors' perceived need to manage the supervision situation formally within accepted parameters. Another emerging theme was the tension that could arise if the student's doctoral study was too closely related to the subject expertise of the supervisor, and the supervisory temptation to encourage the student to reproduce that work or conform on methodological issues. This issue has also been explored by Cryer (2000). The supervisor participants in the study by Delamont et al. stated that students required independence and motivation to be creative and innovative in their doctoral studies, whereas Delamont et al. (2000) identified that the student experience at undergraduate level may not have prepared them for such a radical shift in the academic experience, moving from mastery of knowledge to the development of knowledge itself using creative research approaches.

The development of evidence based practice in health care settings potentially illustrates this point. For example the demand for evidence based practice requires that practice be based on research based protocols, guidelines and empirical evidence. While this may be highly appropriate to care management and delivery, and it is laudable to justify and apply care on the basis of best knowledge and expertise, evidence based practice has its critics. It negates the knowledge and skill acquired through extensive professional practice and experience. In summary, students may be so accustomed to justifying or using the available evidence to practise, that independent thinking and creativity become more difficult or they are not encouraged at all.

The characteristics of supervision

Supervision on any doctoral programme should have potential for the following characteristics:

- Trust, good communication and honesty between student and supervisor
- The potential to enhance student motivation and confidence through supervisor encouragement and coaching
- Regular meetings and tutorials to provide support and guidance through the research process
- Mutual interest, curiosity and enthusiasm for the research topic
- The reading of students' written work and provision of constructive feedback within a mutually acceptable timeframe
- Advice about the student's research training opportunities
- Facilitation and guidance for students to write papers and attend conferences to share/disseminate their experiences with others
- The promotion of student independence throughout the research process
- The student's development of critical thinking, critical reflection and critical analysis during the research process and beyond
- The facilitation of the student's problem solving abilities
- Personal development planning for the student
- The celebration of student achievements
- Preparation for the key milestones of doctoral study: interim review, thesis submission and viva
- Consideration of postdoctoral developments and career planning

   Golde and Dore (2001) identified the key characteristics that doctoral students valued in their supervisors:

- A supervisor with the same or similar research interests to them
- A supervisor who was already involved in interesting research
- A supervisor with an established reputation for student supervision
- A supervisor with knowledge and experience of the research methods to be used
- A supervisor who actually wanted the supervision work!
- A supervisor who ensured the student achieved the best and most rigorous research possible

Choosing a supervisor

At the beginning of the doctoral journey students may not know what to expect or what they require from supervision. Matching as yet unknown student expectations with the experience of a supervisor can be difficult. However, the practical strategies that can help this process will be explored in the following sections. For example McKenna and Cutcliffe (2001) advocate mutual decision making, where the student may enquire about supervisor possibilities and may make a contribution in choosing their supervisor.

In order to do this you should ask about supervision at the informal discussion or application stage for your professional doctorate. Discuss your research ideas and preferences in as much detail as possible with the professional doctorate programme leader and/or postgraduate admissions tutor and in your initial research proposal. In addition you can find out more about supervisor availability by reviewing staff web profiles, research centre websites and university research information. Alternatively reading the professional literature will help you identify who is already undertaking research in similar areas. Another strategy is to ask to speak to another professional doctorate student and find out about their perceptions and experiences of supervision (Phillips and Pugh 2000).

There are four elements to consider in relation to research supervision:

1 The subject/research interests of the supervisor and their methodological interests
2 Your learning styles and preferences
3 The professional experience/professional insight of the supervisor
4 Their knowledge of doctoral requirements

The subject/research interests of the supervisor

This is self-explanatory: your supervisor should be able to demonstrate knowledge of your subject area or at least a shared interest in the research focus. There are positives and negatives associated with having a supervisor renowned for particular subject expertise. For example the supervisor may be tempted to encourage you to replicate their own research or to use a particular research method. In addition an internationally renowned researcher may be simply too busy with an established research programme and other doctoral students.

On the other hand, such a supervisor with extensive research expertise in your topic area will have an excellent command of the literature and current research developments. They are likely to be aware of methodological pitfalls and have access to extremely good learning networks, interest groups or societies that can use their expertise to inform your research and they can help you raise your research and professional profile.

Your learning styles and preferences

It is important to know your learning style and preferences when considering supervision. On the one hand, it could be argued that in such an important relationship there should be synergy between student and supervisor, and there should be shared values and beliefs about the processes of doctoral study. On the other hand, this could potentially contribute to an overly familiar or stable doctoral experience, where the student is not challenged sufficiently in their thinking and research practices. In essence the student may not be exposed to new ideas or practices beyond those already in their subject or professional repertoire. Challenge to accepted values and beliefs may seem destabilizing; however, it will stimulate new ideas and foster creativity.

Also think about your response to study deadlines. For example if you prefer monthly tutorials, produce copious drafts of written work and outline ideas, while your supervisor prefers a more distant, facilitative approach, then there is likely to be frustration for both parties. It is important to discuss your preferences clearly with your supervisor at the outset, and gain a good appreciation of what they also consider realistic and feasible in the time available to them. It may be an institutional requirement that this discussion is acknowledged and shared formally through the mutual development of a learning contract/agreement, detailing expectations and strategies for the supervision processes.

The professional experience/insight of the supervisor

In addition to having a supervisor with subject and methodological expertise it is important to consider their relationships with professional practice. For example what is their knowledge and understanding of your professional context, their understanding of contemporary practice issues, and their experience of undertaking and supervising research in the professional practice setting? Supervisors need to be sensitive to real world research issues and have understanding and experience of the student's challenge of being a practitioner–researcher. This requires the supervisor's ability to acknowledge and discuss professional supervision issues arising during research. It also requires discussion and reflection on strategies for and in action, as they relate to the development and application of research in professional practice. Some subject areas may require a formal supervisor from the student's professional milieu as opposed to informal or advisory requirements. This issue will be explored in detail later in this chapter.

Supervision and socialization within a subject discipline

Delamont et al. (2000) argue that supervision is concerned with more than the acquisition of research skill and emerging original knowledge to satisfy the criteria for doctoral study. They suggest, for example, that the process involves socialization into the prevailing norms, values and beliefs of the discipline. In essence supervision is also concerned with the student's further development and identification with a discipline or subject identity. How this may work for a professional doctorate student, who may already have an established professional identity, is a relatively unknown phenomenon and is worthy of further study.

Trocchia and Berkowitz (1999) employed in-depth interviews with students and academics associated with a marketing doctoral programme to illuminate how students were socialized into the academic world and the factors enhancing student success. Four themes emerged from examination of the formal and informal environment associated with the doctoral programme. The former was concerned with the overall structure of the doctoral programme, while the latter was concerned with communication and interaction between supervisors and students. The four themes identified were:

1 Nurturing
2 Top–down learning approaches
3 Near peer supervisors
4 Platonistic supervision

Nurturing

The first theme explored by the authors related to 'nurturing'. This was used to describe the informal guidance provided by academics, other students and within the wider learning environment. The use of facilitative coaching styles was said to enable students to focus on their research ideas and guide them through a process to clarify their aims. While some students found this experience positive and supportive, others later wished they had utilized more independence in the study process and had less exposure to nurturing characteristics. For example they reflected that independence would have enabled consideration of a wider range of research options and approaches, or that they would have been more adventurous with their research ideas and design.

Top–down learning approaches

Students exposed to the second theme of 'top-down' learning approaches had access to structured, formal studies within their doctorate programme. In this context the students tended to manage themselves and seek more independent learning opportunities with less guidance from their supervisor. Students identified within the second theme tended to have more intellectual independence, and could be critical of the formal taught elements, seminars or training, viewing them as irrelevant and impeding their studies (Trocchia and Berkowitz 1999).

Near peer supervisors

The third theme identified by Trocchia and Berkowitz (1999) was that of the choice of 'near peer' supervisors. These students were said to develop close affiliation with their supervisor or mentor, seeking academics with similar interests and learning from their example, based on the principles of role modelling. In some cases students wished to emulate the supervisor's achievements and developed strong and enduring mentorship based friendships with them beyond the original study encounter.

Platonistic supervision

Finally, the 'platonistic' theme reflected supervision whereby students received very little guidance regarding their research ideas beyond being exhorted to investigate the topic and bring back issues for further questioning and discussion. Such students were described as enthusiastic and self-motivated. The study by Trocchia and Berkowitz provides fascinating insight into the relationship between academic socialization, supervision styles and student learning preferences, not withstanding the fact it is based on interview data – a challenge raised by Delamont et al. (2000). It also raises the possibility of varied supervision styles and how these may influence individual student learning and development.

Exploring professional doctorate supervision

Supervisors or advisers: what is the difference?

The terms 'supervisor' and 'student' are used pragmatically in this chapter, as they are used widely within doctoral studies. However, they are used while taking account of the discussion below. For example given the principles of professional doctorates and the characteristics of many of the students who undertake them, with significant professional and life experience, it is questionable if the term 'supervision', with connotations of overseeing work and hierarchy, is a suitable term or guiding concept. (Green and Powell 2005) argue that the changes in doctoral opportunities and the student population, as explored in Chapter 1, necessitate ensuing changes in attitudes to supervision and actual supervision style. Meanwhile Gregory (1995) also advocates equality between supervisor and student, with an advisory rather than supervisory approach, commensurate with the professional or practice experience of the student. In summary, some may use the term 'supervision', taking cognisance of the discussion above, while others use the term 'adviser' to denote a mutual partnership and collaborative approach.

Supervision teams

The discussion to date has also largely implied supervision as a process between one supervisor and one student. However, McKenna and Cutcliffe

(2001) also acknowledge the increasing use of supervision teams. One supervisor may have overall responsibility for your doctoral studies, while a co-supervisor may provide subject, methodological or professional support. Given the complexity of professional doctorate research – subject expertise, the acquisition of research skills combined with professional knowledge and insight, along with the learning preferences of the student – it is highly unlikely that one supervisor can fully engage with all those elements.

The author's own institution's policy, for example, requires a supervisor, co-supervisor and personal teacher. The former should work together in the supervision process, while the latter, the personal teacher, is concerned with pastoral or welfare issues for the student (University of Salford 2007). Supervision teams are also advocated elsewhere in the literature, for example Maxwell and Shanahan (1997). Kemp (2004) questions the suitability of using a one-to-one model of supervision within professional doctorate programmes, suggesting that this model has originated with and dominated PhD studies.

Facilitating professional doctorate supervision

Evans (1997) implies that for a professional doctorate student supervision should be facilitative, as opposed to directive, helping to clarify the research aims and identify the resources available to undertake the research and supporting the student, particularly with balancing the challenges of professional life, work and study. In summary, the student's personal and professional experience is brought to supervision and will influence the dynamics of that relationship. The common element within the literature explored in this section to date implies difference in supervision style to facilitate the development of professional doctorate students and to take account of the issues implicit within practitioner research. What does not emerge so clearly is what constitutes a model or framework to underpin professional doctorate supervision.

While expertise relating to the research focus, the professional setting and the research methods are clearly important, students appear to want a supervisor who also knows what doctoral study involves, can recognize doctoral level work and can help the student navigate the processes involved. An exploratory study by Lee (2007) found that professional doctorate students with health backgrounds were focused on pragmatic issues when they vocalized their supervision expectations. For example they wanted a supervisor who would help them get through the research, who knew what a doctorate looked like and who was approachable and accessible.

In an earlier study Ellis (2006) also found that nurses undertaking a professional doctorate wanted a supervisor who was accessible, and had high standards and expectations for the student to follow. In addition a supervisor who provided a challenging agenda or helped to drive the research process forward by stimulating and engaging with the student was prefered. The same student expectations have also been identified by Phillips and Pugh (2000).

Lee (2007) found that students worried about being excessive in their use of supervision, being too demanding or needy. One way to overcome this is to explore perceptions and expectations at the outset of supervision, with identification of roles and responsibilities in relation to contact time; what is to be produced prior to supervision meetings; and timely supervisor response and feedback regarding student work. Keeping a supervision log or record is strongly advised, as student and supervisor will inevitably forget the detail of discussion. An electronic record can be shared between all parties concerned and can help open and honest communication.

When embarking on the professional doctorate it is important you understand the relevant institutional codes of practice and research regulations relating to your studies. Do make time to attend institutional induction events, which will outline the role and responsibilities of supervisors and students. Such events are also an important networking opportunity where you can meet other doctoral students. It is tempting to let such events pass by because you are busy in your professional role, don't want to make an extra journey or have a fixed view of what supervision entails. However, supervision is an important process within the study experience and good foundations and planning are important.

Professional doctorate supervision and professional practice synergy

The legitimacy of professional knowledge and practice are implied within a professional doctorate. The student is required to engage with knowledge and expertise derived from the study of the professional context, using this knowledge to enhance practice. This clearly requires leadership and professional skill beyond methodological skill on the part of the student, along with supervisor understanding of the professional context. One means of achieving synergy is to include a professional supervisor or adviser drawn from the student's professional setting within the supervision team.

Scott et al. (2004) describe the engineering doctorate (EngD) where students may have an industrial mentor in addition to an academic supervisor. A professional supervisor may be a requirement in some disciplines, contributing to the overall assessment of the study and participating in key assessment milestones. There is no national or international consensus regarding the use of professional supervisors, and there are arguments for and against their use.

For example a professional supervisor with experience of the organization, who operates at a senior level with a good understanding of the challenges of research in practice, could guide the student through some of the research processes and in some ways help to smooth the pathway for the student. In summary, they could have the potential to act as a champion within the student's professional practice setting. Maxwell and Shanahan (1997) advocate the development of new, collegiate relationships to promote professional doctorate supervision. These require acknowledgement and combination of the research methodological expertise of the academic supervisor with professional understanding of that particular practice context. The authors advocate a collaborative approach to supervision as opposed to supervision in terms of formal oversight of the student's research work.

Evans (1998) suggests that achieving balance and integration between the roles of academic and professional supervisors respectively has the potential for challenge, as the responsibilities for research quality and standards, usually the domain of academia, are shared with an external stakeholder in that situation. Regardless of whether professional supervision or advice is a formal requirement, identification of mentorship and support in professional practice is an important aspect of student support.

Ethical issues in professional doctorate supervision

While ethical principles and seeking ethical approval are explored in detail in Chapter 6, this section will focus on practitioner research and ethical conduct within the supervisory relationship.

The impact of research in the professional setting

Research in the professional practice context raises ethical issues in relation to confidentiality and potential conflict between organizational and research aims, for example. Negotiation and exploration of role and responsibility, and discussion of research ethics are essential regardless of whether professional supervision is a formal or informal process. In addition the management and integration of the roles of researcher and practitioner in the professional context require clarification. For example if the student is involved in an ethnographic study, how will it be made explicit to other colleagues, service users and others, when fieldwork is or is not being undertaken? In meetings, for example, how will it be made explicit when the professional is acting as practitioner–researcher as opposed to professional representative? Importantly, how will poor practice or dangerous practice be addressed, and how is this to be made transparent to participants? Clearly such practice cannot remain confidential or anonymous; there are implications here for your wider responsibilities as a professional. In addition it is possible that the role of practitioner–researcher may be viewed with suspicion by the student's professional colleagues. They may perceive research into practice as negative or a form of checking up. For example Delamont et al. (2000) describe the challenges of gaining or negotiating access to the research setting to explore perceptions of research supervision, even when they were already well known in that context.

Boucher and Smyth (2004) outline other ethical issues in supervision, especially if the subsequent application of research findings will influence the role/experiences of others in that setting. For example, as a result of research, some professional roles may change or disappear completely, while other areas for practice development may be identified, possibly causing embarrassment in the organization if this implies key targets or requirements are not being met. In terms of supervision it is important to explore the supervisor's willingness and capability to reflect on the issues identified above and similarly to explore them in the professional milieu in order to strengthen the professional practice aspects of your research.

In combination, the above characteristics have significant implications for professional doctorate students. Ellis (2006) reports on the findings from professional doctorates for nurses and midwives in Australia. Process issues related to study, such as gaining access to research participants, ethics and even choice of research focus, could be potentially problematic. Clearly the use of a professional mentor or adviser from the practice setting can potentially help in guiding the student through such practice related difficulties, providing of course a suitable adviser could be found. Figure 4.2 summarizes the ethical questions to be addressed through supervisory mechanisms.

- What are the actual or potential ethical implications of professional practitioners researching and influencing their professional context?
- How should sensitive findings, which may impact on professional practice or future organizational arrangements, be managed?
- How will the research process be facilitated? How will sensitive professional issues, dealing with potential resistance, change management, leadership be supported in the organization and through supervision?
- How are the roles of professional practitioner–researcher to be integrated with the student's professional practice?
- How are the respective roles of student researcher and experienced professional to be managed?
- How will the role of practitioner–researcher be perceived by students' professional colleagues?
- How will other stakeholders, service users, clients, consumers and others perceive the researcher–practitioner overlap and ensuing developments generated through professional doctorate study?
- How will the professional doctorate and subsequent research development and application influence the roles/experiences of others in the students' professional setting?
- How will the impact of research in the professional area be managed in terms of future practice?
- How will poor/dangerous practice identified as a result of the student's research activities be managed, and how will this be explained to participants prior to the student's research?

Figure 4.2 Potential ethical questions to be addressed through supervision

The dynamics of supervisor/practitioner researcher relationships

Discussion of ethical issues to date has focused on the professional practice setting, however Boucher and Smyth (2004) also explore the relationships between students and supervisors themselves. On the one hand, it may be positive to work with professionals who have great intrinsic motivation and capacity for learning, combined with significant life and professional experience. On the other, it is possible students in such groups are already known to the supervisors through professional networks or from prior postgraduate study (Boucher and Smyth 2004). Potential tension may develop between personal friendship and supervision as boundaries become blurred.

The authors argue, however, that in professional doctorate supervision the students are less dependent within the supervisory relationship and therefore less open to potential abuse by virtue of being employed externally in professional practice. They are not, for example, research assistants or graduate teaching assistants, dependent on their research supervisors for employment. While ethics relating to role, identity and professional practice have been outlined here, there will be further discussion of ethical issues relating to research in Chapter 6. Meanwhile the case studies at the end of this chapter aim to illuminate some potential issues related to professional doctorate supervision.

Strengths and opportunities within professional doctorate supervision

There are potential strengths and opportunities regarding professional doctorate supervision for students and supervisors. The first and most important is the opportunity for the student to make a real difference to the way professional practice is shaped followed by the opportunity to develop innovative and creative knowledge to underpin that practice. Research and the investigation of practice by the practitioner–researcher themselves has the potential to reduce the theory–practice gap (McKenna 1997).

There is also opportunity for the supervisor to share the process of practitioner research, facilitating its development and experiencing mutual learning and reciprocity. Such exposure to contemporary practice knowledge and skill will enhance the supervisor's own practice as facilitator and supervisor elsewhere, and potentially enhance other aspects of the academic role by keeping the supervisor up to date with cutting edge developments, for example (Evans 1998). Supervision is considered to be a shared learning opportunity as opposed to a one-way, directive learning system. It is also an opportunity for supervision based on equality and partnership. Lee's (2007) exploratory study of supervisor and student perceptions of professional doctorate research supervision found that professional doctorate students regarded supervision as a two-way exchange of learning and ideas. For example Isabelle, one of the participants in the study, commented that: 'It is helping with my research but I think there is also an element of joined up learning . . . if I was research supervisor, the role was reversed, you should both be learning together, that's how I see it.' While this view clearly relates to opportunities within the academic relationship between student and supervisor, there are additional sources of guidance and support that can be used to develop innovative approaches to supervision. Communities of practice, as explored in Chapter 2, and the opportunities to develop cohesive peer support and professional networks are a strong feature of professional doctorates. Considering supervision as multi-faceted strands of research development and learning, drawing on varied expertise and resources rather than reliance on one individual, clearly has an advantage in terms of access to more ideas, resources, support and access to other networks.

Weaknesses and threats within professional doctorate supervision

While the previous section lists possible strengths and opportunities, there are also potential weaknesses and threats within professional doctorate supervision. Evans (1997, 1998) identified the need for an adapted supervision style, when students were equal to the supervisor in terms of professional experience and stature – a point also explored in Chapter 2 in relation to student expectations. Elsewhere it is suggested that students from professional backgrounds have greater needs for varied supervision approaches and for broader interests and styles in their supervisors (Boucher and Smyth 2004; Boud and Tennant 2006).

From both student and supervisor there is also recognition that others must be included in the research process, as professional practice research may impact on service delivery, user experience and other professionals' working lives. In some sectors, for example, the use of participatory action research has the potential to challenge established views of service users and professionals, empowering the former to make an active contribution and determine service delivery.

Lee (2007) found that professional doctorate students in health care did not make sufficient use of professional peers in their practice setting when conceptualizing and designing their research projects. There was a sense that the students were the owners of the research and as such it was their responsibility to achieve the doctorate. While responsibility for doctoral success may ultimately rest with the student and supervisor, it is essential to involve key players from the students' organization or professional practice setting, actively seeking advice and participation.

A key study by Heath (2005) explores research supervision within professional doctorates with specific focus on an education doctorate. Several weaknesses and threats are identified in relation to professional doctorate research supervision. Given the scope of the professional doctorate with research application and development in professional practice, does this require supervision that takes account of and has knowledge of the professional practice challenges? This is especially challenging according to Heath (2005), given that currently most professional doctorate students are supervised by those who have a PhD. Other issues were raised in the study relating to conflict between professional and academic culture. Such conflict could be related to contrasting values and beliefs regarding knowledge, or conflict regarding the practical realities of research in a changing professional practice context.

Kemp (2004) explains that staff involved with professional doctorates should be specialized in the requisite professional practice area. She also goes on to outline some potential issues here, as, given the relative newness of professional doctorates, many research supervisors are steeped in the expectations and conventions associated with the PhD.

Case studies of professional doctorate supervision

There follows two case studies which illuminate the potential strengths and weaknesses of professional doctorate supervision. Use them to think about your expectations of professional doctorate supervision and to develop effective supervision strategies. Discuss your expectations with your supervision team, and develop a clear outline of roles and responsibilities. Many institutions will require that this information is used as the basis of a learning contract or agreement between supervisor(s) and student.

When supervision is positive

Olga's story

Olga is entering year three of a part-time five-year professional doctorate programme. She has established good supervisory processes and wider support networks to address professional issues. She met her academic supervisor during the university orientation days, and was able to discuss her research ideas during the modular components of the programme before starting her research project. This, in combination with discussion in her professional setting and reflection in her student learning group, has helped Olga to realize that her initial research ideas were too broad and that she needed to clarify her focus. In addition the supervisor was able to give her details about a forthcoming seminar related to her research topic.

While Olga has a supervisor and co-supervisor she does not have a formal professional supervisor in the practice setting, drawing instead on close professional colleagues to advise and trouble shoot in the practice setting. In addition she brings significant issues to the student learning group, which meets on a regular basis through the doctoral programme. Olga is examining bullying in secondary schools and is evaluating the introduction of student councils as part of a positive strategy to reduce bullying. She is using a participatory action research approach to establish student involvement in bullying prevention. The research has been discussed and planned in conjunction with student council members, teaching staff and student 'ambassadors', who have a role to play in minimizing bullying on some of the public transport networks to and from school.

Initially Olga's teacher colleagues were cynical about the research, and there was some resistance from the school governors who did not want the school to develop a reputation for bullying. There were also concerns about student involvement in the design and implementation of the research; that it would detract from student coursework, and that they would find it difficult to engage with such a sensitive issue.

Olga initially presented her research proposal to teaching staff and governors, and the supervisor attended both sessions. It was agreed that the study would focus on Year 7 and Year 8 students. In addition there were sensitive issues to be explored in relation to obtaining consent from the students and their parents for participation in the study. With support from the supervisor Olga was able to explore these and wider ethical issues with the head teacher and an education adviser at the Metropolitan Borough Council, where the school was located. There was then wider dissemination of the project within the school and through parental/guardian newsletters. As a requirement for the project to proceed there was emphasis that existing school policies be used within the project should any student disclose that they were already being bullied.

Olga describes the supervisory relationship as open and stimulating. There was initial discussion and exploration with her supervisors regarding feedback, email access and face-to-face contact. She has agreed to meet with her main supervisor on a monthly basis, and to meet with both supervisors every three months. In the interim the supervision team and Olga communicate by email, copying each other into any messages. Olga keeps a record of supervision and tutorials, and emails this to the supervision team after each discussion. There was agreement that any published papers would be authored by Olga, being co-authored by the supervisor if the supervisor was co-writing a substantial piece of the publication.

In addition Olga attended university training days on how to manage the supervision process.

More than the formal issues explored above, Olga is aware that the supervisor

> is interested in her research topic and has specific methodological expertise to offer. The supervisor has been involved in action research projects in primary and secondary settings and appears to have a good grasp of the realities of research in professional practice. She has recommended Olga join the local action learning network and has encouraged her to attend relevant seminars and conferences. The co-supervisor is a former secondary school teacher who has recently joined the academic department where Olga is studying. As such she has a good knowledge of the research setting and has provided practical advice about how to address some of the challenges in the study.

There are some good practices in the above case study. First, there is good communication between the supervisory team and Olga, roles were clearly defined at the outset and there was some agreement about supervision arrangements, notes of meetings and the timing of feedback.

While Olga does not appear to have a formal professional supervisor from within her school, both supervisors have good insight into the practice setting, with experience of researching and working there. In addition Olga has good communication channels within the school and has identified informal support mechanisms there. There is mention of a doctoral student group, who can also provide peer support from a more objective stance as they are not directly related to the professional practice setting or the research focus.

Olga is beginning to widen her networks through participation in a local action research network and attendance at seminars and study days. In addition there is agreement regarding the authorship of publications, a possible bone of contention if not explored openly and honestly, explaining mutual contributions and the roles of student and supervisor.

When supervision is challenging

> ### Paul's story
>
> 'I am an Approved Social Worker within a drugs team, operating within a voluntary agency. The Team Leader wants to further develop outreach drugs services and change some aspects of my role. So far I have resisted as I already have a heavy caseload and find it difficult to integrate my professional role with doctoral study. Consequently this has soured our professional relations.
>
> I am also in the second year of a social work doctorate at the local university where I am an honorary lecturer and where I have previously undertaken a masters' degree. In some ways this is an advantage as I know the professional doctorate team and I work with my personal teacher on other teaching activities, for example the MA Social Work programme. In other ways it is difficult as my personal teacher uses my tutorial time to discuss timetables and related MA issues rather than focusing on my doctoral studies.
>
> As part of the progression from the modular part of the DSW (Doctorate in

Social Work) to the research element I am required to submit a detailed research proposal. I am actually very interested in developing a case study or action research approach to examine the implications of advanced practitioner roles within social work and the team leader is enthusiastic about this focus as the subject links with the development of outreach services. I am also very interested in examining adolescent perceptions of recreational drug use. I have been dissuaded from this focus due to difficulties negotiating access to this group, particularly those under the age of 18.

My research supervisor worked in child protection before their academic career and seems preoccupied with access and ethics issues. This is the second supervisor I have had; the first one went off sick. My teaching colleagues from the MA Social Work programme have said they will "help me all they can" but they seem too busy with their own research activities.

As if this wasn't enough the drugs team is under scrutiny as part of an agency review and a major re-organization is in the offing. I don't know where my professional role will fit into the new structure.'

(Paul)

'I took on Paul's supervision as a favour, as one of my colleagues was off sick. I thought I would just be standing in for a few weeks, but my colleague is off sick long term. I already have five full-time PhD students to supervise; one of them is a research assistant on an ESRC funded research programme. Their research is cutting edge stuff and I am keen to get on and use the research material in my forthcoming book.

Anyway, returning to Paul. I have tried to develop a rapport, but I find his approach to studies haphazard. He frequently cancels tutorials, or just turns up with no development since the last meeting. He has also expressed interest in adolescents and recreational drugs; that interests me as it ties in with my methodological expertise in phenomenology. However, he needs to think this through and clarify his research aim/objectives and subsequent strategies.

Pragmatically Paul will have to decide something as he must submit a detailed research proposal shortly. I have been quite blunt and suggested a phenomenological approach investigating the experiences of adolescent drug users. I have suggested he completes an advanced qualitative research module and attends my forthcoming seminar on phenomenology.

My main concern with Paul is that he seems to lack focus; he is not as independent as my PhD students, all of whom are full-time. He seems to want me to help all the time, rather than him going off and deciding what to do. I have told him that doctoral study requires creativity and independence; he needs to be more autonomous.

Another problem with Paul is that he brings a lot of day-to-day professional issues for discussion. For example he says his role may change in the future and this may impact on his research. I have advised him to discuss these issues with his manager in practice.'

(Freda, Paul's supervisor)

This second case study illuminates communication issues, role and responsibilities, professional boundaries and expectations of part-time students. Furthermore there are issues regarding the allocation of supervisors and workload balance within the academic department concerned, along with the challenges of researching professional practice.

Paul needs to communicate his concerns regarding changes to his role with his team leader in the first instance, and discuss the requirements of his doctoral studies. If he has a mentor or informal professional adviser in practice he should draw on their expertise and consider a range of options. As stated earlier in the chapter, having a mentor or informal adviser is essential with practitioner research. This should be an experienced professional who knows the context well and can provide good support. Such support would be helpful prior to any detailed discussion with his team leader. It needs to be underpinned by Paul's professional reflection on the situation and draw on the views of his professional colleagues, in addition to his reading around the potential research areas.

Professional boundaries between Paul and his personal teacher are blurred as they work together on the MA programme. It may be best if Paul has another personal teacher not connected with his teaching responsibilities in the academic department, and Paul needs to explore his concerns with the personal teacher regarding his tutorial time. Both parties need to develop frameworks and practice whereby personal teacher time for Paul is not contaminated by discussion of other workload issues.

The supervisor should communicate her concerns with Paul and find out his perceptions of progress to date. The case study implies that the supervisor is perhaps not accustomed to working with part-time students and is having difficulty adapting supervision styles to meet his professional needs. There is also a focus on methodological issues that may meet the supervisor's interests rather than Paul's interest. It is not clear what insight the supervisor has in relation to Paul's practice as an approved social worker; it would help if the supervisor had an appreciation of his professional role and how this relates to the development of his research.

In the final analysis the supervisor has taken on Paul's supervision as a favour. Both Paul and his supervisor need to be open and honest about how progress is developing and explore their options with the professional doctorate programme leader and/or postgraduate admissions tutor. If Paul's supervisor has too many students to supervise already this should be explored actively within the academic department concerned.

Even though the supervisor may have felt they were helping with Paul's supervision and they were helping the department while a colleague was sick, they are possibly adding to his problems. While Paul's colleagues from the MA programme are well meaning in their exhortations of help, they are possibly doing more harm than good with their offers of help.

Conclusion

This chapter has introduced and explored the principles of research supervision prior to consideration of supervision within professional doctorate programmes. Some parameters for supervision have been outlined. In some instances a formal professional supervisor from the student's area of practice may be a professional doctorate requirement, whereas informal, advisory mechanisms may be advocated in other areas. Whatever approach is used it is clear that there needs to be transparency of understanding regarding research in professional practice settings, possible ethical issues and challenges of communication.

In addition, given that many professional doctorate students have already accrued professional knowledge and experience prior to embarking on doctoral studies, there are potential ethical issues for student supervisory relationships. Contemporary literature implies that supervisors need to adapt their supervision styles to meet the needs of such experienced doctoral students, who potentially may have as much if not more experience of professional practice than their supervisors may possess.

Student planning for the supervision process is as important as paying attention to the research topic, professional and methodological issues. Evidence indicates that doctoral students are relatively under-prepared for the supervision process and have poorly developed expectations. The use of learning agreements can be a starting point to explore mutual expectations of supervision. In addition institutions offer doctoral training programmes that will include discussion of supervision principles, formal requirements and some pointers on managing the supervision process. For professional doctorate students, a supervisor who has insight and appreciates the sensitivity of research in the practice setting is important.

Some programmes may or may not require the formal appointment of a professional supervisor, from the student's practice area, who will make an active contribution to the summative assessment of student progress. If this is not the case then the use of a professional mentor or adviser is strongly recommended; they should be someone who the student can trust, who knows the student's practice context well and can help them negotiate and explore some of the issues that will arise during the study process. In addition the use of doctoral peers and group discussion to raise and explore supervision issues is important. In the final analysis, good communication is the key to good supervision.

Summary of key points

- Supervision is a facilitative, helping process, based on open and honest communication in the supervision team, and requiring curiosity and enthusiasm from student and supervisor respectively
- The QAA (2004) outline the principal requirements for research supervision, regardless of the nature of the doctoral programme
- Potential ethical issues related to practitioner research require supervisor understanding of professional practice and sensitivity to practice issues. There may be a formal requirement for supervisor involvement from the student's area of professional practice within a professional doctorate. If there is no formal requirement, a professional adviser or mentor is strongly encouraged
- Within a professional doctorate programme supervision should have the potential to be a two-way process of learning and sharing, to take account of the professional experience already accrued by the student
- Remember supervisors are there to challenge your thinking and ideas. Such challenge is an essential part of the doctoral study, as is your ability to debate and discuss critically; don't be offended by challenge

5

Developing a professional toolkit: leading research in professional practice

Ray Stansfield and Nancy Lee

Aims of the chapter

- To critically appraise leadership theories and concepts
- To reflect on the interface between leadership and professional doctorate research
- To consider strategies for leading research in professional practice

---

Introduction

Leadership has a profound influence on our personal and professional lives. Whether we are speculating on leadership skill at the macro level of government influence and decision making or reflecting at the micro level of our workplace practice, everyone has an opinion on leadership. The principles of leadership are presented to us in a variety of ways. Espoused theories are well rehearsed in the academic literature, and the extensive coaching literature explores leadership related to personal success and growth. Elsewhere the underside of leadership has been explored in popular literature, for example the popular political thriller, *House of Cards* by Michael Dobbs. Leadership is also a mainstay of political diaries. In summary, leadership studies represent a complex field for the professional doctorate student to navigate and reflect upon in relation to leading research in professional practice.

Why lead research in professional practice?

It is perhaps more usual for doctoral students to focus on the development of their subject expertise and associated knowledge of research methodology. However, implicit within the professional doctorate is the concept of knowledge, skill and expertise being generated directly in and from professional practice, for use by the practitioners in that area. In order to achieve this, there needs to be reflection and critical consideration of appropriate leadership strategies in addition to research knowhow. It is possible that leadership itself will be a study element within your professional doctorate. Certainly within an education doctorate, business doctorate or marketing, for example, the critical examination of leadership would be a possibility.

Regardless of the professional discipline concerned, there is an important need to consider how the knowledge and skill derived from professional doctorate study will be used to best influence practice. It would be fruitless undertaking a professional doctorate if persistent barriers prevent you from using the ensuing knowledge and skills in practice. Investigating professional issues through research and embedding them in practice presents exciting challenges. For example the values and beliefs inherent in the practice setting, the mindset of the professionals and other stakeholders there, and the overall strategic purpose of the organization need to be conducive to the leadership of research in professional practice.

While the professional doctorate student may be full of enthusiasm for their newly acquired expertise, the research process and findings may challenge others' professional boundaries, or their 'comfort zone' of known experience and routine. Likewise the generation of knowledge from within practice and for practice may necessitate role change, or fundamentally alter others' roles and practices (Boucher and Smyth 2004). Some of these implications have been explored previously in Chapter 4. Leading your research in professional practice is important in order to address some of the challenges identified above.

In order to inform your reflection and prior planning leadership development will now be explored, with discussion and critique of influential theories, past and present. Briefly these will comprise trait, behavioural style and contingency theories. 'New leadership' theories will then be reviewed, for example transformational and transactional leadership, prior to discussion of living leadership. Finally, there will be exploration of the leadership interface with professional doctorate study and practitioner research strategies. This exploration will incorporate reflection on strategies to consider when leading research in practice, with an emphasis on 'zones of choice' developed in living leadership – the work of Binney et al. (2005).

What is leadership?

So what is leadership? Is it an extension of good management? Is good leadership an inherent personality trait or can it be acquired through education and development? Northouse (2007: 3) defines leadership as, 'a process whereby an individual influences a group of individuals to achieve a common goal'. Yukl (2006: 8) also incorporates agreement about the goals and how they are to be achieved: 'leadership is the process of influencing others to understand and agree about what needs to be done and how to do it, and the process of facilitating individual and collective efforts to accomplish shared objectives.'

The above definitions imply activities related to leaders and their followers who, to a greater or lesser degree, may have involvement in the influence and decision making processes. However, in contrast to the idea of leaders as distinct from the followers they seek to influence, Horner (1997) calls for team leadership. This is described as being in keeping with the non-hierarchical, flatter organizational systems in operation in contemporary society as a result of rationalization and downsizing.

Working on leadership as a team issue may have resonance for leading research in practice, when work practices, professional roles or even new knowledge and skills may be generated from practice to underpin and inform future practice. Equally, however, it is possible some of the ideas proposed above have resonance with transformational leadership. It will be demonstrated later in this chapter that this style also embraces a collegiate, collaborative approach based on a shared vision or purpose.

Katz (1955) developed seminal work on leadership identifying three areas of leadership skill:

1 Technical skill: related to a particular work activity or productive activity
2 Human skill: people skills, the ability to work with others, communicate effectively, understand and draw on interpersonal relationships

3 Conceptual skill: the ability to develop ideas or concepts, create vision for organizational goals and develop the strategy to achieve them

Depending on the seniority of the practitioner, some of the skills identified above are considered more important than others. For example technical skill may be important to lower or middle organizational leadership roles, whereas at higher levels the ability to conceptualize, have vision and determine direction is considered more important for effective leadership (Katz 1955).

In terms of the professional doctorate, the development of leadership skills and capability offers the potential to be egalitarian and promote equality in terms of leadership learning throughout an organization or profession. In essence, rather than the notion of leadership being an inherent personality trait, as will be explored in some of the theories and concepts to follow, the skills model suggests leadership expertise can be acquired through suitable support and development. Furthermore some of the skills explored by Northouse (2007) have resonance for the leadership of research in practice, where problem solving, social judgement or decision making skills and knowledge are central. Likewise some would argue that transformational leadership can be developed through appropriate personal development and facilitation (Kelloway and Barling 2000).

Carpenter (2007) undertook a fascinating study of US presidents since Franklin D. Roosevelt. Three categories or themes emerged from content analysis of presidential comments defining or describing leadership. The categories themselves were derived from analysis of the public papers of the presidents of the United States and were:

1 *Vision, values, principles and the common good*: in this context vision was not necessarily in the ownership of one person but was shared within a group
2 *The activity of leadership*: making decisions even if they were unpopular, an activity tested through actions not words; service for others and leading by example illuminated leadership activity
3 *Leading people*: focusing on the needs and wants of people and having a genuine interest in people were characteristic examples in this theme from Carpenter's work

The purpose of Carpenter's (2007) analysis was clearly expressed as the study of presidential leadership, and the study yields important insights into arguably the world's most important role and its associated leadership qualities. Some themes identified in the study have resonance with the leadership theories and concepts to be explored later in this chapter. For example vision, decision making and leading by example are commonly held perceptions of leadership characteristics. However, Carpenter also acknowledges important issues in relation to gender, culture and ethnicity. First, all US presidents to date have been male. Second, Anglo-centric principles and philosophies of leadership are said to be inherent in the study, again due to the characteristics of the presidential sample. Exploration of gender and culture will continue in the following sections of this chapter.

Diversity and leadership: gender

The 'glass ceiling' was originally used to conceptualize the under-representation of women in leadership positions as compared to men. A variety of reasons have been suggested to explain women's comparative absence from leadership roles, for example: gender stereotypes; home/work balance; patriarchy; organizational cultures; career breaks for child rearing and maternity leave. While women now occupy key leadership roles they are arguably comparatively under-represented in the top corporate and political roles.

Catalyst provides research and consultancy regarding business environments (see www.catalyst.org). The organization estimated that half of all management and professional positions in North America are held by women. In comparison, only 7.9 percent of Fortune 500 top earners are women, and 1.4 percent of Fortune 500 chief executive officers are women (Catalyst 2005). Furthermore the above study suggested that men perceive women as having fewer problem solving skills – considered by many to be a key characteristic of leadership. In other areas gender stereotypes persist, for example women and men both considered that women had the attributes for support/reward roles, while women and men equally considered that men are more able at taking charge, delegating and influencing (Catalyst 2005).

While women do occupy key political roles, for example Hilary Clinton and the German chancellor Angela Merkel, they are still under-represented in political and other key leadership positions. Women in high-profile leadership roles are more likely to attract attention in relation to their appearance and presentation rather than the substance of their policies. In 2007 the first woman home secretary in the UK, Jacqui Smith, was subjected to considerable press interest when she made her debut speech in the House of Commons. The interest was not in her political strategy. It was related to the clothes she was wearing. Likewise in 2008 during the run up to the US presidential elections there was much media discussion of Hilary Clinton's personality traits: was she for example a 'cold' person, 'driven', perhaps? Alternatively, did she really 'care' about the US and its future? Possibly such criticism or questioning may have contained a different vocabulary, such as 'focus' or 'energy', if a man was being described in a leadership context.

Some studies have explored women's leadership styles and abilities as compared to men. However, women make equally effective leaders and share the same professionalism and motivation to lead compared to men (Hoyt 2007). Some leadership styles, such as transformational leadership, to be explored later in the chapter, imply inclusive, democratic or participatory approaches.

These styles may be conducive to current societal trends and women's leadership styles in that context may be considered more effective (Northouse 2007).

Diversity and leadership: culture and ethnicity

In the societal context culture is expressed through the beliefs, values, rules and traditions of a group of people. Given the impact of globalization and the need to recognize, respect and appreciate diversity at local levels, it is increasingly important to understand cultural issues to promote equality, to celebrate diversity and to enhance understanding and respect for individuals. It goes without saying that these are important issues if equality of opportunity and respect for diversity is to be fully achieved, while prejudice is minimized.

In relation to cultural interpretations of leadership, Nahavandi (2006) compares and contrasts national differences in addition to ethnicity and other issues such as organizational culture. For example high context and low context cultures are identified. The former emphasize the use of non-verbal cues, reliance on the situation and context, and implied or hidden cues to understand and interpret events. Countries such as France and China are described as high context. Low context cultures by contrast focus on verbal and written communication to understand and interpret events. Scandinavia and the UK are offered by the author as examples of low context environments. It is said that differences between high context and low context cultures can be used to explore communication breakdown, misunderstanding and challenges when communication and leadership are interpreted across high and low contexts simultaneously (Nahavindi 2006).

House et al. (2004) undertook a major study examining culture and leadership in 62 societies. In essence the aim was to examine how different cultures viewed leadership. Six global leadership behaviours were identified and were assessed in different cultural clusters. For example Nordic European leadership profiles were said to advocate visionary and participative approaches. Latin American profiles were said to favour charismatic and value based approaches, with moderate interest in people and participation in decision making. Charisma was generally considered a useful leadership trait in many cultures. Autonomy meanwhile was considered effective in some cultures but not in others. Given the increasing dominance of the knowledge economy and globalization, briefly outlined in Chapter 1, in addition to the diversity inherent in all societies, it is clearly important to acknowledge the cultural construction of leadership if communication and understanding are to be promoted.

Elsewhere Mellahi (2000) undertakes a critical analysis of the leadership development associated with international MBA programmes. He argues that the Westernized approaches to leadership that commonly underpin learning are not always conducive to application and use in the student's own environment. He suggests that MBA programme development should be responsive to the needs of international students, who comprise a significant number of the student MBA population. His analysis was based on a study encompassing 28 business schools in the UK. It was found that literature emphasizing Western industrial models of leadership predominated, while other values and beliefs were often not expanded upon in the MBA programmes.

While the above studies are insightful and illuminate cultural interpretations of leadership, the danger of labelling groups on this basis needs to be acknowledged. Clearly this is a developing and much needed area of research, if ethnocentric views of leadership are to be completely dispelled and a wider understanding of leadership is to be promoted.

Is leadership an extension of good management?

Contemporary literature focuses on leadership knowledge and skill. For example Kotter (1990) makes a distinction between leadership and management. The former is described as providing inspiration, vision and creativity for a group of people. The latter is described as a position of power by virtue of holding a key position within an organization to maintain order and consistency within systems. In contrast Blank (2001) describes leadership as opportunistic: the role being adopted where no formal procedure exists; where there is uncertainty and the need to guide others; to build rapport and trust to influence. Management is described by Blank (2001) as an organizational role within the hierarchy, and used to direct and influence others to undertake their roles in accordance with procedure.

Bennis and Nanus (1985: 1) state that 'managers are people who do things right and leaders are people who do the right thing'. However, in practice the distinction between leadership and management may not be so straightforward. For example a faculty dean may hold a position of leadership as the figurehead for an academic subject group and also have responsibility for staff management, budgetary issues and the achievement of organizational goals and strategy. While others in the faculty may not hold formally ascribed leadership roles when examining their professional title, they may emerge to lead subject groups, programmes of study, meetings or to develop key projects.

This emerging emphasis on leadership styles as opposed to management strategies has been challenged through the critical appraisal of leadership theories and concepts. Teo-Dixon and Monin (2007), for example, argue that such a distinction is a recent phenomenon, which only enhances the mystery of leadership. Within that mystery they suggest there is a danger of viewing leadership as a heroic act. The authors further argue that seminal leadership works such as those by Peter Drucker did not differentiate between leadership and management.

Similarly Bligh and Schyns (2007) critique what is described as the romance of leadership. Attributed to the work of James Meindl et al., the romance of leadership is used to describe the promotion of leadership as a mysterious, charismatic process. Furthermore the authors argue that discussion promoting the romance of leadership fails to address what is essentially a complex interplay between individuals, including leaders and followers, and the variety of organizational contexts. Meindl et al. (1985) found that people used leadership constructs to explain organizational events or outcomes, as opposed to the analysis of wider influential factors. In essence it was suggested that leaders are too often used to explain the characteristics, events and success of organizations. It was argued that leadership had achieved an unwarranted status or significance in relation to organizational outcomes, with the media having a significant responsibility for this situation in their portrayal and discussion of leadership and the roles of key business leaders, for example.

In summary, the title of Ralph Vaughan-Williams' church anthem 'Let us now praise famous men' illustrates some of the challenges described to date in this chapter, in terms of gender, Anglo-centricity and heroism within leadership constructs, for example. Mindful of these issues the following sections will critique a variety of leadership theories and concepts, enabling consideration of their utility when leading research in professional practice.

Leadership theories and concepts

Analysis of leadership theories and concepts warrants study beyond historical interest. Clegg et al. (1999) point out that emerging leadership developments rarely result in the demise of previous leadership approaches. Rather, new leadership styles are integrated with the old ones, but with a change of emphasis. For example the discussion here will demonstrate that current leadership models can be seen to be amalgams of previous ideas in different proportions. The historical development of leadership also offers methodological insights, which may assist in judging the evidence base for current leadership approaches. The four major stages of leadership development to be explored are trait, behavioural style, contingency and 'new leadership', such as transformational and transactional leadership. Living leadership will then be explored in relation to leading research in practice.

Trait approach

Within this approach leadership development was concerned with the personal characteristics and inherent qualities that distinguished leaders from non-leaders or followers. This was predicated on the underlying determinist belief that leaders are born and not made. Therefore managerial education was redundant, or at least marginal, and the emphasis was on the *selection* of natural leaders. Additionally, the identification of those with potential, but as yet unexpressed, inherent leadership abilities was considered worthy of research. Several groups of personal traits were researched as described by Bryman (1986). These tended to be physical – examining physique and appearance or abilities – and intelligence or verbal fluency. Psychological characteristics such as extroversion/introversion or charisma were also explored.

Sometimes combinations of all these groups were studied in a search for what were the *universalist* traits of leaders, that is, those central traits that would be possessed by all leaders. This resulted in the generation of masses of inconclusive and sometimes contradictory traits being identified (Luthans 1989). Only intelligence and height emerged with any consistency; leaders were slightly brighter and slightly taller than those they led. These traits apart, no consistent predictors of leadership could be found. Almost any trait could be used to describe a leader. In addition to these semantic issues, there are other methodological problems. People who were already in positions of leadership were studied and it may be that they were in those positions for any number of other reasons, such as ruthlessness, family connections or sycophancy. Further to this, the research did not allow for the proving of a cause and effect relationship between observed traits and successful leadership. However, there is some evidence to suggest that empathy and self-confidence are desirable leadership traits (Reitz 1987).

Those wishing to embed research in professional practice or generate research based knowledge and skills from within practice may take an interesting perspective by examining the traits and skills of those who fail to construct effective leadership strategies. Such a 'derailment' approach may be seen in McCartney and Campbell (2006). Here the combination of attributes that contributed to leadership success and failure were examined. The authors proposed a model of individual success and failure based on the possession or absence of certain leadership and management skills. Some people with none of the skills are unlikely to be selected as managers or leaders. Those with combinations of low skills are likely to derail. Those with a balance of leadership and management skills may be considered candidates for development and achieve success. Achieving success depends also on being recognized as having potential by the superordinate.

The management skills related to failure were: over-managing, lack of follow through, inability to prioritize and failure to meet objectives. Management skills related to success were: resources, problem solving skills, specialized knowledge, and achievement orientation, skills in directing others, goal achievement and vision implementation. The leadership factors contributing to failure were: abrasive behaviour towards others; appearing cold and aloof; the inability to build a team; inability to resolve conflicts; inability to adapt to changes; and inability to adapt to the boss's style or culture of the organization. Lack of flexibility was a theme that connected many of the derailed subjects (McCartney and Campbell 2006). Some derailed leaders persisted in utilizing approaches that were no longer appropriate. Katz (1955, see above) describes technical, human and conceptual skills: derailed leaders failed to recognize when higher skills were appropriate or if they did recognize this, they did not have them in their repertoire.

Among leadership factors contributing to success were: good interpersonal skills, and idealism in the form of vision and emotional maturity. It should be noted that McCartney and Campbell (2006) considered the balance between adequate management and leadership skills was an important factor. This may be interpreted as the ability to move between transactional and trans-formational approaches (see below).

An influential review by Stogdill (1948), with its attendant criticisms of inconsistency and methodology, had the effect of temporarily freezing trait research. However, as stated above, approaches tend to re-emerge in altered guises. One aspect of trait theory, notably charisma, appears in the early mani-festations of transformational leadership.

Behavioural style approach

In contrast to emphasis on the inborn traits and personal characteristics as described above, the emphasis within behavioural styles relates to actions and behaviours. Implicit in this is the possibility of learning or developing the desired leadership skills. Pioneering studies were undertaken by social scien-tists in the 1930s. Lippitt and White (1960) report upon their crude but semi-nal work with adolescent boys groups in what are popularly known as the Iowa leadership studies. Here sets of boys in hobby groups were subjected to various social conditions to see the effect on behaviour. Most notably observed were the effects on aggression. The manipulated condition was the behaviour of the group leaders.

Group leaders were authoritarian (directive and non-participative); demo-cratic (objective and participative); or laissez-faire in approach (providing no leadership). Satisfaction and aggression were measured in each group, but importantly, productivity was *not*. One definite finding was that the boys pre-ferred democratic leaders. Most disruption was associated with laissez-faire leaders followed by autocratic, with the democratic condition generating the least disruption. Other results were not so clear cut. Autocratic leaders could produce apathetic as well as aggressive responses, for example.

These early studies were extended by what became known as the Ohio and Michigan studies (Clegg et al. 1999). Here the behavioural styles of large num-bers of successful and unsuccessful leaders in many settings were compared.

Leadership styles were identified by a questionnaire survey of leadership followers. What emerged indicated that democratic, participatory leaders were generally considered to be more successful by their followers.

These studies formed part of the evidence offered by the humanists to support their ideas about behavioural styles in leadership. The humanists have an axiomatic position, which holds that democratic, person-centred, participative approaches are always superior in all situations. Rensis Likert, a one-time director of the Michigan studies, has developed these ideas into his four systems of management leadership (Likert 1967). The model describes a range of leadership behaviours ranging through (1) exploitive autocratic; (2) benevolent autocratic; (3) participative; and (4) democratic.

Likert argues that system 4 (democratic) will always be more effective than system 1 (exploitive autocratic). The contingency theorists counter this generalization. Likert and other democratic style proponents have been criticized with regard to methodology. The Ohio and Michigan studies relied upon indirect survey questionnaire measures to the exclusion of more objective analysis and unobtrusive measures. It could be when subordinates described democratic leaders they were in fact describing their personal ideal rather than their leader. The survey approaches taken could demonstrate correlation, but could not prove any direction of causal link. That is to say, the successful group may have caused the leader to be democratic rather than the other way round.

A common misconception surrounds one of the findings of the Michigan studies. Employee satisfaction was measured, but this was not directly related to productivity. As above, it could be that being productive itself generates satisfaction. This is important, as some quality of work life approaches advocate the facilitation of worker satisfaction in order to enhance their productivity.

Contingency approaches

Contingency theorists challenged the assumption that one particular leadership style will suit all settings, and emphasized the importance of situation and context. That is to say, effective leadership was determined by the leader providing what was appropriate in any set circumstance. Prominent among contingency theorists is Frederick Fiedler (1967), largely because his work was some of the first to be published. Fiedler used a 'least preferred co-worker' (LPC) scale to assess the leadership orientation of the leader. In brief, the respondent had to describe co-workers by placing them on a scale of pairs of adjectives such as friendly/unfriendly, distant/close. The score indicated how relationship oriented the leader was. This orientation may be described as their motivational disposition which is either:

- Human relations or lenient (high LPC) or
- Task directed and 'hard nosed' (low LPC)

Fiedler (1967) found that the effectiveness of these types varied with how favourable the situation was. Low LPC leaders were more effective if the task was structured and there was much formal authority used in the situation. High LPC leaders did well in opposite circumstances. The model was developed to account for combinations of variables that in the end made it rather complex. The leader orientations are recognizably similar to the dimensions found in the Ohio and Michigan style studies, for example broadly boss centred or results centred. However, Fiedler considered the orientations to be personality attributes and therefore not amenable to change, which ties his work to earlier trait studies. Thus in order to achieve a suitable match the leader could not change their own behaviour, rather they moved to a more favourable situation. This level of discretion is scarce in most organizations. It may be a consideration when choosing an appropriate setting in which to embed research.

Another approach in which the leader behaviour is matched to the situation is Hersey and Blanchard's life cycle or situational approach (Hersey and Blanchard 1969). This popular model is really an extension of the Ohio State studies and the managerial grid approach. Hersey and Blanchard propose that the effective leader varies behaviour to meet the needs of the followers in the situation. Followers' needs are determined by their current level of maturity and development. As a person develops, they require varying mixtures of support and direction, and these are supplied by the effective leader. This is predicated on the idea that the leader can make an accurate diagnosis of the situation (maturity level) and then can change to the appropriate leadership behaviour from a large personal repertoire. This is in contrast to Fiedler's belief that the leader's orientation was fixed, and to find a match the leader moved to a new situation.

The situational approach was further adapted by Blanchard et al. (1985). This identified the behaviours the leader adopts to meet the need of the variously developed staff as supporting, coaching, delegating and directing.

All contingency models require the two elements of the life cycle model. That is the leader's ability to diagnose the situation and the possession of a gamut of skills or powers of discretion.

New leadership approaches: transformational and transactional leadership

The concept of 'new leadership' is used to describe a range of ideas with some common themes. Areas for exploration here relate to transformational and transactional leadership, for example. Central among these is the leader's ability to articulate a shared vision for the followers. Notably vision was a characteristic emerging from the US presidential study of Carpenter (2007). The leader stimulates followers to change their motives, beliefs, values and capabilities, so that their own interests and personal goals become congruent with those of the organization. In essence transformational leadership emphasizes charisma, the ability to motivate others through the promotion of self-worth and other personal traits.

The use of charisma as a characteristic of transformational leadership and elsewhere has been reviewed with some caution. Marjosola and Takala (2000) argue that charisma has potentially destructive consequences. In extreme cases they argue that reliance on charisma as a key leadership strategy can result in totalitarian regimes as exemplified by the actions of figures throughout history, for example. In other instances they argue that charisma can be construed as manipulation of the truth.

Leadership could then be constructed as the management of meaning, rather than as an influencing process. Cultural alignment is achieved through the application of various components, which is typified in the work of Bass (1985), who proposes the use of charisma, inspiration, individualized consideration and intellectual stimulation. The work of Bass captures transformational leadership. Transformational leadership has become a popular, if uncritically applied approach. It is unquestioningly endorsed in many texts, for example: 'Transformational Leadership is the preferred style in the caring professions' Crowther (2004: 38). The approach can be seen to contain echoes of trait theory with its reference to charisma (although this is de-emphasized in later work and renamed 'idealized influence'). Bass and Avolio (1994) evaluated the leadership performance of large numbers of senior leaders in several settings. They considered that a more effective leader type could be discerned. This type of leader was more effective at bringing about innovation and changing culture. These more effective leaders tended to display what has been described as transformational leadership in addition to transactional leadership (see below).

Bass and Avolio (1994) indicate that transformational leaders employ the 'Four Is', examples of which are illustrated below in Figure 5.1.

- *Idealized influence:* Acting as a role model – leading by example, being admired, respected and trusted. Followers identify with and emulate the leader. Sharing risks with followers and demonstrating high ethical standards are elements of leadership

- *Individualized consideration:* Paying special attention to each individual's need for achievement. Providing a supportive climate: coaching and advising staff to enable them to become fully actualized. Using delegation to aid growth of followers; treating followers in a tailored fashion; giving some staff strong affiliation and others specific directives, depending on their needs

- *Inspirational motivation:* Communicating high expectations and enthusiasm to their followers; sharing their vision with the staff they lead; helping the followers interpret events and provide a version of organizational reality; using symbolic actions to reinforce expectations

- *Intellectual stimulation:* Stimulating followers to be creative and innovative; avoiding public criticism of mistakes; encouraging new approaches whether or not they differ from the leader's approach

Figure 5.1 The 'Four Is' employed by transformational leaders
Source: Bass and Avolio (1994).

Transactional leadership

Effective leaders could also display transactional leadership elements; transaction involves straightforward exchange. The transactional elements are:

- Contingent reward
- Active management by exception
- Passive management by exception
- Laissez-faire

(Bass and Avolio 1994)

Examples are illustrated below in Figure 5.2.

Bass and Avolio's research indicated that transformational leadership tended to be more effective and useful. However, they recognized that transactional leadership, while being used less often, was equally appropriate at times. It must be recognized that this is an element derived from contingency approaches. The authors proposed that transformational and transactional leadership should be used together in different proportions.

Transformational leadership has its critics. For a succinct account, see Pawar (2003). Pawar argues that the writers on transformational leadership do not provide clarity on six conceptual issues:

1 The applicability of transformational leadership to economic organizations is not clear. Much research was undertaken in governmental and political organizations, where outcomes are fluid or vague; not all organizations are like this
2 The relationship between transformational and transactional leadership is constructed differently by different authors. Most writers include transactional leadership, but some consider it to be on a continuum with

---

- *Contingent reward:* This refers to a formal exchange process between the leader and the follower. The leader obtains agreement from followers on what needs to be done and what the payoffs will be for the people doing it. These transactions have also been categorized as constructive transactions

- *Active management by exception:* The leader actively arranges to monitor the follower's performance and takes corrective action

- *Passive management by exception:* The leader does nothing until the follower deviates or makes a mistake, they then take corrective action

- *Laissez-faire:* The leader takes no responsibility and gives no feedback to others. The leader keeps their hands off the situation and has no exchange with the followers

---

Figure 5.2 Transactional leadership elements
Source: Bass and Avolio (1994).

transactional leadership, to be used in a contingent fashion with transformational leadership. Other writers consider transactional leadership to be an entirely separate entity, often to be avoided

3 Charismatic leadership is viewed by some as being synonymous with transformational leadership. Others distance themselves from charismatic leadership because of its connotations of egotism, arguing that real transformational leaders are unselfish

4 There is ambiguity about the focus of the leader in bringing about change. Some researchers propose that the leader uses transformational leadership to install a specific change as opposed to transforming people and cultures

5 The organizational context seems to have been ignored in transformational leadership research. Leaders described as transformational were viewed as successful, but other factors in the organizational environment that may have helped were ignored

6 There is a very broad definition of what transformational leaders are. It is likely that there are a range of leaders that could be fitted into the wide specification given

(Pawar 2003)

Because it covers such a wide range of issues the conceptual clarity of transformational leadership can potentially be lost. The ideas overlap with so many other organizational issues. The issue of 'charisma' is an atavistic echo of trait theory. Indeed, much of what is proposed in transformational leadership is expressed as being 'what a good leader *should* achieve' – how they should do this is given less emphasis (Northouse 2007). Much of the early transformational leadership research was gained from elite, high profile and successful leaders at the top of organizations. There has been a focus on leadership *of* organizations rather than *in* organizations (see Bryman in Clegg et al. 1999).

As suggested earlier, transformational leadership can potentially be constructed as having a manipulative focus. Anyone who is a 'manager of meaning' can abuse followers. There is nothing that makes a transformational leader any more ethical than anyone else. People who define reality for others can be very destructive as Northouse (2007) argues. Being a high profile charismatic heroic leader can be a demanding aspiration, and some more modest yet workable approaches are available. One of these is living leadership, as discussed below.

Living leadership

The previous sections have illuminated the historical development of leadership theories and concepts and have explored the construction of leadership. It can be seen that there are similarities and differences in emphasis and that it is not possible to describe a single, idealized model of leadership. This section explores a contrasting leadership perspective, that of living leadership, as developed by Binney et al. (2005). Living leadership is an 'anti-charismatic' approach which has some contingency elements. The major tenets are that:

1 Leadership happens between people
2 Leading is shaped by the context
3 People are most effective when they bring themselves to leading and match their strengths (and weaknesses) to the organization

Zones of choice

Within living leadership, Binney et al. (2005) recognized that there is not a single organizational reality: the leader has zones of choice in which to act. The leader can work through a continuum in these zones of choice, moving backwards and forwards, positioning their activities according to the individual situation and the activities required. The leader here is not expected to live up to the charismatic hero model but is an 'experimenter', who may try different approaches according to the situation and context. In essence the authors recognized that the leader is not always the dominant visionary who manages the organizational reality. Binney et al. (2005) suggest that the leader 'sinks' or 'swims' (gets by) or 'surfs' (is in complete control) at different times and in different situations.

Binney et al. (2005) developed their work from longitudinal case study research of actual leaders who were found to be struggling in the real world to live up to the ideals of transformational leadership. Those leaders who were successful lived in the moment and experimented within the identified zones of choice. Within the zones there are opportunities for movement within the parameters given, based on an iterative and reflective process of questioning and knowing what the process is. The zones identified by the authors were:

- Understanding: enquiring, while knowing
- Direction: acknowledging limits, while imagining a better future
- Timing: waiting and seeing, while accelerating progress
- Relationships: getting close, while maintaining distance
- Loyalties: putting own needs first, while considering organization needs
- Authority: letting go, while keeping control
- Self-belief: showing vulnerability, while remaining strong

(Binney et al. 2005: 98)

The authors do not suggest a formula to locate leadership practice in the zones of choice. Instead there is emphasis on working within the zones in different ways at different times. The following section illuminates possible interpretations of the zones of choice when they are applied to leading professional doctorate research in practice. You are encouraged to reflect upon the choices on offer in your own professional practice context to determine the zones of choice relating to your own studies. The student activity at the end of this section will assist the reflection process. For further detailed discussion of living leadership, see Binney et al. (2005).

Understanding: enquiring while knowing

As individuals work within practice, they continually build expertise based on experience and reflection in addition to the acquisition of professional knowledge and skill. However, knowledge of practice and knowledge of how to practise are not static. For example an expert professional will have knowledge and confidence in practice, while reflecting on how that practice could be developed further: its strengths and challenges based on influencing factors.

Enquiring while knowing the first zone of choice from Binney et al. (2005), for example, could relate to the development of an initial, exploratory idea emerging from practice and research activity in professional practice. The balance between enquiring while knowing and movement within that zone of choice could also relate to the subsequent clarification and refinement of a focused aim or research question. In essence this zone of choice could have resonance with assessment strategies, and the identification and exploration of research needs in professional practice. There is the potential for critical reflection in and about the practice area; critical discussion with professional colleagues and professional doctorate student peers; critical appraisal of the literature; and assessment of the professional context and the nature of the research issue.

There should be potential for balance between an iterative process of thinking and reflecting while having confidence to progress the ensuing research ideas. This process can only be developed through good communication and collaboration in the professional practice context, drawing on the ideas of colleagues and professional doctorate peers. This zone possibly has potential as a sounding board from which to test out and communicate ideas, and seek the impressions of others.

Direction: acknowledging limits while imagining a better future

Exploration within this zone of choice could relate to the practicalities of research in professional practice. For example are other stakeholders and/or the practice culture ready to participate and generate research in professional practice? Is the time right? Is the proposed study feasible? What kind of impact would the research have in the future? Would there be benefits and/or costs for professional practice? What is the best possibility for leading research in practice, given the resources and time available in combination with organizational and professional priorities?

Pragmatically, work within this zone of choice from Binney et al. (2005)

could involve the scoping of preliminary research ideas to develop consistency and consider the implications for practice. The use of strategies, such as cost and benefit analysis, or examination of strengths, weaknesses, opportunities and threats combined with reading, reflection and discussion with colleagues and student peers should be beneficial in this zone. In summary, how to plan and generate research in the professional context, considering the competing drivers for and against research in professional practice, considering the time span of the study to be undertaken and what is achievable in the time available and the resources available are possible activities within this zone.

Timing: waiting and seeing while accelerating progress

This zone of choice could relate to the research as it progresses in professional practice. For example there could be adjustments to the research process and ongoing communication needs with other professionals and stakeholders. It is possibly a balance between seeing how the research itself unfolds and what issues are identified, and actively moving the research forwards.

Relationships: getting close while maintaining distance

Reflection and action in this zone of choice could relate to the development of a relationship with participants in the professional area that is conducive to research; exploring professional ideas, while maintaining sufficient distance as practitioner–researcher. There is synergy here with the themes relating to the ethics of practitioner research, whether the respective areas could or should be clearly delineated in the practice setting. There isn't a clear cut answer or response here, the actions of the practitioner–researcher depend on the situation in practice at that time.

Within this zone there is an implicit use of reflexivity, which requires the acknowledgement of presuppositions and significant events relating to issues developing from research in practice. Further examples could include collaboration and involvement with others and the use of communication skills. This may be an important consideration if ethnography principles are used, for example where the professional is practitioner and researcher at the same time or at different times in the same professional context, and how that relationship could be managed.

Loyalties: putting own needs first while considering organization needs

There are several possibilities for exploration within this zone of choice identified by Binney et al. (2005). For example it could describe a balance or compromise between the 'ideal' research that you would like to undertake within the practice setting and what is realistically achievable at that time, given resources, organizational wants and needs, and the skills and motivations of other practitioners. There may need to be consideration of priorities and which themes and aspects of practice can be enhanced through professional doctorate research. In essence, this zone may relate to compromise between the professional development and research needs of the individual student and those required by the practice setting.

Chapters 2 and 3 also explored the development of research issues for professional doctorate study. Possibly doctoral students embark on studies with research projects and ideas that are initially too large. Choice may depend on their perceptions of what a professional doctorate involves and notions of depth and detail. Discussion relating to this zone of choice can help to clarify and further develop realistic and timely ideas for practice.

Importantly it could equally relate to negotiating the time required to undertake the professional doctorate, with attendance at workshops and private study combined with activities in the practice setting. This is compared to the time required for professional practice and engagement in professional responsibilities. In summary, it could relate to professional choices; organizational need and personal choices for study; competing demands; and negotiating a balance between professional practice and study needs.

Authority: letting go while keeping control

In relation to leading research in professional practice, this zone could illustrate the balance between enabling the participants and research stakeholders to facilitate the development of the research and take responsibility for its progress, and the practitioner–researcher's wish to keep the research on track and maintain realistic timeframes. This may need to be balanced with issues such as participants' willingness or skills to collaborate in the research process.

An exploratory study of student perceptions of professional doctorate supervision, Lee (2007) found that some professional doctorate students could perhaps have done more to collaborate and involve their colleagues in the initial development and implementation of their research ideas. This strategy would not only have promoted communication and understanding of the research in practice, it would have helped to develop a collaborative approach to the study, and to integrate research and the development of evidence as an integral element of professional practice.

Self-belief: showing vulnerability while remaining strong

This is possibly the most important challenge facing the professional doctorate student. As explored in Chapter 1, many professional doctorate students have already accrued significant professional expertise and are using this to develop their practice through the professional doctorate. As senior and established practitioners there is perhaps a self-expectation, in addition to expectations from peers and others that they are competent, strong and knowledgeable in the practice context. There is perhaps an assumption that they are accomplished practitioners who know what to do and how to do it.

However, practice brings uncertainty. The work of Binney et al. (2005) illustrates that leadership is fluid. It depends on the situation at hand and the context. Acknowledging the doubts and uncertainties of the leadership role in professional practice is one challenge, combining this with research in professional practice is an additional challenge when there may be expectations of competence, knowledge and expertise within the practice setting.

Professional doctorate students may ask: 'Is this right approach for the study? Is this the right focus or research aim? How will I know? What is the best way to lead this?' This may be balanced with self-doubt: 'Can I do this? Can I meet this demand? Am I up to the challenge? Have I the intellectual and professional capacity to achieve these goals?' Working within this zone requires adjustment to acknowledge these issues and discussing them in practice. One positive strategy that can help is to have reference to student peers and discussion with their community of practice.

Reflection on the zones of choice

The previous section has used the zones of choice, identified by Binney et al. (2005) and applied them to the leadership of professional doctorate research in practice.

It is unrealistic to expect that a leader will be able to find a perfect fit in every situation. Binney et al. (2005) recognize that some people are drawn to certain situations in which they feel more comfortable. They suggest that 'inner demons' or flaws in the leader, find a match in the situation and this can create synergy. These inner demons are to be recognized and not discouraged. In the same way, Fiedler believed that the leader may not be able to 'stretch' to fit the situation; there may be situations that you cannot accommodate within professional doctorate research. In that case you have to move on. You cannot be a success in all settings and Binney et al. (2005) suggest that you should not try.

While the zones of choice are considered individually above, there is overlap between the respective zones. While leading research in professional practice, it may be possible to work with several zones simultaneously. In addition the zones of choice suggest that good communication and collaboration at all levels of professional practice are important to develop and apply research within the practice setting.

The relationships between leadership, practitioner research and professional doctorate studies

To date this chapter has introduced and appraised leadership theories and concepts with discussion of living leadership to underpin research in professional practice. The final sections will consider the relationships between professional doctorate studies, leadership and research in practice. There will be specific exploration of leadership at an internal level in the organization and in the external professional world in terms of networking and dissemination of research expertise.

At the internal interface leadership will be explored in relation to the following issues:

- Using leadership to assess and plan research in the professional practice context
- Using leadership to investigate practice in the professional context, for example the process of research
- Using leadership to embed and evaluate new professional practices

At the external interface, leadership will be explored in relation to the use of professional and other networks to help develop research in professional practice and to disseminate the accompanying knowledge and skills.

The internal interface

Using leadership to assess and plan research in the professional context

While overall responsibility for professional doctorate study may lie with the student, success is not possible without consideration of the views and opinions, and ultimately the cooperation of professional colleagues and other stakeholders in the research process. The involvement of key stakeholders at the assessment stage of communicating initial research ideas and using an iterative process of clarification and discussion is important. For example in a feasibility study, analysis of the costs and benefits of the research may need consideration. The success of this depends on the communication skills of the practitioner–researcher; their knowledge of their subject; and the priority of the research in terms of the organizational or professional agenda. Clearly there is overlap here with some of the skills explored in the previous sections. It may be helpful to identify champions or advocates who can help to promote and explore the initial research ideas further. At the stage of assessment, mapping professional contextual issues with findings from the literature, discussion with peers, supervisors and facilitators on the professional doctorate programme is important.

Using leadership to investigate practice in the professional context

The leadership development skills identified above should continue into the research process. For example professional colleagues may need to help identify and recruit participants to the research process, with due consideration and understanding of the ethical issues of informed consent. It may be necessary to observe the work of professional colleagues directly or they may need to adapt the way they are working as part of the research study. Developing cooperation in terms of applying research methods or collecting data will require good communication and thorough explanation and understanding with the participants.

Gaining approval and cooperation of peers may be crucial to the research process, with particular emphasis on involvement and research with stakeholders, not research on or about the stakeholders. At all stages, reflection and learning from the research process is important in the resolution and negotiation of issues. How these may be achieved will be dependent on the leadership styles adopted in professional practice and which of these are appropriate to that particular setting.

Using communication to ensure research is conducted 'with' and not 'on' participants may be crucial to the data collection, giving due acknowledgement and thanks for people who help. In the research process it is also likely that unexpected problems will emerge requiring negotiation and resolution in the practice setting.

Using leadership to embed and evaluate new professional practices

Many practitioners want to embed new practice as a result of research and to evaluate practice. Communicating the research findings and promoting discussion of how they can be best used in practice, or developing new practices as a response to the research is an important consideration. It could involve many aspects of leadership, for example the ability to promote and manage change; to experiment and try different approaches; to involve others; to develop creativity.

The three themes used above to explore the interface between professional doctorate studies and practitioner research have common elements, for example participation in the research process; good communication; problem solving; working with the right people; using influence; and decision making. Suggesting these skills is based on several presuppositions:

- The practitioner–researcher is operating at a professional level with sufficient autonomy to lead change and inspire others
- Other practitioners and stakeholders in the research are in a position to participate
- The practice setting has a culture that actively promotes and advocates such practice, that participatory practices are already in evidence

Jenna is a senior health care professional and is currently undertaking a professional doctorate. The following is her critical reflection on the interface between leadership, professional doctorate study and leading research in practice:

Leading research in practice: an allied health professional (physiotherapy) consultant's personal reflection

'Non-medical consultants are expected to find, appraise and apply research to practice. They are also required to initiate and lead on research projects, and disseminate their work through publication. The focus of the role is "expert" clinical practice but it also demands advanced skills in teaching and education, clinical management, research and leadership. Practice development and evaluation through research requires skills that can only come from a strong academic background, or effective collaboration with academic partners. Sadly, the majority of elite academic clinicians stay in academia and do not return to clinical practice; and senior clinicians may not have the time or necessary skills to engage in research activity.

Although a doctoral level qualification is not a current prerequisite for a consultant post, it is likely to become so in the near future. It is certainly a highly desirable qualification for such a role. Collaborative working between senior clinicians and those working in a research capacity is to be encouraged if we are to bridge the practice–research gap. Potential barriers to practice based research include a lack of support, supervision and funding, multiple demands on clinicians' time and insufficient research skills – and practitioners' resistance to change. Practice based research is central to ensuring that research evidence embeds itself in practice, and that it remains clinically appropriate and patient focused. Evidence based practice is the new paradigm, but this evidence must be of high quality, clinically applicable and appropriately utilized.

Clinicians must juggle empirical evidence with experiential knowledge and clinical judgement. Research has a daily impact on clinical practice in the form of national guidelines and standards of best practice. However, this does not obviate the need for clinical judgement and transparent clinical reasoning processes. In fact, if clinicians were to follow research based guidelines with an unquestioning mind, it could lead to the kind of recipe driven practice that such guidelines are meant to challenge. Clinicians are generally uncomfortable with a Procrustean approach to health care, especially where it may be politically driven. Like it or not, the NHS has finite resources and guidelines are invariably linked to targets, and where this is the case, evidence is more likely to be implemented. In short, leading practice based research requires the acquisition of the necessary skills and the opportunity to collaborate with professional researchers, higher education and research institutions. Research activity requires time and investment. For the consultant practitioner, leadership and communication skills are important in aligning research and development with commissioners and other stakeholders. At a strategic level, an awareness of the political influences on practice and research become an integral part of researching the quality and cost effectiveness of our practice.'

The external interface

The use of professional and other networks to lead research in professional practice

There is some overlap here with the information presented in Chapter 7, 'Sharing your expertise with others', and the final chapter, 'Life after your professional doctorate: what happens next'? The over-arching message is that professional doctorate students need to consider their external leadership profile, in addition to the leadership skills and strategies encompassed within their practitioner role. For example while leadership is important to the generation of research knowledge in practice, it is important to share your knowledge and expertise with others, and to find colleagues and networks with similar interests who can help you further develop your professional doctorate research and your professional profile in the wider professional context beyond the workplace.

Chapter 7, for example, discusses the strategies for disseminating research in practice through writing in academic and professional journals. In addition there are other means of disseminating work – using the media, for example. Similarly, the final chapter details the kinds of strategies to raise your professional profile externally, through membership of professional groups and committees as they relate to your research and professional practice interests.

Student activity 5.1

The following activity provides the opportunity for you to reflect on the information presented in this chapter relating to leading research in professional practice. You are encouraged to think about your current leadership knowledge and skills and how these could be enhanced for research in the practice setting. Use the themes below to think about your own professional practice context; what you would like to achieve through professional doctorate research; and your current leadership expertise and how this could be developed further. Zones of choice from Binney et al. (2005: 98) have been applied within the activity to inform your reflection.

Zones of choice (Binney et al. 2005: 98)	Your current leadership expertise	Your desired expertise for leading research in professional practice
Understanding: enquiring while knowing Direction: acknowledging limits while imagining a better future Timing: waiting and seeing while accelerating progress	How does your current professional context enable your practice within the zones of choice? What current leadership skills underpin your practice? How have these been determined?	How do you envisage working within the zones of choice when leading research in practice? What further leadership expertise would you like to develop for research in your professional practice setting? What further leadership expertise do others consider important for leading research in your professional practice context?
Relationships: getting close while maintaining distance Loyalties: putting own needs first while considering organizational needs Authority: letting go while keeping control Self-belief: showing vulnerability while remaining strong	How do you evaluate their effectiveness? How do others evaluate their effectiveness?	How can you develop these leadership skills? What do peers, colleagues and others also need to develop? Who can help with their development? What else would help you? How will you and others evaluate the effectiveness of your skills for leading research in professional practice?

Conclusion

This chapter has attempted to introduce and critically appraise the historical evolution of leadership theories and concepts. This has been combined with exploration of the complex and highly skilled activity of using leadership capacity to lead research in professional practice. There is no formulaic approach; the strategies to successfully lead research in professional practice are dependent upon the professional culture and context of practice, organizational priorities and organizational learning ability.

It can be seen that consideration of approaches to lead research in practice is potentially time consuming. However, attention to leadership related to the professional context and the participants therein is equally, if not more, important than consideration of the research methods to be used to develop research within the professional practice setting. In the final analysis, it will be difficult to lead research in practice without the effective use of interpersonal skills and leadership strategies. Within the professional doctorate developing knowledge and expertise related to practice is one element, its successful use in practice is the other.

Earlier in the chapter, Jenna reflected on her leadership role in the context of health care practice. Here, she reflects again on issues related to leading research in practice:

> I think it takes a liberal kind of leadership, the kind that encourages the development of others. One that is collaborative and strategic in thinking. It's about leading people yet also leading the service and engaging multiple stakeholders. And knowing that you are just one of many leaders all working to achieve the same end. It's about being happy with sharing leadership with others, without losing sight of one's own leadership remit in the process. And that is very difficult. The most difficult thing for a clinician (me, for example) is that I am expected to lead with very little management training behind me, and I don't have the authority of a management position (or a budget, which many people seem to equate with leadership, power and authority). So, leading is a challenge. But then managers aren't necessarily leaders and vice versa.
>
> Leadership training is essential to the person who is leading (or expected to lead) on research. Otherwise, all the expertise and knowledge in the world may fall on deaf ears. I guess another way of putting it is 'having influence'.

Summary of key points

- Varied leadership theories and concepts have been appraised and their respective strengths and weaknesses for leading research in practice have been explored
- Development and enhancement of your leadership repertoire can be achieved by critical reflection on instances where 'derailment' has happened, and the leadership approaches have not been successful (McCartney and Campbell 2006)
- Assessment of your professional context and culture combined with identification of your current leadership skills and those you require to lead research in practice are important considerations within the professional doctorate process. This assessment is time consuming but important if the research relating to professional practice is truly to have impact and generate knowledge and expertise directly from practice
- Binney et al. (2005) offer the notion of zones of choice, providing flexibility of leadership within identified parameters. These may allow the practitioner to operate within parameters or boundaries of practice, offering scope for flexibility according to context rather than consideration of fixed leadership approaches
- An important element of leading research in practice relates to the external interface and raising your profile through publications, professional networks and other strategies. (These will be considered in detail in Chapters 7 and 8)

6

Professional practice, knowledge and ethics

Aims of the chapter

- To critically reflect on the changing nature of professional practice and the knowledge required for professional practice
- To discuss ethical principles and their application within professional doctorate research
- To review the strategies required to obtain ethical approval for professional doctorate research

Introduction

The practicalities of achieving your professional doctorate have been explored thus far. Throughout there has been an emphasis on processes: to manage your personal study time; to maximize good supervision; to use reflection and reflexivity and illuminate the professional practice context; and to lead research in professional practice. Central to the discussion has been the implication that knowledge and expertise associated with professional doctorates and professional practices are developed 'out there' within the professional context, as opposed to 'within' the academic setting.

This chapter has two elements. The first element will explore the nature of professional practice and the nature of professional knowledge to underpin practice. The changing context of professional practice and the characteristics of professions will be explored. The intention is to prompt wider discussion among professional doctorate students about the similarities and differences in their practice. It will be demonstrated, for example, that issues such as professional dominance, the blurring of professional boundaries and the emergence of new professions is influencing contemporary professional practice.

The second element of the chapter will explore the related issues of ethics and practitioner research. Ethical principles will be considered, accompanied by discussion of good practice for professional doctorate research projects. The overall aim is to demystify ethical principles in relation to research and professional practice, and to reflect on what constitutes ethical research in professional practice. In doing this there will be some reference to research in health and social care settings. That is not to say that such information is irrelevant for other professionals, there are many examples of good practice that should underpin any research in professional practice.

Student activity 6.1

Use the questions below to prepare for discussion with your student peers regarding the nature of your practice and influencing factors. See what similarities and differences you can identify:

- What is your professional practice area?
- How has this area of practice been determined?
- What kind of education underpins preparation for professional practice?
- What codes of conduct or professional guidelines underpin your practice?
- Where have they originated?
- Who applies them and how?
- What influence has research within your professional practice?
- What factors are influencing your current professional practice?

The nature of professions and professional practice

The characteristics of professions

Professional work has been the focus of sociological interest and analysis for a considerable time, Friedson (1970) undertook detailed examination and critique of the medical profession, for example. He also describes the earlier seminal work of Herbert Spencer and other founding sociologists, regarding the emerging professions of the nineteenth century. For example Spencer, even then, considered professions were privileged by their position in society, with unique knowledge and skills that set them apart from other members of society and that were required within society (Friedson 1984).

Such status or distinction is reflected later by Reeder (1972) who also described professionals as autonomous practitioners controlling the production and use of their knowledge in a way that those outside the profession could not access. Furthermore professions were self-regulating, with codes of professional ethics.

The ensuing critique of professional status and role has resulted in identification and discussion of the following characteristics:

- Specialized knowledge, which is subsequently enhanced and developed through research (Wilkinson and Miers 1999)
- A monopoly of the professional practice area with registration being required for practice
- Professional practice governed by a code of ethics or practice, administered by professional associations (Wilkinson and Miers 1999)
- A concern for the general good: public service rather than individual gain
(Giddens 2006)

While much of the discussion challenges professional dominance, Carrier and Kendall (1995) offer a balanced approach to professions. For example they suggest professionalism can have positive aspects when used to improve and develop services, and it can have a negative impact when underpinned by privilege and exclusive claims regarding expertise. Meanwhile Eraut (1994) argues that an all encompassing definition for the professions is impossible, preferring instead to use the notion of professional ideology, focusing on three central features:

1 Specialized knowledge
2 Autonomy of practice
3 Service provided to those who have need of the profession's particular knowledge and skills

Eraut explores the rise of aspirational professionals, described by Etzioni (1969) as semi-professions, such as teachers and social workers. Practitioners in these areas may view themselves as professional, and be considered so externally, yet they do not possess a unique body of knowledge and they may also be subject to considerable government regulation. Historically some of the semi-professions have striven to improve their status by improved education – examples include nursing and other health professions.

While some professions, as above, are striving for enhanced status and are aspirational, other professions have emerged out of technical considerations, developing knowledge and practice under the aegis of established professions, and have now become almost independent of those original professions. Here Eraut (1994) describes the ascent of professions related to construction as an example, with surveyors and engineers now practising independently, as opposed to within the sphere of influence of the architect, for example.

It can be seen that there are over-arching themes in discourses about professional practice; however, it will be argued in the following section that the changing nature of economics, stakeholder/public opinion, technology and work practices are transforming the meaning and nature of professional practice.

The changing nature of professions and their practice

Transdisciplinarity

Historically professional characteristics have focused on autonomous practice within a specific and closed sphere. However, for many years there have been successive calls for the revision of practice with professional collaboration. These have been reflected in calls for multidisciplinary teams, interagency working, interprofessional education and collaboration and transdisciplinarity, for example.

Since the 1970s, health and social professionals have been exhorted to communicate, collaborate and work as effective teams. Such exhortations have been important pillars of professional practice. The failure of such practices is illustrated with regard to key enquiries into child abuse and neglect (Colwell Report 1974; Laming 2003). Early calls for collaboration can be seen as part of a continuum which now calls for the full integration of health, social care, education and an increasingly wide range of services for stakeholders.

Leathard (1994: 6) uses the phrase 'terminological quagmire', and comparison and contrasting of the complex terminology has been well rehearsed elsewhere (Leathard 1994; Barr 2005; Meads et al. 2005). This discussion is likely to be familiar to professional doctorate students, given their professional experience and knowledge, and is not the focus of discussion here. However, in order to progress with this chapter, the following are offered in clarification:

- Multiprofessional is considered to be when two or more professions learn side by side, for whatever reason
- Interprofessional is considered to be when two or more professions learn from and about each other to improve collaboration and the quality of care

(Barr 2005)

Leaving aside the semantic challenges of professional practices, the emerging issue for reflection and analysis here is the notion of transdisciplinarity. Transdisciplinarity focuses on the generalities of professional disciplines – for example knowledge that can be shared between disciplines and the overarching elements or themes that professions can use to address their work.

For example Klein (2004: 516) cites the definition of transdisciplinarity by Nicolescu: 'the science and art of discovering bridges between different areas of knowledge and different beings.' In essence the complexity of challenges facing societies, themselves underpinned by uncertainty and change, and recognition that there are several ways of interpreting and understanding these issues is reflected by the need for transdisciplinary approaches.

Nicolescu (1999) argues that transdisciplinarity is 'the transfer of methods from one discipline to another . . . transdisciplinarity concerns that which is at once between the disciplines, across the different disciplines and beyond all discipline'. Arguably professions (and the institutions that educate them) need to recognize transdisciplinary approaches if they are to have an impact on societal developments and challenges.

Klein (2004) gives examples of the need for transdisciplinarity in the areas of interchangeable social, technical and economic developments – for example energy, housing, sustainable development, environment and health care. The author illustrates this point through discussion of an innovative learning programme, where medical students collaborate and work with a wide range of the above disciplines to understand and appreciate the patient/client experience of health breakdown. Furthermore Klein argues that this is not a passing fashion, transdisciplinarity is essential if societal challenges are to be fully appreciated and addressed.

Transdisciplinarity as a means of professional practice is not a new idea. While it may have re-emerged at the forefront of contemporary societal complexity, Piaget discussed the concept in the 1970s, identifying over-arching themes and commonalities for disciplines to explore and address (Klein 2004). In essence it can be seen that the themes and common elements of transdisciplinarity question and indeed challenge the established notion of professions operating within a unique body of knowledge, and the perceived insularity of professional practice. Furthermore if stakeholder involvement and active stakeholder contribution to decision making and planning are to be achieved, then professional language and communication needs to be accessible to all.

Transdisciplinarity is in itself a complex field of study and has been explored here in the context of the changing nature of professions and their practice. In summary, that change is represented by convergence and identification of common themes in subjects and disciplines. However, transdisciplinarity as a response to the challenges facing societies is one measure of the changing nature of professional practice. Other possibilities will now be explored.

Critical scrutiny of professional practice

The professions, once perceived as omnipotent and superior, are under increasingly critical scrutiny from governments and stakeholders. Their fall, almost from grace, is exemplified in a project undertaken by the Royal Society for the Encouragement of Arts, Manufactures and Commerce (www.rsa.org.uk/). Entitled Exploring Professional Values for the Twenty-First Century, the project culminated in a series of discussion papers critically analysing the professions' situation.

For example Perkin (2003) reflects on the prodigious growth of professions through history and the development of learned societies to promulgate their development. In this context the university is seen by Perkin as the 'key' to professions; catering for educational knowledge as preparation for professional practice. He continues by exploring some high profile examples where the trust, indeed reverence, for professions has been breeched, resulting in contemporary cynicism and a dubious response to claims of professionalism.

Examples related include the Bristol Royal Infirmary Inquiry. This investigated issues around the care management and delivery for children who were in need of complex cardiac surgery. The subsequent recommendations were focused on good leadership in health care; respect and honesty from professionals; the safety and standards of care; public involvement; and the care of children (Bristol Royal Infirmary Inquiry 2001). Other examples of the demise of professional trust and responsibility are illustrated with reference to the clergy, scientific research, environmental sciences, business and financial services (Perkin 2003).

Friedson (1984) argues that professions have traditionally been self-regulating, dealing with members' shortcomings by the threat of removal of professional privileges such as the license to practice as a professional. However, previously Friedson (1970) contended that professions have systematically not controlled their members in a just or systematic manner; this belief is also evident in the timbre of Perkin's paper. Consequently the reputation and standing of professions are in disrepute and subject to increasing scrutiny at the micro level of public opinion and at the macro level of government policy and practice. There are, increasingly, directives for regulation beyond professional self-determination, with lay members joining regulatory bodies and councils; government inspection and regulation; and legislation and targets relating to how practice is conducted and in what format. Accounting and financial services are examples of areas where the over-arching scrutiny for professional practice has occurred.

It can be seen that such scrutiny and critique has critically undermined some of the characteristics and prestige of professions described earlier, fundamentally altering the shape of professions and the nature of their practice. This has implications for the professional doctorate student, not only how they are, but how they have been admitted into their profession. It has implications for how they practice, their autonomy and how they investigate and/or influence practice.

The location of professional practice

Professional practice is also changing its location, and medicine illustrates this. As a child I can recall visits to our family doctor who worked from a surgery in the front room of his own home. There was no receptionist, people moved around the straight-backed dining chairs that lined the walls of a green and brown waiting room. By consensus everyone understood when it was their turn to see the doctor. There was no appointment system, people simply turned up between the stated hours and waited their turn to see the doctor.

The doctor sat in front of a roll-top desk to address health problems. (Interesting to recall that his wife periodically popped in with his cup of tea and any woman who was doctor and not tea person at that time had the respected prefix of *lady* doctor.) I can recall a memorable incident when I had severe whooping cough and the doctor came regularly during his morning rounds to visit our family home. This was quite an event: our home was in a remote rural area and the doctor's small car could be seen from miles away. In summary, this doctor was a single-handed practitioner, a respected professional who knew all about our lives and business, an exemplar of benevolent patriarchy, dedication and vocation.

Today his equivalent would work out of a fully equipped medical centre with a team of practice nurses, a computerized appointment system and a multidisciplinary team. While the family doctor of my childhood era was working within the professional codes of the General Medical Council, as do contemporary doctors, today there are also superimposed targets: waiting times, health service targets, frameworks and clinical excellence guidelines to govern general practice and wider health care practice.

Leicht and Fennell (1997) analyse the shift in professional practice as described above. For example they argue that there is a change in the dynamics of professional work through its relationship with the workplace. As in the medical illustration above, professionals can now be found in a variety of organizational settings as salaried employees. The authors use the legal profession as an illustration: rather than the link between the business customer who has built up a relationship with an external law practice, businesses increasingly have legal departments with inhouse professionals to address issues.

Furthermore the grouping of professions in such organizational settings confers opportunity and need for additional supervision. This is related to professional work and hierarchal supervision within the organization by the managers of the organization, according to the organization's priorities and needs (Friedson 1984; Leicht and Fennell 1997). In essence, professionals are accountable to the supervisors and hierarchies within their employing organization in addition to the increasingly rigorous and external parameters of practice. There is potential for conflict of interest, then, if organization drivers, such as the economy, increased business throughput and productivity, are at variance with professional ideals of service.

Deprofessionalization

Prior to the contemporary scrutiny of professions, Haug (1973) suggested that professions were losing their mystique as their unique knowledge base and rites disappeared. More recently 'new' professions, initially subsidiary to established practice, have subsequently emerged as producing practitioners who are professionals in their own right (Eraut 1994). Furthermore, professional practice is increasingly supplemented by support workers or assistants who undertake tasks usually perceived as requiring lesser expertise, but which are possibly central to the professional practice.

Nursing provides a fascinating example, with support workers or health care assistants transformed into the trainee assistant practitioners within nursing and now other health professions. Likewise teachers have assistants in their classrooms to develop students' reading skills or to provide additional assistance for those who need it. The police have community support officers. Such examples are characterized by their possession of competence based skills and training.

Deprofessionalization can perhaps also be illustrated by the phenomenonal growth of the Internet, where information on a wide range of subjects is now achievable for anyone with access to a computer and computer skills. Friedson (1984) argues that professional knowledge has lost its 'esoteric' character as it can be accessed by anyone. On the one hand, this relieves stakeholders of professional dominance, as others also can be as well informed as (if not sometimes more informed than) the professionals. On the other hand, it leaves the stakeholder open to more spurious Internet claims regarding professional knowledge and skill. In that case access to knowledge is not enough: appraisal skills to determine the salient knowledge and information are also required.

The changing nature of professional practice as portrayed above has the potential to be doom laden and to result in poor morale for professional practitioners. Certainly in terms of recruitment and future admission to professional practice adverse publicity may result in a negative response, especially when other employment opportunities are increasingly available and attractive. On the one hand, the changing nature of professional practice could be constructed as a diminution of professional expertise and gravitas and the 'deskilling' associated with Braverman (1974). On the other hand, nothing in society is static, and if professions are to be responsive to societal need they need to use research to evaluate and engage in stakeholder dialogue regarding professional work. This is necessary not only to enhance the quality of professional work but to improve trust, and to promote partnership and public understanding. Furthermore the redistribution of professional knowledge and skill could provide more opportunities for research and development.

The changing nature of professional knowledge

The nature of knowledge and how it is constructed has been the subject of complex philosophical discussion for centuries and is beyond the scope of this chapter. Texts such as Cottingham (1996) and Gribbin (2002) illuminate epistemological and historical debate concerning the meaning and origins of knowledge and science. Furthermore Taylor and Hicks have previously alluded to epistemological and methodological issues, within their excellent Chapter 3, in this book.

Professionals usually have acquired their knowledge through a university education. Such education conferring status on the profession by the nature of the qualifications required to enter university and the qualifications and licence to practise on completion of studies. Such knowledge has been described as propositional knowledge, with a basis in fact, theory and association with empirical research. Propositional knowledge is based on rationality and transferability from one context to another (Eraut 1994).

Eraut (1994) contends, however, that the knowledge used by professional practitioners is different to propositional knowledge. It is based on experience, judgement, trial and error, or intuition. The notion of tacit knowledge as developed by Polanyi has been used in detailed discussion of professional practice (Polanyi 1967: 2003). In contrast to the rational and methodical nature of propositional knowledge, tacit knowledge is difficult to explain, being based on the thoughts and experience of the practitioner; as Polanyi states 'There are things that we know but cannot tell' (Polanyi 1962).

Such practice based knowledge, emergent from practice and for practice, is also to be found in the work of Schon (1983, 1987) and the development of reflective practice, to examine, evaluate and critically develop professional practice. Elsewhere the notion of expertise has been used to reflect on the nature of professional practice and the acquisition of professional knowledge (Selinger and Crease 2006).

Changing approaches to professional knowledge: the professional doctorate

The brief exploration above has encapsulated discussion of the meaning of knowledge for professional practice, with some comparison and contrast of types of knowledge and its development for professional practice. Meanwhile an emerging debate has critically examined the location of professional knowledge development.

In relation to professional doctorates the typology of knowledge developed by Gibbons et al. (1994) is often applied to underpin the characteristics and nature of the ensuing knowledge. For example the authors contend that Type 1 knowledge is related to the convention of university based and acquired knowledge: students generally acquiring knowledge within universities and applying it within their chosen discipline or practice sphere. Such characteristics were reviewed in Chapter 1 in relation to the nineteenth-century development of the PhD, with an emphasis on scientific method to meet the needs of industrialization. Type 1 knowledge also resonates with the principles of propositional knowledge.

Huff (2000) argues that such knowledge has characterized education in the post-World War II era, with connotations of scientific truth, a unidisciplinary basis, and positivistic or mechanistic underpinnings. This situation has been the ideal; however, there has been no guarantee that the desired knowledge application in practice would happen. Indeed Eraut (1994) suggests that some academic knowledge may be considered overly theoretical and not easily transferable to the practice setting. In this case, the development of situated or practice based knowledge may emerge to better explain and underpin actions in professional practice.

In summary, the parameters of knowledge within the respective disciplines have been controlled by the academy. Furthermore this system is said to reflect the interests of academic development in terms of reputation and status, with journals catering for the needs of academics rather than knowledge users (Wood 2002).

Student activity 6.2

1 What examples of situated or practice knowledge relate to your area of professional practice?
2 How is propositional knowledge determined in your area of professional practice and how is it used?

Gibbons et al. (1994) offer, by contrast, Type 2 knowledge production. This is characterized by a collaborative approach between knowledge users and the academics. Such knowledge is likely to be derived from and within practice by practitioners. As such this approach best reflects the situation for the professional doctorate student, where supervision as discussed in Chapter 4, for example, is viewed as a reciprocal partnership between university supervisor and professional. In essence, knowledge is derived from the immediate realities of practice and is likely to be context based within that practice.

In their discussion of Type 2 knowledge, Scott et al. (2004) emphasize transdisciplinarity (see previous section), with professional practice developments being found in the practice milieu as opposed to the academic setting. The authors also contend, however, that Type 2 knowledge is complementary rather than completely replacing Type 1 knowledge sources (Scott et al. 2004).

The complementary nature of Type 1 and Type 2 knowledge also resonates for Huff, who argues that Type 1 knowledge will not become obsolete, there being an important contribution for both Types. However, Type 2 knowledge is perhaps more ably shared by virtual groups enabling rapid development and adaptation. There is a cautionary note in the debate, however. Huff (2000) argues that the student population is increasingly sophisticated and discerning, and may find Type 1 knowledge too slow and introspective for the needs of professional practice. Given the professional maturity and experience of many professional doctorate students, this is a possibility and warrants further study and evaluation.

This section has attempted to encapsulate a complex discussion, starting with the nature of professional knowledge and the acquisition of knowledge for professional practice. Within the discussion it is suggested that Gibbons et al.'s (1994) typology of knowledge best illustrates the professional doctorate's underpinning philosophies. The focus for knowledge generation and development is shifted from within the academic setting to that of the professional practice setting. The relationships between academic and student also adjust, and are associated with partnership and reciprocity. The following section will explore some of the implications of practitioner research and knowledge development within the practice setting in relation to ethical issues.

Ethics, professional practice and research

Research ethics will now be explored as they relate to the process of professional doctorate research. It is acknowledged at the outset, however, that not all professional doctorates are concerned with research involving human participants. For example the development of original artwork, sculpture, design portfolios, creative writing or musical compositions may not involve the viewpoints of other participants at all, being derived entirely from the intellectual and creative repertoire of the professional doctorate student. However, research involving animal experimentation and all research involving human participants needs ethical consideration; this section will focus on research involving human participants. Such participants could involve service users, stakeholders, other professionals, their managers, professional regulatory bodies or the general public.

The following themes will be used as a basis for exploration:

- Contemporary issues and ethical research
- The ethics of researching practice/practitioner research
- The ethical principles of informed consent and doing no harm (non-maleficence)
- Confidentiality and anonymity
- Mental capacity
- Data protection issues
- Research in the health care setting

- Research in the social care setting
- Research in other settings

Regardless of the profession concerned, ethics, ethical practice and ethical research should underpin professional doctorate study; however, research relating to health and social care by virtue of the sensitive nature of this practice, would appear to have been the subject of considerable media and professional attention. For this reason it is easy to think that principles of ethics, ethical approval policies and procedures only relate to health and social care stakeholders, as they are perceived as more vulnerable by virtue of the services they receive (or deliver).

If your professional practice does not fall into these disciplines, then please do not sigh and turn to the next chapter: ethical principles should underpin all practice and especially so when research is being used to explore and develop professional practice. Questioning practice has the potential to generate knowledge and expertise from practice, but only with good communication, leadership and consideration for others who may be affected. The previous chapters have detailed some of the challenges relating to research and professional practice:

- Research supervision for professional students: the blurring of boundaries between friendship; professional collaboration; and professional doctorate supervision requirements
- The implications of research located in professional practice: for the researcher; the supervisor; other practitioners; other stakeholders; and the organization or practice context

Contemporary issues and ethical research

Ethics could be described as a set of rules or guidelines which influence behaviour on a societal and individual basis. They underpin notions of what is right or wrong, and are derived from the norms and values shared within societies. Similarly professional practice is governed by specific codes of professional conduct, which may make reference to ethical issues.

The Nuremberg Code 1947 developed in the aftermath of World War II detailed the following areas in relation to the conduct of research:

- The voluntary consent of participants
- Participants should have the power to choose without being placed under duress
- Participants should have knowledge to understand and decide if they want to get involved

- Participants need to understand the nature, duration and purpose of any research

(http://history.nih.gov/laws.pdf/nuremberg.pdf)

Ethics and ethical practices must underpin all research: demonstrating that researchers undertake their work in a way that is open, honest and does no harm to the participants and others. Society is increasingly critical of the power and status held by professionals and the research they undertake, as implied in the first section of this chapter. People want to know (and have a right to know) what is being done in the name of research and/or professional practice, how and why. Such questioning and challenging possibly stems from the availability of information on the Internet and individuals' ability to access vast amounts of information and practices once held firmly in the professional domain. Furthermore controversies involving high profile international research have prompted questioning and challenge of the nature of research.

Many professionals would concur with Miller and Boulton (2007) and argue that they would undertake research based on their professional integrity and judgement, with due respect for those involved in the research. However, in contrast, Braxton and Bayer (1996) argue that public trust of research communities has been challenged by a series of high profile cases in the US. Their study found that a sample of US senior academics had personal knowledge of scientific misconduct.

Sir David King, Chief Scientific Adviser for the British government has outlined the following seven principles for researchers to follow; they have also been endorsed by the Royal Society of Chemistry:

1 Act with skill and care, keep skills up to date
2 Prevent corrupt practice and declare conflicts of interest
3 Respect and acknowledge the work of other scientists
4 Ensure that research is justified and lawful
5 Minimize impact on people, animals and the environment
6 Discuss the issues science raises for society
7 Do not mislead: present evidence honestly

(BBC 2007)

Ethical approaches to research are paramount regardless of the location of research. Professional doctorate students may undertake their research under the auspices of their university, a research council, another funding body or as part of their professional practice, in all of which cases there will be an ethics framework. Furthermore these organizations will not want their reputation threatened by poor research practices. Some areas of research, for example health care research involving patients and others who are ill or vulnerable, require that stringent ethical approval is sought prior to conducting any study. Arguably all human participants in research are subject to the same anxieties and vulnerabilities, especially if their own professional practice is under scrutiny.

The ethics of researching practice/practitioner research

The ethics of practitioner research have been explored briefly in relation to the student supervisory relationship in Chapter 4. Practitioner research is not unique to the professional doctorate: professionals can and do undertake such research as part of PhD, masters' level studies or within their professional role. However, as suggested in Chapter 1 of this book, practitioner research is central to the philosophy of the professional doctorate. The key processes and outcomes for the professional doctorate relate to research knowledge and skill generated from and within a practice setting, by the practitioner as opposed to by an independent researcher.

These characteristics confer benefits to professional doctorate study: insider knowledge of the professional practice setting; understanding of the roles and responsibilities of those within practice; and knowledge of professional practices and organizational cultures. They can also bring potential costs or risks, for example the research may raise sensitive issues about practice, and there are issues about the status and power of the practitioner–researcher and their ability to influence or coerce others. Such concerns have been analysed by Costley and Gibbs (2006).

For example the authors argue that practitioner–researchers are unable to distance themselves from the research context in the same way that an outside researcher invited into a specific professional context could. Prior to their research they already have a relationship with the stakeholders in that setting, which will continue during the research process and may be adversely influenced by the aims of the research, the research process and the subsequent findings. This, Costley and Gibbs argue, creates particular tensions and issues for the researcher and the context, if not explored from the outset from philosophical and pragmatic viewpoints. Here are some other tensions raised by the authors:

- Those giving information within a practitioner–researcher study may do so not knowing that they are at risk of exposing their own shortcomings and those of the organization
- Participants may not know that observations of their practices are being undertaken for the purposes of research. For example if ethnography is used in a practice setting, at what point does the practitioner–researcher change between active professional and active researcher? How are these roles to be managed and made explicit?
- The above may potentially result in changes to individual practice or the overall organization of the professional practice context. For example there

may be role changes or job losses, a point also raised by Boucher and Smyth (2004). The research may illuminate sensitive areas of professional practice, poor practice or shortcomings, which may be embarrassing if made public. Ellis (2006) reported that some professional doctorate students who held senior positions in the health sector faced resistance to their research on that basis

Furthermore Costley and Gibbs (2006) argue that the practitioner research scenario can lead to a triangulation of competing tensions between the professional development and learning of the researcher; the academic expectations of doctoral study; and the viewpoints or beliefs underpinning the professional practice context. Some of these tensions relating to the nature of knowledge for professional practice have already been explored in the earlier stages of this chapter. The authors argue for an ethical process of 'being' and regard for others, rather than simple adherence to ethics as a methodological procedure. In essence, they advocate the issues of reflective practice and reflexivity appraised by Taylor and Hicks in Chapter 3.

The ethical principles of informed consent and doing no harm (non-maleficence)

Informed consent

In order to avoid the tensions illustrated previously in relation to transparency of research purpose and method in the practitioner setting, the principles of informed consent require due consideration. As with research conducted in any context, participants need to know why and how the research is being conducted, and by whom, before they can make an informed decision about participation. Informed consent may be obtained in several ways, for example using written information and a written consent form; using verbal explanation or implication, as in the return of a postal survey or questionnaire; participation in a conversation (if the purpose relating to research is explicit); or through participation in an online survey, again if the purpose is explicit.

Even if research is being undertaken with an organization's permission or at their behest, then participants at fieldwork level must still have full details of the research before they can decide whether to participate or not. Withholding information and explanation could be construed as a form of coercion or bullying and would not be in keeping with the principles of informed consent.

In summary, informed consent requires the practitioner–researcher to consider how they will negotiate access to research participants and how they will explain their intentions at a professional/organizational level and at the level of individual practice. For example what kind of explanation will be used to illuminate the study and enhance informed consent? Information for participants needs to be accessible to that particular group. This does not necessarily mean using the kind of academic language used within the doctoral thesis, doctoral portfolio or within academic or professional journals. As part of informed consent it is also important to state how information and data will be discussed in the thesis and elsewhere, including how it will be shared in the professional context, through publications and conference presentations, for example.

Participants in your research study should have enough information from which to make a decision whether or not to get involved. They should be able to understand the purpose of the research, what is involved in the research and what is required of their participation, including any benefits or potential risks. Participants should have enough time to make a choice about their involvement in the research and this should include time to change their minds if they wish, without any of their rights being affected. This is especially so if they are receiving professional services, such as counselling, health or social care.

Miller and Boulton (2007) concur that informed consent is an important aspect of the relationship between those involved in research activities and participants. However, they raise questions about excessive bureaucracy and regulation, purely as a reactive response to societal concerns about the nature and purpose of research.

Doing no harm (non-maleficence)

It is not always easy to guarantee that harm will not ensue from practitioner research. For example discussion of sensitive issues, reflection on past events, or discussion of sexism, harassment in the workplace or other abuse can potentially cause distress to the participant. However, not undertaking research on the basis that it will cause harm, raise controversy or expose sensitive issues means that potentially under-explored areas of professional practice or social processes are overlooked. In this case it is best to raise awareness of the potential for distress and have mechanisms in place to help the participant. These could include referral to others for further support and guidance. It is not advisable to blur the roles of researcher and professional by offering counselling and support yourself, even if this constitutes part of your professional practice. It is far better to refer the participant to others, should support be needed.

Remember Olga in Chapter 4? There was potential for students to disclose issues relating to bullying. It will be recalled that one of the stipulations for the research to proceed at the school was that mechanisms were in place to counteract bullying should this be identified during the research process. The fine line between acting as a professional, and giving advice and guidance, as opposed to acting the independent researcher is blurred in practitioner research. Doctoral students may find that clients may ask for their advice or opinion in the context of the research study. Sensitive discussion and referral to the appropriate resources is important.

An increasing area for concern is the harm that may result to the researcher, especially if fieldwork is being conducted away from their practice setting. Ideally interviews or discussions should not take place offsite, or should at least be undertaken in public places. Anyone working offsite should inform a colleague of their whereabouts, phoning them once their research activities have been completed. At the stage of ethical approval, whether this is formalized through an ethics committee or approval within an organization, a risk assessment should be undertaken to look at the consequences of the research. Not only should this highlight the issues above, risks to the researchers and others should be considered in relation to health and safety, exposure to chemicals and other substances.

Confidentiality and anonymity

Issues such as confidentiality and anonymity require reflection. While it is taken as given (and routinely written on ethics approval forms) that both these principles should be adhered to when researching professional practice, the realities may reveal challenges. Assurances of confidentiality are often given on participant information sheets, suggesting information will not be disclosed outside the research team. However, if the practitioner–researchers are professionals with a particular code of practice or conduct, there may be professional, legal, if not organizational reasons why information relating to dangerous practice, financial irregularity or child abuse, for example, should be disclosed to others. In summary there may be a professional responsibility to disclose and act upon this information and as such this needs to be made explicit to any research participants in the practice setting as part of their decision to take part in the study or not.

Anonymity, safeguarding the names, identities or roles within an organization, may pose challenges too. Individuals may be identifiable within a small study by virtue of the role they hold, comments they have made or actions they have taken, even with the use of pseudonyms or other descriptors. If this is the case then permission to identify participants and/or the organization must be obtained.

The Mental Capacity Act 2005 (England and Wales)

While this legislation relates to England and Wales there are wider considerations for research undertaken in other countries too. Capacity relates to the ability to make individual decisions on the basis of information presented. The

Mental Capacity Act relates to those adults over the age of 16 who may not be able to give their consent to participate in any research study. It must be acknowledged that the Mental Capacity Act applies to *all* areas of research and not just that undertaken in the health service or social care contexts (for comprehensive information see: www.dh.gov.uk/en/PublicationsAndStatistics/Publications/PublicationsPolicyAndGuidance/DH_074491).

Data protection issues within the conduct of research

During their practice many professionals are given access to sensitive information: personal health information, personal financial information or personal social information, for example. The Data Protection Act 1998 confers legal responsibilities in the UK in relation to access, storage and disposal of personal data and this includes that used for research purposes. Similar legislation has been developed in other countries. While professionals may routinely have access to this information as part of their professional role, its use for additional research purposes is strictly proscribed without explicit permission. In essence, the processing of an individual's personal data and information, if the person is living and identifiable, is subject to the Data Protection Act.

Within the Data Protection Act there are eight principles:

1 Data should be fairly and lawfully processed
2 It should be processed for limited purposes
3 Data should be adequate, relevant and not excessive
4 Data should be accurate and up to date
5 Data should not be kept for longer than necessary
6 It should be processed in accordance with the individual's rights
7 It should be secure
8 It should not be transferred to countries without adequate protection

The above principles help to illuminate the role and the responsibilities of the practitioner–researcher. You must seek advice from your supervisors and the professional context regarding data protection. There will be named individuals in your place of study and within your practice setting who can provide detailed and specific advice on your research and the data protection implications. Further guidance can be sought at the Information Commissioner's Office (see: www.ico.gov.uk/).

Storing information and data

The storage of personal information and research data is a key issue during any research process involving human participants. Participants often give personal details, trusting in the researcher's ability to handle and store this appropriately. During your research design and certainly when seeking ethical approval in your professional context or elsewhere, you will be asked to explain the arrangements for the storage of data. Research council funding may require adherence to their policies regarding research data, requiring that it be stored for a particular length of time once the research is complete. Certainly storing research data until the completion of your doctorate and through the dissemination process is a minimum requirement. Personal data such as names, addresses and other personal details should be separated from the research data and stored securely in locked cabinet or a password protected computer in a secure setting. Remember that laptops and home computers may have less security. Personal information may not be disclosed to a third party or used in any way unconnected to the research in hand.

Data protection exemptions

There are some exemptions within the Data Protection Act. For example assessment marks and examination results may be used for research purposes even if this is not made explicit to the people concerned. Furthermore if information was collected and it was not known at the time that it may potentially be used for research purposes later, and if it is not practical to contact the individuals concerned, then permission to use the information for research purposes may be given. Personal information may not be published unless it is anonymized or the participants have given specific permission for its use.

The use of sensitive personal information may only be approved for research purposes if any one of the conditions in Schedule 3 of the Act is satisfied, examples include the following:

- Explicit consent is obtained in writing from the individuals
- If the researcher has a duty of confidentiality as in medical research and this is adhered to
- If information is used for equal opportunities, or monitoring of racial or ethnic origins

The Data Protection (Processing of Sensitive Personal Data) Order 2000 allows for sensitive data processing if the research is in the substantial public interest. Clearly issues such as the public interest and sensitive information are open to wide interpretation and debate. If in doubt you must seek clarification as above. In summary, data protection is an important issue and you must seek advice from the appropriate people on this matter.

The following sections explore research in the health and social care settings where studies are likely to involve people who are vulnerable or anxious. While the discussions below relate to the policies in the UK there will be equivalents in other settings. In addition, even if the study is not being under-taken in health or social care sectors, there are some transferable lessons in relation to research ethics.

Research in the health care setting

In April 2007 the National Research Ethics Service (NRES) was launched in the UK to streamline ethical approval in the health care setting using one approval mechanism. The overall aim is to protect the rights, safety, dignity and well-being of research participants, and to promote ethical research. A website provides detailed information and guidance notes in addition to an online application form (see: www.nres.npsa.nhs.uk/).

The Integrated Research Application System was operational from 29 January 2008. The application form is completed and then considered at the relevant local research ethics committee.

In summary the application form is based on the following themes:

- The title of the research study
- Who has overall responsibility: the chief investigator
- An overview of the research
- The aim or purpose of the study
- The research methodology
- Data collection, analysis, storage and retention of data
- Recruitment of participants to the study: inclusion and exclusion criteria
- Consent, confidentiality and anonymity issues
- Risks, including risks for the researcher
- Ethical issues
- Advertising material, participant information if applicable
- Duration of the research study
- Liability issues
- Dissemination of findings

When the application is completed a telephone booking service is in oper-ation which enables allocation to the relevant local research ethics committee for consideration. It is possible to attend the research ethics committee meet-ing on the day your proposal is being considered. It is helpful if your supervisor can attend with you to help you clarify any of the issues raised.

While the system above relates to the UK, there will be equivalents in other countries. The application process may sound daunting for the professional doctorate student; however, it is there to be rigorous, to safeguard health service users and to protect the rights of individuals. A satisfactory outcome with this ethical approval is affirmation that your research study is of good quality, as it has been assessed by experienced researchers, health service personnel and lay members of the committee.

There are several positive things you can do to ensure your ethics application is of the highest quality. First of all, seek the advice of your research supervisor who should have insight into the health service requirements for gaining ethical approval. In addition, attend any training or workshops provided relating to research ethics. It is also valuable to speak to other professional doctorate students who have been through the process, and develop insight into their experiences. It is quite acceptable to contact the chair of the local research ethics committee for advice and guidance, and of course you must familiarize yourself with the extensive information provided by NRES itself. Allow sufficient time to complete the ethics approval form: make a draft copy first and then complete the online process. It is not helpful to rush the process and then realize you cannot obtain the signatures required or other information relating to liability, for example. Do your homework and preparation first and only go through the ethical approval process when your research design is clear and coherent. In the final analysis, if you are not clear about the scope and purpose of the study, others will not be able to understand your ideas intuitively and so your application will require further work.

Here are ten top tips to facilitate positive ethical approval processes and outcomes for health services research:

Top ten tips to facilitate positive ethical approval

1 Involve your research supervisor, who should have experience of health service requirements
2 Attend local training or workshops related to research ethics
3 Speak to other professional doctorate students who have sought ethical approval and discuss their experiences with them
4 Contact the chair of the local research ethics committee for advice and guidance
5 Familiarize yourself with the extensive information at www.nres.npsa.nhs.uk/
6 Allow enough time for the application process, plan ahead and ensure you have all the information and authorizations to hand
7 Do your homework: preparation is essential, so start early
8 Only apply when your research design is clear and coherent
9 The ethics application process is not there as an extension of your supervision or as a reflection on your proposed study
10 If you cannot explain the scope and purpose of your study clearly then more reading and preparation is needed: go back to the drawing board, as the ethics committee cannot work on their own intuition and interpretation

---

Research in the social care setting

Research conducted within local authorities in England with responsibility for social care has been required to demonstrate adherence to research governance frameworks since 2005. This requires that the researcher discusses their proposal with their manager in the first instance and then submits a detailed research proposal for consideration at the appropriate level within the local authority.

Pahl (2007) explores this in *Ethics Review in Social Care Research*. It was found that much social care research was carried out under the aegis of existing ethical scrutiny, in relation to funding councils, for example, university ethics committees and NRES, and that some local authorities already had mechanisms to review research applications involving service users and other staff. At the first level it was suggested that ethics review in social care should operate within local councils or across local government alliances. At a second level a social care research ethics committee was proposed to approve research involving more than one site or crossing national boundaries. This committee would be comparable to NRES (Pahl 2007).

Research in other settings

One much cited criticism of the procedures for seeking ethical approval in the health care setting is that the system is bureaucratic and slows down the research process. However, the ethical approval procedures are there for a specific purpose, and there is significant good practice and transferable learning that can enhance research in other settings. When your professional doctorate work is completed you want to have a clear conscience that the work has been undertaken with integrity and that ethical issues were foremost in your mind. Even if you are not working in health or social care settings you will still need to consider issues of informed consent, doing no harm, and data protection and mental capacity. You will certainly need to seek permission from within the context you are practising or researching in, and this must include permission at strategic and operational levels, as described earlier.

In addition, most universities now have their own procedures for ethical approval and may require you to submit a research proposal for perusal by their research ethics committee or equivalent. Even if this is not the case then your supervisor should insist on discussion of research ethics and evidence demonstrating that you have considered and adhered to ethical principles at all times.

Here are some common misconceptions relating to ethical considerations in professional doctorate research:

Some misconceptions relating to ethics and professional doctorate research

- *'It is only health service research that requires ethical approval'*: All research requires consideration of ethical issues in design and implementation. While the health services and local authorities have stringent procedures to protect the vulnerable, all research requires approval at strategic and operational levels of professional practice and this must include that of the participants
- *'My workplace has said I can go ahead'*: Is this in writing and on what basis was permission given? A conversation in a lift or on the corridor does not constitute full discussion. You need to detail your proposed research in the organization or practice setting and consider how you will inform all participants
- *'It's already part of my job. I have access to this information already'*: Maybe, however you are using your role for another purpose when undertaking professional doctorate research – gaining your doctorate and disseminating information with others – your research may expose sensitive issues about practice. Explicit permission in writing to use the information for research purposes is always required and must take account of informed consent and data protection issues

---

Conclusion

This chapter has attempted to explore the complex areas of professional knowledge development and the ethics of practitioner research. The task has been made especially difficult as the subject matter is not tangible or precise, being subject to different interpretations and opinions. It is hoped that a foundational outline of issues germane to professional practice knowledge and accompanying ethics have been given, with considerable scope for further reading and detailed discussion with your professional doctorate peers.

It can be seen that the development of knowledge and its meaning has a long philosophical and historical tradition. Views about the nature of knowledge and understanding may underpin choices relating to your choice of doctoral study route, and the research approaches to examine professional practice. In Chapter 3, Taylor and Hicks identified some of these discourses in relation to theoretical and methodological perspectives underpinning research.

The main contention in this chapter has been that professional doctorates offer new opportunities for knowledge development based on the Type 2 knowledge suggested by Gibbons et al. (1994). This emphasizes knowledge derived from within practice itself, led by the practitioner and involving collaborative partnerships with the academic community. In essence, academia is exhorted to develop partnerships to generate ideas and solutions for practice without the university, as opposed to relying on the development and transmission of theoretical and propositional knowledge to the student community.

The second part of the chapter considered the principles of ethics in professional doctorate research, drawing together earlier discussions in Chapters 3 and 4, for example. While research in health care settings has been accused of stringent, some would say Draconian, methods for obtaining research approval, there are principles of good practice for transfer into other settings. While national and international codes of ethical conduct focus on health care research, all human participants in research have the right to informed consent and to make their own decisions whether to participate in research.

The second section has aimed to demystify some ethical principles, with consideration of informed consent, doing no harm, mental capacity, confidentiality and anonymity, and data protection. Professional doctorate students can benefit from peer support and discussion in their communities of practice at all stages of decision making in relation to research ethics, and especially in relation to the realities of researching their practice context. Finally, it is acknowledged that the section on ethical approval is drawn from examples of English practices; however, there are standard over-arching ethical principles even if the procedures are slightly different in other countries.

Summary of key points

- The nature of professional practice is changing and adapting in the light of societal concerns and increasing scrutiny and challenge to professional power
- The nature of knowledge required for professional practice is subject to increasing academic and professional debate. There are moves towards Type 2 knowledge (Gibbons et al. 1994) as the basis of professional doctorate study, with emphasis on the practitioner leadership and generation of knowledge from within the practice context
- Ethical principles, such as informed consent and doing no harm, should underpin all research involving human participants. This is evident regardless of the research setting and does not apply solely to health and social care settings
- Mental capacity is a key factor to consider in relation to decision making and informed consent. This applies to all research as above and not solely to that which is conducted in health and social settings
- Stringent legislation protects the storage and use of personal and other data; students should ensure their research meets these requirements

7

Sharing your expertise with others

Aims of the chapter

- To explore professional doctorate requirements: the thesis and its alternatives, for example the portfolio
- To discuss effective strategies for viva preparation
- To critically analyse the writing styles required for different audiences: writing for academic purposes, professional reports, conference abstracts, journal publications and alternatives

Introduction

As part of your professional doctorate studies and postdoctorate you will write for different audiences for different purposes, communicating work in progress, collaborating with colleagues and others, for thesis presentation, report writing, and abstract writing, for example. The variety of audiences requires a variety of writing styles and language. In the professional doctorate thesis or equivalent there is a need to demonstrate confidence and expertise with your work; to present your research and outcomes in the best way possible; to emphasize your ability to think critically; and to develop an original and creative piece of work.

Just as master cabinet makers were accustomed to developing miniatures of furniture to showcase their talents; the professional doctoral thesis should showcase your knowledge and skill: your ability to engage with the advanced development of professional practice along with your professional expertise. Professional report writing by contrast should be succinct and factual, emphasizing the key points of your work and how it was developed, and suggesting future recommendations for professional practice.

This chapter will explore a variety of writing issues to help you share your expertise with others. It will help you further develop and enhance your writing and maximize the impact of your work. Initially the meaning of the word 'thesis' will be considered, and there will be exploration of thesis submission. Viva requirements will then be considered, along with various styles of professional doctorate portfolio presentation. Some writing issues will be explored, for example the use of the first person and how best to contextualize research within the professional setting. Finally, the chapter will consider professional report writing, conference abstracts, writing for publication and other creative forms of presentation as ways of sharing your expertise.

Illuminating the thesis

The word 'thesis' has Greek origins relating to the fundamental question, aim or standpoint to be analysed. Asking, 'What is your thesis?' could be equated with the question, 'What is the argument or question you are going to discuss?' In the academic context the word 'thesis' is used to describe the substantial piece of written work submitted, by the student, for examination by a panel of accomplished experts. In the UK the thesis is also critiqued and discussed through a viva voce or oral examination; however, this does not happen in all countries. The thesis is substantial: the culmination of several years of study to develop your professional knowledge and methodological expertise; to critically generate a research issue pertinent to professional practice; and to provide original and creative insights for professional practice.

Thesis length

Individual universities will have guidelines regarding word limits. The average PhD thesis can range from 80,000 to 100,000 words; although a much shorter thesis may be advocated in mathematical or biological disciplines, for example. The word limit for a professional doctorate thesis is usually shorter to take account of the assignments or other coursework submitted during the professional doctorate journey. The word limit may range from 40,000 to 60,000 words, while shorter works may be advocated in some areas.

Some subjects may not have a thesis at all, for example music may require a musical composition, while art and design professional doctorates may require a portfolio of artwork. While a shorter professional doctorate thesis may seem more appealing, remember that considerable skill is required to demonstrate critical analysis and evaluation within a shorter word limit. Word limits tend to evolve as part of academic or subject conventions, constituting what is acceptable and recognized within a particular discipline. It is important there-fore to read a variety of doctoral theses within your own subject area and elsewhere, to gain an appreciation of style and content. If possible compare and contrast PhD and professional doctorate theses.

Thesis content

As stated earlier the thesis is an important piece of work, demonstrating the original knowledge gained as part of the professional doctorate process, along with critical analysis of theoretical perspectives, relevant literature, justifica-tion and critique of the research processes. It critically analyses the funda-mental question or research aim and germane literature, and other knowledge and evidence, in addition to justifying the research methods used to conduct the study. The thesis gives a detailed account and analysis of the research findings, reflection on the study limitations and suggests areas for future study.

For the professional doctorate all the above are located within the context of professional practice. There should be a clear introduction to the professional practice setting and analysis of the key issues to be explored through profes-sional doctorate study, including how and why the study issue arose and how it will be addressed. While the discussion here lays out the general principles of the professional doctorate thesis, there are other influencing factors: the role of the practitioner–researcher, and critical reflection and analysis of significant events pertaining to research conducted in the professional practice setting. These themes will be considered later in this chapter in the subsection 'Locat-ing research within a professional practice context'. Reflection and reflexivity have previously been explored in detail in Chapter 3.

Thesis presentation and submission

Presentation of the professional doctorate thesis is in accordance with uni-versity guidelines and codes of practice. These typically require a title page; an abstract or summary of the research within a particular word limit; a contents page along with a list of tables and figures used; chapter headings; references and bibliography; along with relevant appendices. In addition to an abstract there may be a requirement for an introduction signposting the overall aim of the study and introducing briefly the content and layout of the chapters within the thesis. Commonly an acknowledgements page is incorporated at the beginning of the thesis, outlining the key people who have supported the student through the research process.

The information above provides an overview of thesis contents. However, the exact order and requirements will be governed by particular university con-ventions, along with those of the academic discipline or subject. The university guidelines can be very specific, down to the type of font, font size, word spacing, the size of margins and even the binding requirements. It is important to check the exact details prior to submission of your work and ensure you leave enough time at the submission stage to deal with unexpected editing. You must also leave sufficient time for checking and double-checking the bound copies of your work. Occasionally chapters can be in the wrong order or pages missed completely. It is your responsibility to check the final piece of work; finding missing pages or chapters the day before viva will add significantly to your stress.

Most universities will require formal notification in writing within a specified time period prior to submission, and this should detail the exact title of the work, the name of the author and identify who is to examine the thesis. The process for submission will be laid down in the university code of practice and a good supervisor will be fully conversant with the requirements. It is not unusual for the thesis title and the examiners to be ratified or approved by an internal panel of academics within the university. Initially the thesis may be submitted as soft bound copies for the respective examiners. A hard bound copy is produced following the viva, giving time to incorporate any changes required as part of the examination and viva process.

Examining the thesis

The written thesis does not usually receive a percentage or grade during the examination process. Decisions are generally based on the following areas, loosely adapted from the University of Salford (2007):

- Pass with no corrections required within the thesis
- Pass subject to minor corrections: these are usually related to specific paragraphs, or adjustment of minor typing and spelling errors along with referencing style. Usually a time limit to attend to minor corrections is stated, so work in this category must be developed comparatively quickly, within a four- to six-week time period, for example
- Pass subject to major corrections: these require more substantial changes to the work – the redrafting of chapters, the development of new chapters or the expansion of discussion points. Major corrections are achieved within a longer time limit, for example six months or longer
- Resubmission: in this instance the thesis requires much more detailed development, as the work produced is not of the standard commensurate with doctoral requirements. Resubmission may take place within a 12-month period, for example.

Once the relevant changes have been made and approved by the examiners, hard bound copies of the thesis are made and placed in the university library. Increasingly an electronic repository may be used as an alternative. At this stage the thesis is in the public domain, which is why you should have paid stringent attention to anonymity in your work. Remember that as part of the ethical approval process you have given assurances to the research participants, the professional practice setting and others that individual comments and the research location will not be identifiable.

The viva voce

The viva voce constitutes a verbal examination of the research work and the term is derived from Latin. In the UK the viva is a private process between student and examiners. One examiner will be identified from within the university department where the professional doctorate was studied. The second or external examiner will be appointed from another university, on the basis of their expertise in the thesis area. The supervisor may be present at the viva but does not usually contribute to the proceedings. In addition some universities appoint an internal independent academic to act as chairperson, especially if a member of staff is undertaking viva. The chairperson's role is to make sure the viva runs smoothly, the environment is conducive to discussion and that the viva is fair, consistent and conducted in accordance with university guidelines. As such they are not there to ask direct questions regarding the thesis itself.

In other countries, for example Scandinavia, the viva is an open event where other academics and members of the public may be invited to attend and participate. In this instance the thesis is publicly critiqued or examined, while the student is invited to defend the thesis. Members of the audience are also invited to ask questions. Elsewhere, for example Australia, there is no viva, the thesis being reviewed in private by the examiners.

Preparing for viva

The viva is the culmination of years of work so participants are understandably very nervous, feeling that it is a make or break situation. Many participants cannot remember the questions asked in any detail as they are concentrating at such a high level. In addition many myths abound regarding vivas that lasted for hours or where the examiners argued among themselves! However, with good planning and preparation these things should not happen. During the process of developing the thesis it is likely that there are staged, internal reviews where you undertake a mini viva. In addition many supervisors will organize a mock viva for their student, or groups of students can develop the expertise among themselves and from speaking with other students.

The viva is undoubtedly an assessment situation; however, the examiners are there to ensure your professional doctorate is within the parameters of doctoral requirements: original, creative and yours, demonstrable by your ability to discuss the work in detail. Remember that they are genuinely interested in your work, which is why they have been appointed as examiners. While questions will be detailed, remember that you are the one who has devoted considerable time to the subject under study, subsequently developing knowledge and expertise. Be confident while avoiding arrogance. Do not be angry if your work is challenged and do not be defensive. Explain your viewpoint and justify your approaches while recognizing any limitations. Be prepared to reflect upon things that did not go to plan and your learning from the situation. The unexpected things that happen are often important sources of learning for students and others.

Usually examiners have introductory questions, asking for an overview of your professional background and reasons for choosing your study. At the introductory stage examiners will usually outline the areas they wish to discuss, for example one may focus on the research methods employed, and another may focus on the literature review and other elements. They will have had the opportunity to meet prior to the viva and discuss your work, developing an outline of the questions they wish to ask. You should also be given the opportunity to ask questions, so it is advisable to plan some beforehand, or be prepared to clarify and expand on the points raised in the viva itself. You can take a notebook with you and a copy of your thesis. You should not be expected to discuss your work completely from memory.

Usually the viva will last one to two hours, and once started the time will pass quickly. As explained previously, the chairperson is there to ensure you are treated fairly, subjected to rigorous discussion but not placed under extreme pressure by a lengthy viva or aggressive questioning. Examiners will challenge your ideas to determine the quality of your response and debate; however, this should be professional as opposed to overly intimidating. Your supervision team should have discussed possible examiners with you, and you should know their own research interests and publications. It is usual to inform the student of the viva outcome on the day, once examiners have had some discussion in private.

Dinah successfully completed her viva in 2007; here are her top ten tips:

Dinah's top ten tips for viva

1 The best piece of advice that anyone gave me was to treat the viva as if you were going to an interview
2 Dress in something you feel smart in, or comfortable
3 Try to skim read your thesis and think about likely questions
4 Talk to other people who have successfully survived their viva. All are different but there are often common themes or similarities, which can help
5 Would your supervisor be able/prepared to do a mock viva with you? For me, this was invaluable

6 Is your supervisor invited to come to the viva? Both my supervisor and co-supervisor came to mine and I found this very helpful. They did not participate but I could feel their silent support. The notes they made were really helpful as I found the experience so stressful that I can remember very little of the content! I also really appreciated their company while waiting for the examiners' verdict

7 Stay calm – don't get angry or aggressive!

8 Try and keep the balance between being assertive when defending your thesis and coming across as arrogant

9 Admit if you don't know something!

10 Ask the examiners if they can rephrase a question, if you don't know what on earth they mean.

Good luck!

Table 7.1 provides a list of guidelines on what you should and should not do at viva:

Table 7.1 Viva do's and don'ts

Do	Don't
Dress professionally, greet the examiners with a confident handshake and a smile	Arrive late and flustered
Speak confidently and clearly	Argue or engage in heated debate
Take a notebook *and* your thesis	Speak from memory; if asked about a particular page or reference look it up in your thesis
Listen carefully and take time to clarify questions before you respond	Make excuses or obfuscate; if there are limitations say so, explaining your learning from the situation
Have some questions for the examiners at the end of the viva	Give the impression you have not prepared for your viva or you are not confident with your thesis

Other ways of submitting doctoral work: portfolios

While most professional doctorate programmes will follow the PhD convention and require submission of a thesis, professional portfolios are increasingly used within professional doctorate programmes. They could be used to demonstrate the impact of research in professional practice and to illuminate any smaller projects undertaken. They may include professional reports, other evidence relating to professional practice or journal publications. In some cases a critical reflective commentary will be used within the portfolio to integrate the ensuing knowledge and expertise with professional practice.

If the professional doctorate requires the direct assessment of practice, being part of admission to professional practice, then specific guidelines will relate to the assessment process. For example the British Psychological Society has guidelines relating to the supervision of practice within the doctorate in clinical psychology. Elsewhere the requirements for portfolio submission will be explained in the programme regulations and proforma relating to assessment practices. The following section gives examples of portfolio requirements as identified from contemporary professional doctorate literature.

For example Martin (2006) discusses professional doctorate portfolios and the tutorial strategies to facilitate their development. Professional doctorate portfolio requirements at the University of Essex are described, where portfolio work must illuminate the students' expertise in professional practice while demonstrating the outcomes of the professional doctorate programme. Within the accompanying critical commentary there is specific emphasis on linking the processes of research and study with the commensurate development of professional practice, recognizing and acknowledging the development of the student's expertise in practice. Such a portfolio clearly moves beyond the theoretical interpretation of literature to reflect on how the literature may have informed practice, and to incorporate strategies the student has used directly within professional practice.

Earlier discussion by Doncaster and Thorne (2001) emphasizes the importance of professional reflection and planning within the generic professional doctorate programme at the University of Middlesex. Here students undertake critical reflection on their professional practice and prior learning in order to develop an individual and detailed learning plan which will help them facilitate development in their professional practice settings. As such the students' professional doctorate programme is explicitly linked to their professional practice. They need to demonstrate specific professional capabilities within subsequent written work. The authors describe Part I of the programme as preparation, where students reflect and plan for the subsequent project development of Part II. Throughout there is an emphasis on critical reflection; knowledge of organizational change; the personal capacity to manage learning; and the professional ability to practise at the limits of current professional knowledge and expertise.

Elsewhere O'Mullane (2005) explores other professional doctorate requirements. These may include a shorter thesis and other elements of assignment or coursework produced during the programme. The use of portfolios to showcase particular aspects of art and design and accompanying commentary are also highlighted. Meanwhile Neumann (2005) describes the use of a portfolio to demonstrate published works, papers and journal articles sustained over the period of professional doctorate study. Within a doctorate in musical arts, for example, originality may be demonstrated by a new musical composition, with or without an accompanying critical commentary.

Professional practice and the impact of research in practice: the generation of new knowledge, skills and practices are unifying factors within portfolio submission. However, there are varied interpretations of how this should be achieved. Students should have clear and transparent discussions with their supervisory team regarding requirements, and pay clear attention to any guidelines or frameworks that are provided. For example the approach described by Martin (2006) implies a narrative, reflexive approach within the portfolio, as the student's 'story' of practice unfolds. By comparison Doncaster and Thorne (2001) suggest parameters for Part I and II of the portfolio requirements, with clear indication of the ensuing knowledge, skills and professional attributes to be demonstrated.

Developing an appropriate writing style for the professional doctorate

As the professional doctorate concerns research generated in a professional setting it is axiomatic to fully acknowledge and explore that setting within any written work. For example given the interaction between the practitioner–researcher, the professional practice setting, the participants in that setting and the available literature, it would appear common sense to incorporate these elements within professional doctorate writing. This would enhance reader understanding and demonstrate the development and application of research relevant to practice. However, writing style can be contestable. Requirements may be dependent on the subjective preferences of the supervisor, wider subject or disciplinary conventions, and the nature of the study. For example some disciplines may prefer a neutral, impersonalized presentation of experiments or facts and figures. Others may require critical commentary and reflexivity as explored in Chapters 2 and 3. This may be particularly so when the research is based in a real world professional practice setting, subject to the vagaries of professional and/or organizational cultures, policies and the actions of the professionals within the setting.

How then can the essence of professional practice be captured within professional doctorate writing? This section now analyses a variety of writing styles which may help to underpin the professional doctorate thesis or portfolio. The following elements will be considered:

- An overview of doctoral writing skills
- Dealing with writer's block

- The use of the first person in professional doctorate writing
- English for academic purposes
- Locating research within a professional practice context

An overview of doctoral writing skills

To suggest professional doctorate writing is an academic activity is an oxymoron. Such programmes focus on the legitimacy of professional practice developed by practitioner–researchers, as opposed to the tradition of research developed by independent researchers. However, the term 'academic' is used here to differentiate the writing requirements and styles for formal thesis or portfolio submission from those required for other purposes: the development of professional reports and executive summaries. This section will explore the foundational skills that students should consider when developing professional doctorate writing for formal assessment purposes.

There is perhaps an assumption that professional doctorate students will come to their studies with an advanced repertoire of academic skills, such as writing and critical thinking. However, many (not all) students are mid-career, possibly returning to study after a significant study break, or are simply more accustomed to writing professional briefs and reports, which do not require expansion and underpinning debate. Lloyd (2007) developed a helpful guideline relating to the development of written work as part of a programme of study. This includes strategies for planning written work, referencing and use of grammar and proofreading.

Others suggest that it is the collective mindset of the profession rather than the individuals within the profession that poses challenges. Some of the emerging professions do not have an established history of academic development or doctoral level study. Academic presentation from these professions may be less confident compared to the established disciplines. Sellers (2002) describes this situation in relation to the nursing context. Traditionally vocational, it is argued that the nursing profession attempts to copy or emulate the characteristics of professions that are well established in their university traditions of education and research. This emulation or wish to replicate what others do is used as a strategy to gain acceptance within the academic community and enhance their academic status (Sellers 2002).

So what are the components of doctoral level writing? The QAA (2001) doctoral descriptors introduced in Chapter 2 indicate the desired level and outcome: originality and contribution to knowledge. However, demonstrating originality of knowledge and innovation are themselves dependent on writing style. The following list is based on discussion with professional doctorate supervisors and illustrates some of the elements they consider essential within professional doctorate writing:

1 Introduction to the self and the practice setting: analysis of the issue to be explored

2 Use of salient literature as opposed to inclusion of all literature regarding the research topic

3 Links between the topic as presented in the literature and its practice in the professional context: identification of strengths and weaknesses from the literature and in relation to the professional context; critical appraisal of both

4 Critical thinking, critical stance or viewpoint: appraisal of information, for example comparison and contrast of varying points of view in the literature; analysis of ideas; development of alternative explanations

5 Emerging ideas: moving beyond the opinion or viewpoint of the student to a sophisticated way of viewing the world of professional practice and the related research theme, drawing on professional reflection and literature critique

6 Challenge to conventional thought: emergence of new ideas and perspectives for professional practice

7 Confident articulation of research methods chosen using philosophical concepts as an underpinning framework

8 Justification of research methods used: consideration of others explored and not used

9 Ability to evaluate and critically reflect on the research undertaken in professional practice: moving beyond discussion of events to demonstrate critical analysis and evaluation of events; analysis of role of self and others; discussion of theory used to underpin and illuminate

10 Implications for future practice: critical reflection on the research process; future areas for research and development

Dealing with writer's block

All writers look at the computer screen, either willing the words to appear or struggling to express an idea or viewpoint. Dealing with writer's block is a subjective area and the following section outlines some potential strategies. Anderson (2006) describes the struggles of Thomas Hardy, who is said to have had difficulty writing in the latter years of his life. Just knowing that distinguished writers experience block can be a revelation. When writing my PhD thesis and compiling this book I can only affirm that writer's block exists and causes panic when deadlines are looming.

However, it can be managed. For example gathering information and developing confidence in writing before writing 'it': a thesis chapter or an important report is a useful technique. This is one reason why contributors to this book encourage you to make notes or write things down in a notebook. From this process of notetaking it is possible that ideas will emerge for development. While the thesis has to be written at some point, thinking about it too soon, developing draft chapters too early in supervision can stifle creativity and cause anxiety. However, wider writing about your ideas, your professional practice and your progress with research is beneficial for discussion in supervision and in student and peer discussions. Learning journals as advocated by Moon (2004) are extremely helpful for recording ideas and also for reflecting on the process of learning.

If you really cannot write at all, then put the activity to one side and go and do something else. When exploring originality in Chapter 2, it was acknowledged that some kind of 'struggle' is often experienced before a breakthrough with ideas. Putting the work to one side and doing something relaxing, such as walking the dog or even doing housework, is a useful distraction. Sometimes thoughts will emerge during these activities. Take a notebook and pen everywhere. Ideas can emerge at anytime; it is amazing how a train journey or even waiting in the dentist's surgery can help. Keeping a notebook and pen at your bedside is handy for those thoughts that emerge in the middle of the night.

Christopher Thomond, Professor of Philosophy at Manchester University, described the development of his ideas thus:

> It's also hard graft. When you're writing something up you've got to just apply the seat of your trousers to the seat of your chair and keep hacking away. But sometimes you just think, well, I'll take a break. So I'll ride my bicycle or go out for a walk, and sometimes something happens. Things sediment, and then you go back and they become clearer.
>
> (Thomond 2007: 3)

If you really cannot tear yourself away from the study, then organizing your notes, tidying up references and papers can be therapeutic. On a serious note the use of free writing may be a helpful mechanism. With this technique Anderson (2006) suggests the selection of one idea and ten to fifteen minutes spent writing the first associated ideas that come into your head. These could even include why you are struggling; what you really want to say; what is stopping you. Alternatively you could simply start again with a blank sheet of paper. Explore the area of challenge beginning with one word and let your writing simply associate with the theme. Just write: there is only yourself and the computer there. Likewise using mind maps or spider diagrams can help. In summary, here are some useful ideas for combating writer's block:

- Use distraction: go for a walk, do anything that you enjoy
- Focus on something you can do: write a reference list; tidy up
- Use free writing: another dimension may emerge; other helpful tools are brainstorming and mind mapping
- Talk your ideas over with your supervisor and student colleagues
- If you have access to a virtual learning environment post something there, remember, however, that you won't have an immediate answer
- Turn the idea on its head: maybe you are examining the issue in the wrong way
- Tear up the draft and start again: persisting with one approach, cutting and pasting can lead to a real block. Sometimes it is better to just start again

Finally, the best advice comes from Anderson (2006: 21): 'Postpone perfection.' While you want to produce the best work possible, the doctorate is never going to be perfect. Constantly striving for perfection and profound debate is going to lengthen your period of study considerably, if not kill your enthusiasm stone dead.

The use of the first person in professional doctorate writing

Using the first person remains controversial: it is predicated on the accepted form in the various subject disciplines and the preferences of the supervisors guiding the student. Hyland (2001) explores two views relating to the first person. First, he considers the traditional view of academic writing as a neutral, objective discussion perhaps associated with positivism and the so-called 'hard sciences'. In this context events are observable through the use of experimentation or other methods, which accommodate the control of variables and/or the lack of human role or involvement. Ironically Hyland (2001) also outlines use of the first person across a variety of subject disciplines, finding that reference to self was most common in biological disciplines. Second, Hyland (2001) explores the notion that authors must not give an account of themselves in their writing, if they wish their published papers to be acknowledged.

However, qualitative approaches, particularly those that involve research in the practice setting, and that require the direct involvement and action of the researcher, necessitate an alternative form of content and writing which includes the first person. For example within a professional doctorate the practice context requires an introduction, along with an outline of the role of the practitioner–researcher and their relationship to the research study and key events. Such information is required to orientate the reader, and at a higher level it is an important aspect of reflective analysis. Continual uses of terms, such as 'the author' or 'the researcher', sound clumsy within academic writing. It may be easier to simply use the first person, 'I', especially where there is reference to personal thoughts and feelings during the research process. Similarly the use of the first person may be more appropriate when identifying researcher presuppositions, ideas and beliefs regarding professional practice and the research study.

Student activity 7.1 **Compare and contrast the two examples below:**

- 'The author's area of work will now be described. For five years the author's place of work was a busy Human Resources Department . . .'
- 'I worked in the Human Resources Department for five years . . .'

Furthermore Hyland (2001) suggests that academic writers inadvertently give their own voice in writing anyway. This is based on the language and expressions used, regardless of whether writing is in the first or third person. Within the genre of creative writing, for example, the development of 'voice' is strongly encouraged in order to develop creativity (Anderson 2006). Both authors are possibly using voice as a concept to illustrate how written words may convey personal traits in the same way as does face to face communication. In essence 'voice' may indicate a personal style or preference in writing as in speech.

Using the first person needs to be balanced in order to avoid a chatty, conversational approach or the use of professional colloquialisms, abbreviations or jargon, which cannot be understood by others. However, in avoiding the colloquial there is a tendency to use convoluted language and inaccessible words, simply because they appear more academic. Fairburn and Winch (1991) suggest that the first person can be used effectively, providing it is not used to excess or to the point of becoming intrusive within the writing. They provide examples of the first, second and third person and their use in academic writing. If you are not sure whether to use the first person, here is a reflective activity which may help:

Student activity 7.2

1 What kinds of writing style are you comfortable with? What kind of feedback have you received about your written work?

2 What kind of research methods are you using? Those associated with reflexivity and/or narrative indicate the use of the first person

3 Are you writing about your own experiences? If yes, then it is likely that the writing will have authenticity if you use the first person

4 Would you like to try a different writing style? If yes, then *write*! Get into the habit of writing from an early stage of your studies, discuss your writing constructively with your supervisor; if they do not see examples of your writing from an early stage they cannot facilitate development

5 How do others within your professional discipline write in journals and elsewhere?

The following extract is from Lee (2002). Independent learning techniques in nursing education were under discussion, particularly the use of action learning to enhance students' critical thinking skills, confidence and autonomy. To give context there was reflection on my rather Draconian experience of nursing education, where autonomy was not encouraged. This was illustrated using literature in order give a backdrop to the changes proposed. It has been used here, as many people can identify with the traditions and hierarchy inherent in nursing:

The character of training and the training of character (Rafferty 1996: 23)

'Rafferty (1996) offers an historical analysis of nursing that reinforces the principles of discipline and obedience. As demonstrated in Chapter one these principles were certainly reflected in my night duty experiences as a student and staff nurse. However, while I found the experiences had a negative impact, I have colleagues and friends who are positive about their nurse training, relishing the whole experience. The discipline and obedience never bothered them. In fact their reminiscences suggest that the rigid framework of nurse training was preferable to the contemporary liberalisation of nurse education.'

(Lee 2002: 26)

For further discussion please refer to Taylor and Hicks in Chapter 3, this volume.

English for academic purposes

Universities offer English for academic purposes training along with other courses in preparation for academic writing. While these courses are primarily for students whose second language is English, grammatical issues and written expression can cause problems for native English speakers too. In relation to grammar and spelling, proofreading from friends and colleagues is essential for all students, and especially for those who are not native English speakers.

The following is not strictly a writing issue, being more of a content issue. Some academic concepts can be taken for granted, for example the use of reflection or critical thinking. However, these ideas have various cultural permutations. A conversation with a visiting academic some years ago revealed that reflection was a spiritual rather than professional construct for them. Similarly the notion of challenging conventional wisdom or critical analysis of the literature may be considered unacceptable even disrespectful in some cultures. This was illustrated when a student was asked to critically compare and contrast theories of leadership and management. Even the idea of being critical, of questioning academic writing was unacceptable to them. Discussion of conceptual issues in student groups and with supervisors is important, alongside reading and writing.

Locating research within a professional practice context

As suggested in the opening part of this chapter, it is important to locate professional doctorate research within the relevant professional setting. A good writer will move beyond introduction and description of the professional practice context to integrate theory and practice perspectives within their writing. This may include separate chapters devoted to reflection on professional practice issues or, ideally, the seamless weaving of professional practice elements in all elements of the written work.

Within the professional doctorate literature, at least, there is consensus that the above are important elements. For example Yam (2005) suggests that nurses undertaking professional doctorates should explore and analyse professional issues and challenges pertinent to their sphere of practice, identifying how these can be examined or developed further. Furthermore he suggests students challenge their thinking by working beyond the conventions of research and knowledge, using their own professional experience to examine critically and develop practice research issues. Literature should be used to underpin research or, indeed, to challenge what is known and to develop alternative explanations and practices. These elements are in keeping with the originality and creativity associated with doctoral level study (Yam 2005).

San Miguel and Nelson (2007) concur and suggest the following should be evident in professional doctorate writing:

- Introduction and exploration of the practice setting where the research will take place
- Analysis of the issue under research, linking the practice setting and the challenges presented with those identified in the literature
- Discussion of the role of the practitioner–researcher and other participants

While the above elements are achievable there are some challenges to consider. For example the majority of supervisors have themselves undertaken a PhD, and subsequently may have different expectations of doctoral level writing. Indeed Heath (2005) identified that one challenge for professional doctorate students was their supervision, development and examination by those more conversant with the requirements of the PhD. Until such time as professional doctorates are better understood and there is a growing number of professionals and academics with such awards, there needs to be academic discussion, transparency and evaluative research as regards writing style and submission requirements.

San Miguel and Nelson (2007) used a case study analysis of the writing styles of two professional doctorate students and the feedback of their supervisors. The case study was accompanied by data from student and supervisor interviews, analysis of writing workshops and seminars, and student writing styles/ supervisor feedback over a two-year period of a professional doctorate programme. While it was acknowledged that students should 'frame' their practice issue within the current literature rather than analysing the literature and identifing gaps in provision, the case study revealed that the latter rather than the former achieved more positive feedback.

Where does this situation leave the professional doctorate student and their writing? It should be used as an opportunity to further develop originality and creativity. At a practical level, programme facilitators and supervisors should collaborate in order to ensure consistency of approach and to develop understanding for themselves and their students. This should extend to discussion with examiners and orientation to programme issues before viva. Some practical strategies are given below to help the development of writing style:

Strategies to develop writing style

- Use a notebook to record thoughts and impressions and to develop confidence with writing and critical analysis. Go back to Chapter 2 for revision
- Share examples of writing with student peers; compare and contrast writing style; and develop peer assessment of written work to inform and develop writing
- Develop your written work in discussion with your supervisor; try different styles of writing
- Ensure there is clear dialogue and there are guidelines from the supervisors and programme team about particular programme requirements, including discussion regarding similarities and differences of approach, attitudes and beliefs as compared to the PhD
- Read examples of doctoral work, PhD and professional doctorates to gain insight into writing style
- Read widely in relation to your professional practice setting and the research topic
- Attend writing workshops within the doctoral studies programme, and debate the inclusion of professional practice within the written work and the use of the first person
- Refer to the programme handbook and guidelines for writing at doctoral level pertinent to your particular programme

---

Writing for other audiences

So far there has been exploration of writing for the academic audience. Some of the principles introduced, for example note taking, drafting and dealing with writer's block, should also be considered when writing for other audiences. However, the writing style will vary depending on the audience, and the next section will explore writing for professional and other audiences.

Report writing

Your thesis or equivalent is used to demonstrate depth and breadth of knowledge and your ability to critically analyse and reflect on the professional situation in order to effect innovative and original changes. While you have undoubtedly toiled with this masterpiece, it is highly unlikely that the volume of words and chapters will be studied assiduously by other professionals. Alternative forms of writing are used in the guise of professional reports and other media to share your expertise with others. Reports may be used to discuss work in progress, or to provide a summary of key findings and recommendations for future actions at the end of your studies.

As such reports serve a completely different purpose. They are used to inform, as opposed to discuss or analyse; to explain, rather than to compare and contrast or to invite further debate. There are many texts and web based materials that can enhance report writing skills. Bowden (2002) and Bailey (2003) provide concise examples, as does the Plain English Campaign (see: www.plainenglish.co.uk/reportsguide.pdf).

Any report needs to be accessible, use clear language and avoid jargon and academic terms, which have the potential to mystify or infuriate the reader. The report is an important way to present your work, to further influence practice and to develop further collaboration with colleagues and others. Especially in some of the newer professions, there may be scepticism or resistance to professional doctorate study or any higher level study, as being unwieldy, inaccessible and unrelated to the realities of practice (Yam 2005). You do not want to reinforce this attitude through the presentation of your own work.

The typical report may comprise the following:

- Title page
- Contents page
- Acknowledgements: important if the study has received funding from the organization or from external sources
- Abbreviations/glossary, if appropriate
- An abstract, also known as an executive summary
- Introduction
- Discussion of the work undertaken: who, what, where, when and how
- Findings/outcomes
- Conclusions
- Recommendations for future action
- References/bibliography
- Appendices

Language should be formal and professional, as opposed to colloquial or overly academic. Headings and subheadings should be used to organize the key sections of the report, and help clarity and understanding. The presentation should be attractive, using good line spacing, white space and relevant diagrams and tables.

The report writing checklist below has been reproduced with permission from Dr Ela Beaumont of the Education Development Unit at the University of Salford:

Report writing checklist

A report is different from an essay. It usually has sections similar to the ones below BUT check your assignment brief and handbook (and clarify with your tutor if necessary) to make sure you are using the format required. Use this checklist to make sure you have included all the information needed.

1 *Title page*
  Does this include the: Title? Author's name? Module/course details?
2 *Acknowledgements*
  Have you acknowledged all sources of help?
3 *Contents*
  Have you listed all the main sections in sequence?
  Have you included a list of illustrations?
4 *Abstract or summary*
  Does this include:
  The main task?
  The methods used?
  The conclusions reached?
  The recommendations made?
5 *Introduction*
  Does this state:
  Your terms of reference?
  The limits of the report?
  An outline of the method?
  A brief background to the subject matter?
6 *Methodology*
  Does this include:
  The form your enquiry took?
  The way you collected your data?
7 *Reports and findings*
  Are your diagrams clear and simple?
  Are they clearly labelled?
  Do they relate closely to the text?
8 *Discussion*
  Have you identified key issues?

Have you suggested explanations for your findings?
Have you outlined any problems encountered?
Have you presented a balanced view?
9 *Conclusions and recommendations*
Have you drawn together all of your main ideas?
Have you avoided any new information?
Are any recommendations clear and concise?
10 *References*
Have you listed all references?
Have you included all the necessary information for locating each reference?
Are your references accurate?
11 *Appendices*
Have you only included supporting information?
Does the reader need to read these sections?
12 *Writing style*
Have you used clear and concise language?
Are your sentences short and jargon free?
Are your paragraphs tightly focused?
Have you used the active or the passive voice?
(www.edu.salford.ac.uk/academic-learning-skills/report-writing/report-writing-checklist.doc)

Conference abstracts and presentations

During your studies you will certainly want to share your preliminary work with other professionals at conferences. Conference presentations have a two-fold purpose. First, they enable you to obtain feedback about your work, or discuss and address challenges that you have encountered. Second, conference participation enables you to develop collaborative links with mutually interested professionals while establishing your own expertise.

Poster presentations, concurrent sessions, workshops or symposia are possibilities. Posters are usually displayed in the conference communal area, so that delegates can review them as they wish. Concurrent sessions are used to provide as many delegate choices as possible with several sessions running at once. A workshop may be related to a particular skill or knowledge development, and is usually longer than a concurrent session. A symposium is a collection of papers relating to one topic and providing different perspectives on the topic. Most people start with poster presentations and concurrent sessions, working towards longer workshops to train others, and symposia. Your professional doctorate programme or postgraduate studies programme may offer workshops on abstract writing and provide a student conference, where confidence can be developed before exploring external conference opportunities.

This section will consider abstract writing for conference presentations. These are generally a precursor to journal publications. The first step is to choose the conference that will attract like-minded professionals and others, perhaps organized by a professional body, professional council, voluntary agency or interest group. Usually conferences have a clear title and purpose with three or four subthemes, so ensure your ideas for presentation relate to one of the conference themes and the overall title and purpose of the conference. Most conferences require online abstract submissions and will provide guidelines for authors regarding word limit, use of references, style and layout. Read these carefully and work within them, using the word limit to the full but not exceeding it. The average abstract word limit is 200 to 300 words. It may help at the planning stage to read previous conference proceedings and develop ideas regarding style and language. Show your abstract to more experienced conference presenters to clarify and refine your ideas.

Developing the abstract

Pay particular attention to the title. An overly 'creative' title that gives no indication of the purpose of your session is not helpful. Remember that this abstract, as for your thesis or a journal publication, should summarize your discussion and indicate clearly what can be expected. Professional conferences usually have a chairperson for concurrent sessions to facilitate questions and keep proceedings to time. You will not be popular with the audience or other speakers if you go over the stated time. When planning and writing your abstract be mindful of the time allotted for your session. Consider one or two elements from your doctoral studies, as it will be impossible to detail your entire thesis in a short time period.

When planning and writing the abstract, use precise language to describe the content, and avoid opening sentences such as, 'The aim of this paper is to explore doctoral supervision requirements . . .' Such style wastes valuable words and gives no indication of what exactly will be explored. Instead use an eye catching, confident opening statement, such as, 'Good doctoral supervision is the key to successful student completion. Five components of good supervision will be discussed and these are . . .' Two or three references can be used to give a general overview and introduction to the topic. Choose references that are contemporary and relevant, and have resonance with the audience. For example in relation to doctoral supervision, key references about student experiences or policy requirements would be beneficial. Use the references to set the scene, explain the key challenges and the issues you wish to discuss.

Once you have introduced the topic, explain how your presentation will address the issues raised. Give details about how you will explore, discuss and develop your presentation. Finally, you need to return to your overview and reinforce how your presentation has addressed the key issues, identifying any limitations or challenges within the work.

Submitting an abstract

There will be a submission deadline for abstracts. Ideally you will work to this deadline; however, if there are difficulties it is worth contacting the conference organizers, as sometimes the deadline can be extended. Online submissions usually trigger confirmation of receipt and a reference number in case there are problems in future. Your abstract will be considered by a conference scientific committee, and in some cases feedback is provided on your abstract. A date will be given for confirmation of acceptance; do follow this up if you don't hear by the specified date.

Writing for publication

Writing for publication is an important and accepted method of disseminating your knowledge to others. It is part of the process of establishing your research profile during the professional doctorate and beyond. Quality journals have an impact factor: this gives an indication of the quality/standard of the journal based on how much the journal is cited in other academic journals. However, the impact factor can be misleading as specialist subjects may have a low citation frequency. Good journals are peer reviewed: independent reviewer(s) have read your paper and commented on its suitability for publication. This is usually an anonymous process; however, some journals use an open process. Information about peer review will be found on the journal's website.

Writing for a professional journal is an alternative. This may mean your work is read by more frontline professionals; however, the esteem in which the journal is held may not be as high. Deciding which journal to write in and for what purpose is the first factor to consider when writing for publication. The quality academic journals may give you presence and establish your reputation as a credible practitioner–researcher, while professional journals may help your research reach a wide professional readership. Your choice will influence your writing style and content. It is advisable to start your writing career by contributing to a modest professional newsletter, for example, before progressing to professional and then to academic journals, as confidence develops. It is also extremely helpful to work with experienced writers, as they can guide you through the stages of writing for publication.

Having decided where to write, read the instructions for authors carefully. Peer reviewed journals will have web based guidelines for authors, indicating word length, the style and format of submissions and the content preferred.

Student activity 7.3 **Compare and contrast the instructions for authors from the following journals:**

- *Nature* at: www.nature.com/authors/author_services/index.html
- *International Journal of Marketing Research* at: www.ijmr.com/
- *Reflective Practice* at: www.tandf.co.uk

For copyright reasons you must never submit the same article to more than one journal at the same time. It may seem an efficient use of time and resources; however, it is not allowed. During the publication process some journals will ask you to sign a declaration that the paper is your work and has not been submitted elsewhere. If the journal does not have instructions for authors, contact the editorial team and discuss your ideas. If you are a student writer they will hopefully be encouraging and provide constructive feedback.

Planning the article

Plan your writing using the principles you would for any other form of writing. For example think about the structure of the writing, which subheadings you should use, the intended content and its suitability for the intended journal. Some journals are specific about the structure required. It is extremely helpful to read the journal and appreciate its writing style and tone. The content of your paper will depend on the journal and intended audience: it could be an editorial or comment about something previously published in the journal; or it could be a paper outlining your literature review, research findings, reflection on the study process or related aspect of the implications of researching professional practice. It should be possible to select at least two or three themes from your professional doctorate as you progress and use them for publication. Match your writing style to the contents of the journal. This means that essays or thesis chapters will need revision, as their style will not be appropriate.

Authorship and published work

When planning your article or paper, allow others to read drafts critically and give you feedback. In particular seek the opinions of experienced writers and your supervisor. As suggested earlier, working with an experienced writer as co-author is a good learning experience. Generally people should not simply put their name to your work, so decline politely and firmly if this is suggested: authorship requires substantial input. Once a good draft has been developed, and this may take months remember, put the paper away for at least another month and work on something else. When the paper is read again you will be surprised at the changes required.

Submitting the paper and peer review

When you are submitting the paper consider the instructions for author's submission carefully. For example find out where and how to send your work, to whom, the format and layout, the referencing style, the use of keywords. You should be familiar with these requirements during your writing process as you don't want to waste time reformatting your work. Sometimes there is a requirement to send the title page with your contact details, abstract and paper as separate files in order that anonymity can be maintained in the review process.

Once submitted you should receive an email acknowledgement and a reference number, which you can use for queries. Good journals will stipulate how long the review process will take, for example six to eight weeks. Some journals are disappointing and do not have this transparency, leaving writers waiting months in some cases for feedback. It is a good idea to compare other writers' experiences as you embark on the writing process. When the feedback arrives, do not take umbrage at the comments. They are there to help you refine your work to the highest standard. While most reviewers will offer constructive feedback, there are some whose comments seem rather sharp: your professional involvement with an issue combined with your enthusiasm may mean that important explanatory points have been overlooked.

Make any changes with an accompanying commentary as a separate file, thanking the reviewers for their feedback. If you really don't want to respond to some of the comments then you don't have to do so. It is possible to explain or justify the position you have taken. It is important, however, not to become involved in an argument with the reviewers. At the end of the day you want to publish your paper, if the reviewers are not happy it will not be published. If there is continued disagreement you can contact the editor and ask for discussion, although this scenario is comparatively rare. Hogg et al. (2007) give a detailed account of the peer review process.

Preparing for publication

Once the paper has been accepted for publication you will receive a confirming letter. Prior to publication it is usual to sign a copyright form. Your work then becomes the property of the journal and permission is required for its reproduction. Waiving copyright is a regular occurrence and helps protect you from writers who want to use the work without due acknowledgement. Before publication you will be sent proofs; these are a draft copy of the paper as it will appear in print or online. You will be required to read the proofs carefully and make any corrections to punctuation and grammar, for example. Redrafting is not welcomed at this stage, as it can slow down publication and increases the costs for the publishers. Murray (2005) provides further detailed guidance on writing for academic journals.

Finally, writing for publication is an exciting aspect of the study process.

Having your work published gives credibility and enhances your confidence. It demonstrates the work has been read by experienced peers and is of a good standard. If you are writing for academic publication you must allow sufficient time to draft ideas, plan your work and redraft before submission. Writing for publication is a lengthy process and it can take up to 12 months to produce work of a suitable standard.

Alternative means of dissemination

Sharing your expertise through conventional academic and professional methods has been explored thus far. However, while these methods are important, the sharing of information and expertise remains within a particular expert rather than wider lay or public audience. There is an emerging body of knowledge concerning alternative methods of disseminating research findings.

Figure 7.1 illustrates the possibilities for sharing your expertise with others. These are not represented in a hierarchy, instead the pyramid represents those strategies most commonly used. For example the foundation of sharing expertise lies with the development of conference papers and journal publications. These are located at the bottom of the pyramid and are the most popular ways of sharing expertise. At the second level of the pyramid there are, however, researchers who will use reflexivity: the use of self, biography and narrative in keeping with developing ideas about knowledge, ownership of research and the interaction between the researched context and the researcher. Also within that area are those who advocate action research approaches, who may or may not involve participants in the dissemination or sharing process. These approaches predominate in the qualitative tradition and have greatest use in relation to the social sciences.

The third level of the pyramid comprises those commentators who fully acknowledge journal publications, conferences and the like, while analysing and exploring alternative means, such as dance, drama, poetry (Keen and Todres 2007). In this context research findings may be turned into a dance or a play which is then performed as opposed to a verbal or written presentation.

At the next level are others, for example Bagley and Cancienne (2001), who have incorporated dance and drama into dissemination strategies to highlight parental experiences of school choices when their children have special educational needs. In this situation a choreographer was used to help portray the experiences of parents, as derived from interview transcripts developed during the original research study. Background policy context and information were also provided in order to help the development of dance and drama. The authors reflect honestly on their practical experiences and challenges with this activity, while reflecting on the limitations and power inherent in the use of the more conventional written media.

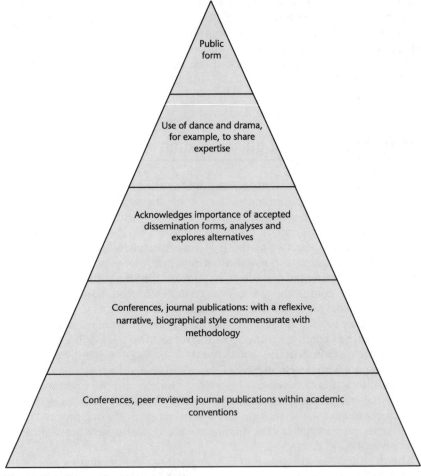

Figure 7.1 Dissemination strategies

The top level of the pyramid demonstrates the interest in alternative dissemination which has grown from increasing debate regarding the hegemony of emerging knowledge and evidence, and the control exerted by those in production of knowledge. For example Barnes et al. (2003) argue that research dissemination should not be considered as the final stage of a linear research process, demonstrating how research activities at all stages are a potential means of dissemination to a wider audience. As one example the conducting of an interview between researcher and participant could be construed as being beyond data collection and reinterpreted as representing the mutual development of knowledge, insight, the sharing of ideas and views, in keeping with dissemination practice (Barnes et al. 2003). Furthermore the authors suggest that journal editors and referees potentially enhance a gatekeeping function whereby research presented beyond the norms of academic conformity may be challenged, having restricted or even no access at all. Eisner (1997: 4) states that: 'one of the basic questions scholars are now raising is how we perform the magical feat of transforming the contents of our consciousness into a public form that others can understand.'

Arguably some of the ideas above are beyond the scope of the emerging professional doctorate researcher, who needs to develop confidence and expertise with existing dissemination methods before considering more innovative means of informing others of their work. These ideas are introduced here to broaden your understanding. On the other hand however, the professional doctorate journey should demonstrate creativity and innovation. Practitioner–researchers working with service users or under-represented groups in society or examining societal taboos may wish to think about the best means of raising awareness of the key issues. Alternative dissemination also opens up possibilities for transdisciplinary collaboration, notably with experts from media, music and performance, who can use their skills to develop and maximize dissemination materials.

There are other means of dissemination depending on the audience you would like to target. For example while publication in a peer reviewed journal will add gravitas or presence to your research work, an opinion piece, editorial or news item in a professional or news magazine may reach a much wider audience. In addition if help is required with a project, such as professionals with similar interests or networks or study participants, then discussion of your research ideas within a professional weekly magazine or other media will be valuable.

If your sphere of professional practice is related to work in the public sector or if it involves other service users, then again you may want to share your findings in the wider domain beyond the academic or professional audiences. For example you could approach voluntary agencies or key action groups and charities to share information. Similarly organizations and clubs in the community may be looking for speakers. For example developing models or frameworks to enhance marketing may be of interest to the Chamber of Commerce and other places where small or medium-sized businesses may be represented, for example the Soroptimists. Public speaking might be especially helpful if you want to share your research with participants or recipients of services, to obtain their opinion or to widen participation in the study. The language and style used will need to be entertaining, while communicating a clear message. In these contexts PowerPoint presentations will not suffice at all.

Alternatively, if your work is relevant to a particular community or geographical area, you may consider taking part in an interview for a newspaper, radio or television. You should seek the advice of the communications office, or press office within your own organization at the outset. They can provide expert advice about the best means of sharing information and use their professional contacts to access the media and advise you about presentation and style. They may also be able to write press releases for you. Importantly they will want the organization to be presented in the best possible light. If you do not have access to such resources then some of the following websites or their equivalent will be helpful to you:

- www.senseaboutscience.org.uk
- www.mediaguide.org.uk
- www.news.bbc.co.uk

When preparing for a media interview the following may be a useful aide memoire:

Media interview aide memoire: SPEECH

Speak clearly: nerves may make you gabble, avoid 'urm, er' in the conversation

Prepare: what do you want to say? What is your main message? Ask about the opening question and prepare a good, clear answer; never speak on the hoof

Explain: your story, relate your experiences and how your work is innovative and relevant to others in the community, why is your practice and research of such importance?

Etiquette: smiling will help you appear friendly and approachable and it will help to control butterflies; listen carefully to the interviewer, do not interrupt and keep calm; don't be put off by a difficult question

Contact details: telephone number or website/email are important if you are looking for participants or to provide further information and follow up; never disclose home numbers or personal details

Help your message: it will have more impact if you are smart and business-like, you want to present a positive image. If the interview is for television, ensure you are in an attractive background environment that reflects the themes of your discussion; ensure you will not be interrupted by telephones or excessive background noise. Finally, help yourself: the information given in this section is intended as an introduction, seek the advice of experts first

---

Conclusion

While there may be specific parameters for the assessment of practice expertise within a professional doctorate, there are comparatively few guidelines governing requirements for the submission of written work. Although there is consensus regarding the need for originality and creative or innovative contributions to knowledge, there are varied interpretations of how this should be presented. Requirements are often prescribed by accepted convention within the respective disciplines. Perhaps implicitly there is a belief that professional doctorate students should rise to the challenge and utilize their intellectual capacity and creativity to the full, as opposed to following prescriptive guidelines.

This chapter has explored some methods of sharing your expertise with others. These have ranged from thesis and portfolio development to preparation for the viva. While these focus on academic discussion of expertise in order to successfully complete the professional doctorate, there are also measures, such as conference presentation and journal publication to reach a wider professional audience. Similarly you may be required to write a professional report for your workplace, detailing the research undertaken and considering the implications for future practice. Innovative methods of dissemination, such as dance or drama, have been explored too.

Given the interest in reaching wider audiences with research and development, particularly user or consumer involvement, there are also other non-academic ways of sharing your expertise. These could involve radio or TV interviews and press releases, for example. Whatever method you choose, it is important that the style of writing and presentation reflects the method and the requirements of the intended audience. Effective writing style can only be developed with practice. Drafting, planning and redrafting help you develop a writing style, while using notebooks or journals to record your thoughts and ideas during the developmental process is invaluable.

Summary of key points

- Writing for formal assessment of your professional doctorate should demonstrate depth and breadth of professional knowledge, research skill and an emerging original contribution to knowledge
- Integration with professional practice, the generation of knowledge from practice and the use of critical reflection should underpin the above
- Writing for the professional audience, for example report writing, will require a more succinct, factual approach
- Presenting your work at conferences and for publication in journals is essential to clarify ideas, network and raise your profile
- Alternative means of sharing your expertise are likely to reach a wider audience, for example use of the media

Useful websites

- www.senseaboutscience.org.uk
- www.mediaguide.org.uk
- www.news.bbc.co.uk
- www.plainenglish.co.uk/reportsguide.pdf

8

Life after your professional doctorate: what happens next?

Dr Carol Haigh

Aims of the chapter

- To discuss strategies to enhance your postdoctorate professional career profile
- To consider opportunities to participate in postdoctoral research activities
- To consider the optimum presentation of your professional knowledge and skills through effective CV development

---

Introduction

When you are engaged in professional doctorate study, a certain amount of tunnel vision can be said to develop. Pursuing a professional doctorate means that increasingly large areas of your life are spent immersed in the topic and process of doctoral study. Very few students look beyond professional doctorate completion, and the viva if there is one. It is not unreasonable to suggest that for many students the achievement of a professional doctorate is an end in itself. In reality, however, this is far from the truth and the new doctoral graduate may find that the expectations of both employers and the academic community are that there is an immediate priority for them to consolidate and enhance their position in the professional and academic domains.

The provision of postdoctoral training varies from discipline to discipline and from country to country (Thompson et al. 2001; Dietz and Bozeman 2005). Often the doctoral graduates are left to work out what happens next and to discover for themselves what actions can enhance their future prospects. The purpose of this chapter is to explore the activities that the new professional doctorate graduate is encouraged to undertake as ways of strengthening their position in the professional research world.

Within the chapter we will explore four domains of activity that all new doctoral graduates will encounter. These are as follows:

- Developing a publications profile
- Developing 'presence'
- Supervision and examining
- Postdoctoral research

Each of these is vital if the professional doctorate is to be used to enhance your position in your chosen professional field. Each can be used in different ways and may be given different priorities at different times, but all are important.

Developing a publications profile

In many respects this is one of the 'easier' of the activities since most doctoral supervisors expect some publication activity from their students during the lifetime of the study. In addition some people achieve doctoral status through the PhD by publication route. This requires a significant body of published work to be submitted as part of the doctoral portfolio, often accompanied by a critical commentary linking the respective publications. However, for many doctoral graduates, writing for publication is generally the first thing they do, primarily because they have a thesis, which contains new knowledge that must be shared with the wider academic and working community. This situation applies to professional doctorate students. The practicalities of publication have been dealt with in detail in the previous chapter. However, some supplementary issues surrounding the development of a publications profile are presented here.

Who am I writing for?

Every professional discipline has its hierarchy of journals, some of which are mainstream, populist and journalistic, and others that are specialized, highly 'academic' and intellectual. To take an example from health care, some of the most widely read journals have a strong clinical focus; they appeal to students and newly qualified staff; they usually have a significant jobs section; and articles are generally journalistic and short but very informative. At the other end of the spectrum are more learned journals: still with a strong clinical focus, articles tend to be longer research reports, and clinical innovations in such journals appeal to experienced practitioners and to students undertaking graduate study. The question that the postprofessional doctorate author may need to pose themselves is, 'Why am I writing and who am I writing for?'

On completion of the professional doctorate students have produced new insights or new knowledge to particularly practical elements of their profession. They may choose to publish their work in professional journals, which are widely read by those people who work at the 'sharp end' of the discipline in question. On the other hand, the developments of new theoretical perspectives are better presented in the academic journals in the first instance. Of course, there is a case to be made for publishing in both domains: the professional and the academic, and the decision to be made is which domain you publish in most. If you have ambitions to work in an academic environment then you may be best advised to put most of your writing energies into the learned journals. On the other hand, if your career plans involve progression of skills in the professional practice environment, then you may wish to develop a publications profile that will allow you to influence a greater majority of practitioners.

What do I want from my publications?

While most authors write because they feel they have something to share with the wider community, the honest ones will also admit that they write because it will strengthen their curriculum vitae. Therefore, in addition to deciding what audience you want to inform or influence, the novice author should decide what they want their publication to do. If you are planning to develop your career in the practical application of your discipline, you may decide that publishing in mainstream professional journals will be the best way to enhance your reputation in the wider discipline specific community. Conversely, if you wish to develop your standing in the academic disciplines, then you will wish to submit your work to higher impact, peer reviewed and academic journals.

Who can help me?

There are a number of people who are able to help you as you take your first steps towards developing a publication profile. In the first instance, you may want to talk to your doctoral supervisor, particularly if your first publications efforts will be drawn from your thesis. Be aware that sharing authorship with your supervisors is a possibility and this is something that should be discussed early on in the supervision process. Some students maintain their links with their supervisors long after their professional doctorates are completed and work with them upon collaborative research projects. Other may wish to seek new collaborators or new mentors to support them.

In addition, journals (especially those that are peer reviewed) often send their editors to various research and professional conferences to run publications workshops. It is always worthwhile making contact with journal editors, not because they are more likely to publish your work if they know you, but because they are able to provide useful tips and hints that will strengthen your writing.

Key messages on developing a publications profile

It is clear that, for your professional and academic career to continue to evolve on completion of the professional doctorate, the development of a publications profile is essential. Whether you choose to publish in the professional or the academic domain is incidental, what is important is that the rationale for that decision must be carefully considered and form part of a personal and professional development strategy. There is a critical mass of expertise in the publications field that postdoctoral researchers or practitioners can access to support them with their profile development.

Developing 'presence'

One of the more challenging aspects following professional doctorate study is the development of 'presence'. While being seen as the key to professional career progression, a concrete definition of presence is yet to be satisfactorily articulated, making the quest for it somewhat difficult. A working definition of the concept, adopted for this chapter is:

Presence is a measure of an individual's visibility in their chosen field.

Thus it can be seen that part of the postdoctoral activities for the professional doctorate graduate must be aimed at raising their profile in the wider professional and academic arena. Although the overall aim of presence development could be argued to be international recognition, most people are content to begin at the local or national level before venturing into the international arena. There are a number of ways in which an individual can raise their professional and academic profile.

Committees

One way of enhancing your professional profile is to participate in carefully chosen committees. There is a temptation for some people to join anything and everything, but this can send the wrong sort of message to the wider professional and academic community. Local branches of professional organizations are usually keen to recruit people who are willing to get involved with their activities. Not only can this provide a useful platform for further dissemination of your professional doctorate findings, it can raise your profile locally and, in some instances, nationally.

As well as professional organization committees, there are a number of national groups and committees who regularly advertise for experienced and well qualified individuals to participate in their activites. Local research ethics committees, national institutions such as the National Institute for Clinical Excellence or international organizations, such as CORDIS, which is the research arm of the European Union, offer opportunities, not only to contribute in a meaningful way to the development and progression of an individual's profession, but also to allow them to showcase their expertise and skills to the wider community.

Conferences

There are two ways of using conferences to enhance your presence. The first and most obvious is to put your work out there in the public domain by presenting it to your peers at a conference. For some individuals the thought of standing up in front of a large audiences is particularly intimidating; however, thanks to the way that many conferences are structured this is not actually likely to happen. If you choose to present your paper during a concurrent session, it will be one of many being delivered at the same time. This means that you may be sharing your work with a handful of people in a fairly relaxed and intimate environment. Another frequent concern that affects the novice conference presenter (and occasionally the experienced one too) is the thought that the other people attending the conference are all better informed about the topic under discussion. While it must be acknowledged that it can be quite daunting to find that the 'great and the good' are in your audience, more often than not they are attending your session out of genuine interest rather than out of any petty motivation to highlight deficiencies in your work or your thinking. This point notwithstanding, if you decide to present your work in the public domain you should also expect to participate in critical debate.

Some conferences invite poster presentations. Until recently posters were often viewed as a sort of conference consolation prize. However, many conferences now expect that the poster author will make themselves available at break times to discuss their poster contents with delegates. For novice presenters, this more informal presentation style may be a good first step into the public domain.

One way to prepare for the public arena, whether national or international, is to start off with local study days or research seminars, presenting your work for colleagues before exposing your work to a wider range of peers and professional colleagues. It should be remembered that it is good practice to turn your conference presentations into journal papers as often as possible.

As well as simply presenting at conferences, your presence can be enhanced and consolidated by something as simple as acting as a session chair. The session chair plays a key role in keeping speakers to time and managing the audience's questions (Haigh 2007). However, especially if you manage to be a good and efficient session chair, this activity is a very effective one for raising your profile among your professional peers. Furthermore seeking opportunities to participate in the scientific committees of specific conferences often results in being invited to introduce keynote speakers to the entire conference audience. Although this does involve standing up in front of potentially hundreds of people (and so it not without its terrors for some) it allows your colleagues to put a face to your name and helps consolidate your presence.

Consultations

Every year numerous policy documents are disseminated by government departments for comment by professional groups, interested parties and individuals with suitable expertise. For example, the Department of Health (DoH) in the UK and the Higher Educational Funding Council for England (HEFCE) regularly invite comment on their proposed policies and many other government departments and professional organizations do the same. If you are part of a national or professional committee you will doubtless be involved in these consultations; however, you are equally eligible to comment as an interested practitioner or professional. If you are part of a professional context, such as education, business or health, you may want to forward your comments to the chief executive or equivalent, or you may wish to submit your comments as an individual. This will again have the effect of enhancing your public profile and consolidating your contribution to your chosen area of expertise.

Journal/conference reviewer

Another useful way of enhancing your presence in the wider disciplinary and academic community is to volunteer to be a reviewer for professional journals. Most peer reviewed journals have an open invitation on their website to would-be reviewers. As part of your postdoctoral development, it is a good idea to choose a 'high impact' journal since such journals are most likely to publish rigorous research papers and conceptual reviews. Although there is a degree of debate surrounding the notion of impact factors, which are calculated on, among other things, citation rates, the way things stand at the moment the most highly regarded journals are those with high impact factors.

As a reviewer you will be expected to comment, within a specific time frame, on the suitability of submitted papers for inclusion in the journal. Different journals have different review criteria, but they are all very similar. You will be able to specify your areas of expertise so you are unlikely to be asked to review papers on topics about which you know nothing. Many journals publish an annual list that records the names of all of the reviewers who have contributed to the journal in the previous 12 months. This, again, can help to raise your professional profile, not only with the journal readership, but also with your fellow researchers.

Another aspect of the reviewing process that is open to the postdoctoral graduate is participating in scientific review of submitted conference abstracts. As with journal reviewing, the important skills that you can bring to this activity are impartiality, objectivity and the ability to work to a deadline.

Key messages on developing presence

It can be seen that professional presence is somewhat difficult to define precisely. The activities presented here are not exhaustive but are offered as examples of the type of undertaking that can contribute to developing or consolidating your reputation in the wider field of your chosen profession.

Supervising and examining

Traditionally the role of the doctorial supervisor and that of the thesis examiners have been firmly grounded in academia. A minimum standard in most universities is that the supervisor should have a doctorate themselves. Traditionally this has been the PhD. However, as the range of doctoral opportunities has grown, as explored in Chapter 1, and in conjunction with the growth in professional doctorate provision, it is not unlikely that supervision opportunities will exist for professionals outside of the university system. Indeed this possibility would bring a wealth of professional insights and expertise to supervision from the reality of the practice setting. It would also enhance the skill mix available for doctoral supervision, especially for professional doctorates.

Supervising

Although participating in the doctoral journey as a co-supervisor and then supervisor may seem daunting, be reassured that this is not a journey you will be expected to take on your own. It is good practice to ensure that doctoral candidates have access to a supervisory team of which you will only be one. Now that doctoral studies have moved outside the boundaries of the university and into the professional practice arena, it makes good sense for the methodological and academic skills of university personnel to be complemented and enhanced by those of discipline specific graduates.

Although participating in the supervision process as a work based supervisor can be seen as a good way of enhancing your profile, it is presented as a third option within this chapter deliberately. Unless you have started to build a reputation via your publications, conference activities, and your reviewing activities, you are unlikely to be invited to contribute to supervision.

Another way to get involved in supervision is to maintain your links with your own supervisory team after graduation. They are likely to be the local people interested in your area of expertise (after all you must have picked them as your own team for a reason) and they may well be able to offer you some appropriate supervisory experience. In the academic world, although getting some supervision experience is very important, what really counts are 'completions': seeing a doctoral student through to satisfactory completion of their study. Be aware that completions are usually badged to the first or main supervisor. However, in the worlds of service delivery or industry, this may not be as important as being part of the team itself.

Examining

Like the memory of pregnancy or a bad accident, the memory of your own viva mercifully fades fairly quickly. Nonetheless, you may feel that you retain enough recollection of the experience to contribute in a meaningful way to the viva of other professional doctorate candidates in your field. The comments made earlier in this chapter regarding the importance of publications and presence if you want to be part of a supervisory team are even more crucial if you wish to become involved in examining theses. This is particularly critical if you remain in your practice context rather than migrating into academia. The academic world tends to be fairly small and, if everyone does not know everyone else, they probably know of them or know how to find out about them. Industry and service delivery do not really lend themselves to this type of intellectual incestuousness and so to be seen as a potential supervisor you have to stand out from the rest in your professional discipline.

Generally speaking, examiners are required to demonstrate examining experience. However, the potential advantages that the professional doctorate graduate may possess relate to their extensive discipline specific knowledge, knowledge of the professional setting and the skills related to leading research in practice. These can bring additional dimensions to examination of the thesis, or equivalent, and may complement the methodological expertise of other examiners. The role of the examiners is not necessarily to critique every tiny aspect of the candidate's thesis until it (or they) bleed, but to assess whether it is comparable with other doctoral work and worthy of the doctoral award. This is not to say that poor work should be accepted, but rather it is to highlight the importance of fairness and placing the work in the overall context of higher degrees.

Key messages on supervising and examining

As more and more doctoral students undertake professional doctorates and pursue doctoral study in the work environment, supervisors and examiners who can bring that work focused expertise will be in great demand. Keep in contact with your own supervisors if this is an area in which you wish to contribute. Most universities run education sessions on how to be a doctoral supervisor or examiner and it may be worthwhile exploring these options even before you complete your own studies. Remember, if you are invited to supervise or examine a doctoral thesis, it is because the student or the other supervisors are confident you have a contribution to make that is important.

Postdoctoral research

As mentioned at the beginning of this chapter, professional doctorate study is considered an end in itself for many students and represents the ultimate achievement. However, doctoral education is widely held to be preliminary training for a subsequent research career, and there is no reason to think professional doctorate studies differ from this expectation. There is a probability that, within six to nine months of achieving a professional doctorate, you will be expected to actively canvass for other research studies: to contribute to as a collaborator or to seek postdoctoral funding. This will allow you to consolidate the skills developed during your professional doctorate and also to advance your professional knowledge and expertise through further research.

For example there could be additional developments or dimensions relating to your professional doctorate that you would like to pursue. In Chapters 2 and 4 it was suggested that many students commence their doctoral studies with projects that are simply too large to be managed within the time available, or projects that are too complex to be managed by one individual. In summary, those elements could, or should, be amenable to postdoctoral study. Similarly, your professional doctorate studies may reveal interesting themes for future development.

Joining in with other people

This is probably one of the best ways to dip your toe into the bidding waters, especially if you consider yourself to be a novice in the wider world of funded research. If you can join either an established research team or be invited to join a team that is being put together in order to bid for specific project funding, you can watch and contribute to the entire process from start to finish. In this respect, your professional expertise and knowledge, networks and contacts would be invaluable and sought after within a research team.

As with any of the activities outlined in this chapter, it is important that you are clear, not only what you can bring to a research team, but also what you expect from your colleagues. Research teams have to meet short deadlines and cannot afford to take on any one who will be 'dead weight', so it is useful to be able to make clear to them exactly why you will be an asset to their project. As with all publication scenarios it is worth negotiating issues, such as first authorship, right at the beginning of the process in order to avoid acrimony later.

Going it alone

One of the most common questions asked at doctoral viva, usually toward the end of the ordeal is, 'How will you take this work forward in the future?' After a brief period of celebration you may well find that there are some further avenues of enquiry that will support your previous study and you may wish to seek funding to explore them.

For a novice researcher, getting funding to go it alone can be quite difficult. This is partly because funding bodies do tend to take experience and reputation into account when handing out significant amounts of money (which is a bit of a catch-22 situation – you can't get money without a reputation and you can't get a reputation without the money!), and partly because research is, in reality, a group activity requiring a team approach, if it is to work.

The best way to seek funding for your own project is to seek out postdoctoral funding opportunities. In the UK, the research councils all offer postdoctoral fellowships in their associated disciplines. These are:

1 *Arts and Humanities Research Council* (www.ahrc.ac.uk/). The Arts and Humanities Research Council (AHRC) supports research from traditional humanities subjects, such as history, modern languages and English literature, to the creative and performing arts
2 *Biotechnology and Biological Sciences Research Council* (www.bbsrc.ac.uk/). The Biotechnology and Biological Sciences Research Council (BBSRC) is the UK's principal funder of basic and strategic biological research
3 *Engineering and Physical Sciences Research Council* (www.epsrc.ac.uk/). The Engineering and Physical Sciences Research Council (EPSRC) are the main UK government agency for funding research and training in engineering and the physical sciences covering a broad range of subjects – from mathematics to materials science, and from information technology to structural engineering.
4 *Medical Research Council* (www.mrc.ac.uk/). The UK Medical Research Council (MRC) promotes research into all areas of medical and related science with the aims of improving the health and quality of life of the UK public and contributing to the wealth of the nation
5 *Natural Environment Research Council* (www.nerc.ac.uk/). The NERC's mission is to gather and apply knowledge, improve understanding and predict the behaviour of the natural environment and its resources
6 *Science and Technology Facilities Council* (www.scitech.ac.uk/). The Science

and Technology Facilities Council funds the best research within astronomy and nuclear and particle physics

(Research Councils UK: www.rcuk.ac.uk)

These research councils have a combined budget of £2.8 billion to invest annually in research. In addition, the European Union (EU) has launched its Framework Programme (FP). This initiative is the EU's main instrument for funding research and development. It is designed to build on the previous research achievements of the EU towards the creation of the European Research Area, and carry it further towards developing a knowledge economy and society in Europe. The FP is supported by the European Research Council (ERC). This council is the first European funding body set up to support investigator driven frontier research. Its main aim is to stimulate scientific excellence by supporting and encouraging the very best, truly creative scientists, scholars and engineers to be adventurous and take risks in their research. The scientists should go beyond established frontiers of knowledge and the boundaries of disciplines (more information can be found at http://erc.europa.eu/index.cfm).

Be aware that if you are planning to go for a postdoctoral fellowship, time lines are usually quite tight. In most cases you will need to have identified a research mentor and a host organization in which to place your fellowship work. Competition for these fellowships is fierce, so you have to have a very well crafted project that makes a clear contribution to your discipline. Postdoctoral fellowships are also designed to give new researchers team leadership and management experience, so when you put your proposal together you may want to think about constructing a study that will require input from a research assistant.

If these fellowship programmes seem too ambitious, and there is nothing wrong with starting your research career modestly, you may wish to seek out smaller pots of funding. For example some hospital research and development departments offer small grants of between £5000 and £10,000 to fund specific, practice related projects. In addition you can sign up for email alerts from funding databases, such as RD Info (www.rdinfo.org.uk/), an organization which is part of the National Institute for Health Research in the UK and which offers information for those researchers in the field of health and social care. Similar schemes are in existence for other professional groups, such as the Joseph Rowntree foundation (www.jrf.org.uk/) for social policy research.

Whichever route you choose to follow for your postdoctoral research activities there are certain things that you must be aware of:

1 You will need help with the costing of the bid. Universities in the UK cost out their research activities using a full economic costing model (FEC) which costs space drivers (such as offices, etc.) as well as an individual's time. Some funding bodies do not pay FEC and you need to be clear about this when you start your bid

2 You should always cost dissemination monies into your bid (unless specific-
   ally prohibited), as these will fund your conference attendance when you
   start to publicize your research
3 Research will *always* take longer than you think so it helps to factor in some
   'slippage' time to cover you if the unexpected happens. In the UK, just
   obtaining research governance approval can take months in some instances
   (Howarth et al. 2008)
4 Make sure that everyone included on the bid is clear about what their role is
   and what they will deliver. Try, if you can, to get a mix of experienced and
   novice researchers. The experienced researchers are a useful resource and
   mentoring a novice is good postdoctoral development for you

Key messages around postdoctoral research

It can feel like quite a challenge when you start to bid for monies to fund your
future research activities, and it may take a while before you actually manage
to get your first grant. However, it is important to remember that there are
experienced people around who are able to help. Most grant making trusts
have advice on their web pages for would be applicants, and many university
based researchers will be willing to help and support you as part of their
research team.

Putting it all together: enhancing your CV

So far, this chapter has concentrated on an examination of the four key
domains of postdoctoral activity, namely:

- Developing a publications profile
- Developing 'presence'
- Supervision and examining
- Postdoctoral research

However, no matter how successful your endeavours in each of these key areas
may be, unless you present them well on your CV they are unlikely to impress
potential employers. To that end, the final element of this chapter will outline
some of the useful strategies that can be used in order to 'sell yourself' via your
CV. You will probably find that you end up with several different versions of
your CV, which you will use for different occasions. The short version CV, which
you are expected to include with research bids or ethical review applications,
will not be sufficient to support a job application, for example. It is always a
good idea to have a full and comprehensive CV available from which you can
extract relevant data for specific circumstances.

The full CV

A full CV will clearly outline your education and professional experiences. The full CV is the one you will use when going for a job interview, and its primary purpose is to get you shortlisted. It gives you the chance to 'sell' your skills and experiences to the potential employer. You should use it to emphasize your strong points – to make your application stand out – but you shouldn't use it to lie. A number of recent surveys have suggested that as many as a quarter of job seekers deviate from the truth on their CV. The common distortions include bogus or exaggerated qualifications, changing the dates of employment to hide career gaps and exaggerating the pay received in a previous job (see: www.startups.co.uk and http://jobsadvice.guardian.co.uk).

Obviously information such as your name, current position, educational qualifications, professional qualification and previous posts need to be on your CV but other key headings to use include:

- Membership of learned societies
- Positions of responsibility
- Research funding
- Research reports
- Doctoral supervision
- Doctoral assessment
- Editorial activities
- Reviewing
- Books
- Chapters in books
- Peer reviewed publications
- Peer reviewed conference presentations
- Invited conference papers
- Professional publications and professional conference presentations
- Other media activities
- Teaching activity

Membership of learned societies

If you are a member of a society, for example the Royal Statistical Society or the International Association for the Study of Pain, and especially if you hold a position on a committee or working party in such a society you should make that clear on your CV.

Positions of responsibility

Some people, when writing their CV, mix up all of the activities and positions of responsibility into one long list. However, if you consider the points made earlier about 'presence' on the international and national platform, you will see that it makes sense to present such responsibilities under those headings. You should also emphasize your local and work related obligations. Therefore this part of your CV will have four subheadings under the main one and these will be

- International
- National
- Regional
- Internal[1]

Research funding

As you develop funding activities it's a good idea to record them on your CV. In the early stages of research career development, you may wish to record your bids (whether you get the funding or not) in order to demonstrate that you are actively seeking research funds. When you have one or two funded projects to your credit you may wish simply to record your successful bids.

Research reports

When you have completed a research project, it is expected that you will produce a final report for the funding or supporting body. It is good practice to record these on your CV close to your funded projects so that potential employers can see that you have delivered completed work.

Doctoral supervision

It is a good idea, if you are involved in doctoral supervision, to record the name of your student, the title of their work and their expected date of completion on your CV. This shows prospective employers, not only that you are contributing to the research community, but also it provides an idea of your current workload.

Doctoral assessment

As with research funding, when you record all of your bidding activity in the first instance, so when you are new to doctoral assessment you might want to record all your activities. Most doctoral programmes have specific progression points at which candidate progress is assessed. Being involved in such assessments is a good way of developing your examination technique and recording them on your CV shows that you are working to enhance these skills. However, once you are taking part in doctoral vivas then you can remove these preliminary activities from your CV and just record the formal end-point examinations you have done.

Editorial activities

If you are on the editorial board of a journal, you should ensure that is featured on your CV. Likewise if you publish any editorials, they should be presented under this heading. Being actually invited to submit an editorial is quite an honour so if you are invited to submit one you might want to out it under a separate heading of 'Guest editorials'.

Reviewing

Earlier in this chapter it was noted that a useful way to enhance your presence in the wider disciplinary and academic community is to volunteer as a reviewer for professional journals. Your CV should clearly record all of the journals that you review for.

Books

If you have a book, either in print or in press, you should say so in your CV. As with book chapters and journal papers, it is a good idea to have 'in print' and 'in press' subheadings so that you cannot be accused of making false claims on your CV.

Chapters in books

Possibly one of the first postdoctoral book opportunities offered to you will be to contribute a chapter to an edited book. This is a useful way into the book publication field and as such deserves to be recorded on your CV. As suggested above, papers must have 'in print' and 'in press' subheadings.

Peer reviewed publications

A peer reviewed publication is one in which submitted papers are subjected to evaluations (usually blinded) by other experts in the field. Although the quality of peer review varies widely across the publishing arena, generally speaking the high impact journals tend to have the more rigorous review procedures. As before, separate your papers into the 'in print' and 'in press' subheadings. To be clear, 'in press' means accepted for publication and submitted to the publisher, but that the work is still in production. It does not mean submitted but under review, since there is a possibility that the reviewers may reject the paper. However, if you want to demonstrate that you are actively writing, it is in this instance permissible to have an 'in progress' subheading where you can outline your work in progress.

Peer reviewed conference presentations

Any conference at which you present that uses a peer review system of abstract selection should be recorded on your CV. It is a good idea to reference them as you may any other published work, for example:

> Haigh, C. Johnson, M. and Yates-Bolton, N. (2007) Student nurses values: a three centre study. Paper presented at the Nurse Education Tomorrow Conference, Cambridge.

Invited conference papers

As your reputation and presence grows, you may find that you are approached to present your work at conferences as an invited speaker. As with invited editorials, this is a good indicator of presence and should be recorded under a separate heading on your CV.

Professional (non-refereed) publications and professional (non-peer reviewed) conference presentations

Although non-refereed publications and presentations are considered together here, on your CV they should be under two separate headings. These give you an opportunity to demonstrate your input into local study days and non-peer reviewed publications. As with most other things, you may wish to review the inclusion of these activities in comprehensive detail as your list of more robust activities grows with your experience. You may still wish to keep the headings but confine yourself to statements such as '21 non-peer reviewed publications since 1990' or '11 non-peer reviewed conference presentations since 1998'.

Other media activities

If you are approached by the media to talk about your work – and it happens more than you may think since conference organizers usually try to identify presentations around which there may be media interest – you should record it in your CV. If you have your own website or work/research related blog then it is also worth recording that fact here.

Teaching activity

If you routinely contribute to teaching or training other people then you should record it. Obviously how much depth you go into depends upon whether teaching activity plays a big role in the job you are seeking, but at the very least it is a good idea to list the topics to which you could contribute. For example:

- Research methodology to master's degree level
- Research methods
- Literature search and review
- Research ethics and ethical approval
- Quantitative methodologies
- Qualitative methods
- Supervision techniques

In the early stages of your postdoctoral career, you are unlikely to be able to use every heading suggested above. However, it is not a good idea to leave headings on your CV for which you have no content, as this highlights what you have not achieved more than what you have actually achieved. It is entirely appropriate to remove headings and then re-insert them when you have something to put under them.

The research CV

The full curriculum vitae as outlined above is likely to run to many pages as your postdoctoral career develops. When submitting a CV for research funding you may find yourself restricted to one or two pages at most. Certainly the content will be available for you to take from your full CV, but generally funding bodies are most interested in your previous funded projects and any publications that are relevant to the field for which you are seeking research funding. Sometimes they want to know about your research training and your employment history. Some funding bodies have specific CV templates for you to use and it is always a good idea to check for these before you submit your bid.

Key messages about CVs

There are numerous CV websites available that can give you information about the nature and structure of a satisfactory CV, if you want further help. It is important to note that rarely are prospective employers or fund makers interested in how many children you have, what your hobbies are or in any voluntary work you do, and these are not things to have on your CV. A CV is about your *professional* life and that is all.

Conclusion

This chapter has explored the ways in which the doctoral graduate can enhance the professional reputation and further their career prospects, with the notion of four key domains of activity, namely:

- Developing a publications profile
- Developing 'presence'
- Supervision and examining
- Postdoctoral research

These domains have been fully examined and suggestions for meaningful involvement in each of them have been presented. It should be noted that the suggestions made within this chapter are neither exhaustive nor comprehensive, and it is up to the individual to find their own ways of raising their profile within their own specific field or discipline. The importance of a comprehensive and accurate CV has been discussed, and suggestions have been made for content headings that allow the postdoctoral individual to best showcase their achievements. Career enhancement and presentation of self are both important elements in the postdoctoral world. Although it seems hard to believe on the day of your viva, achieving your doctorate is really only the very first step on a very long journey!

Summary of key points

- Achieving your professional doctorate is not an end in itself: use this effort as a springboard for career planning and enhancement
- Publications are essential to getting your work out there: carefully consider who you need to share your research with, why and how
- Maintain your academic and professional networks and use them to develop experience of bidding for research projects. Contribute to a bidding team and gain valuable experience before you lead your own bids
- There are many ways of enhancing your professional presence: contribution to local and national committees and networks; chairing conference sessions; becoming a member of a conference scientific or planning committee
- Finally, after all this hard work, don't let your CV let you down: good presentation is essential to career development, take time and care over its content and layout and keep it up to date

---

Note

1   This will include any work related activities such as working parties or committee membership.

References

Alvesson, M. and Skoldberg, K. (2000) *Reflexive Methodology: New Vistas for Qualitative Research*. London: Sage Publications, p. 39.

Anderson, L. (ed.) (2006) *Creative Writing*. Abingdon: Routledge and Open University.

Atkinson, P. (1995) *Medical Talk and Medical Work*. London: Sage.

Back, L. (2007) *The Art of Listening*. Oxford: Berg.

Bagley, C. and Cancienne, M. B. (2001) Educational research and intertextual forms of (re)presentation: the case for dancing the data, *Qualitative Inquiry*, 7(2): 221–37.

Bailey, S. (2003) *Academic Writing: A Practical Guide for Students*. London: Taylor and Francis.

Barnes, V., Clouder, D. L., Pritchard, J., Hughes, C. and Purkis, J. (2003) Deconstructing dissemination: dissemination as qualitative research, *Qualitative Research*, 3(2): 147–264.

Barr, H. (2005) *Interprofessional Education: Today, Yesterday and Tomorrow*. Occasional Paper No. 1, revised edition. London: Learning Teaching and Support Network Centre for Health Studies and Practice, Kings College.

Bass, B. (1985) *Leadership and Performance Beyond Expectations*. New York: Free Press.

Bass, B. and Avolio, B. (1994) *Improving Organisational Effectiveness Through Transformational Leadership*. London: Sage.

BBC (2007) UK science head backs ethics code. Available at: http://news.bbc.co.uk/ (accessed Oct. 2007).

Becker, H. S. (1986) *Writing for Social Scientists: How to Start and Finish Your Thesis, Book, or Article*. Chicago: University of Chicago Press.

Becker, H. S. (1998) *Tricks of the Trade: How to Think About Your Research While You're Doing It*. Chicago: University of Chicago Press.

Behar, R. (1996) *The Vulnerable Observer: Anthropology that Breaks Your Heart*. Boston: Beacon Press.

Bennis, W. G. and Nanus, B. (1985) *Leaders: The Strategies for Taking Charge*. New York: Harper, p. 1.

Binney, G.,Wilke, G. and Williams, C. (2005) *Living Leadership. A Practical Guide for Ordinary Heroes*. Harlow: Prentice Hall.

Blanchard, K., Zigarmi, P. and Zigarmi, D. (1985) *Leadership and the One Minute Manager: Increasing Effectiveness Through Situational Leadership*. New York: William.

Blank, W. (2001) *108 Skills of Natural Born Leaders*. New York: Amacom Books.

Bligh, M. C. and Schyns, B. (2007) The romance lives on: contemporary issues surrounding the romance of leadership, *Leadership*, 3(3): 343–60.

Bolton, G. (2005) *Reflective Practice: Writing and Professional Development*, 2nd edn. London: Sage.

Boswell, T. and Kemp, G. (2001) *Critical Thinking: A Concise Guide*. London: Routledge.

Boucher, C. and Smyth, A. (2004) Up close and personal: reflections on our experience of supervising research candidates who are using personal reflective techniques, *Reflective Practice*, 5(3): 345–56.

Boud, D. and Tennant, M. (2006) Putting doctoral education to work: challenges to academic practice, *Higher Education Research and Development*, 25(3): 293–306.

Bourner, T., Bowden, R. and Laing, S. (2001) Professional doctorates in England, *Studies in Continuing Education*, 26(1): 65–83.

Bowden, J. (2002) *Writing a Report: How to Prepare, Write and Present Effective Reports*. Oxford: How to Books Ltd.

Bowerman, J. (2000) Strategizing at work: practitioner perspectives on doctoral set working, *Journal of Workplace Learning*, 12(3): 124–30.

Braverman, H. (1974) *Labour and Monopoly Capital: The Degradation of Work in the Twentieth Century*. New York: Monthly Review.

Braxton, J. M. and Bayer, A. E. (1996) Personal experiences of research misconduct and the response of individual academic scientists, *Science, Technology and Human Values*, 21(2): 198–213.

Brechin, A. and Sidell, M. (2000) Ways of knowing, in R. Gomm and C. Davies (eds), *Using Evidence in Health and Social Care*. London: Sage.

Brinkley, I. (2006) Defining the knowledge economy. Available at: www.theworkfoundation.com (accessed Sept. 2007).

Bristol Royal Infirmary Inquiry (2001) The inquiry into the management of care of children receiving complex heart surgery at the Bristol Royal Infirmary. Available at: www.bristol-inquiry.org.uk/index.htm (accessed Mar. 2008).

Brookfield, S. (1987) *Developing Critical Thinkers: Challenging Adults to Explore Alternative Ways of Thinking and Acting*. Buckingham: Open University Press.

Bryman, A. (1986) *Leadership and Organisations*. London: Routledge and Kegan Paul.

Bryman, A. (2004) *Social Research Methods*, 2nd edn. Oxford: Oxford University Press.

Bulman, C. and Schutz, S. (eds) (2004) *Reflective Practice in Nursing*, 3rd edn. Oxford: Blackwell.

Burgess, R. G. (1984) *In the Field: An Introduction to Field Research*. London: Routledge.

Burman, E. (2006) Emotions and reflexivity in feminised education action research, *Educational Action Research*, 14(3): 315–32.

Burr, V. (2003) *Social Constructionism*, 2nd edn. London: Routledge.

Carpenter, D. M. (2007) Presidents of the United States on leadership, *Leadership*, 3(3): 251–80.

Carrier, J. and Kendall, I. (1995) Professionalism and interprofessionals in health and community care: some issues, in P. Owens, J. Corner and J. Horder (eds), *Interprofessional Issues in Community and Primary Health Care*. Basingstoke: Macmillan.

Catalyst (2005) Women 'take care', men 'take charge': stereotyping of US business leaders. Available at: Exposed@http://www.catalyst.org (accessed Mar. 2008).

Charmaz, K. and Mitchell, R. G. Jr (1997) The myth of silent authorship: self, substance and style in ethnographic writing, in R. Hertz (ed.), *Reflexivity and Voice*. Thousand Oaks, CA: Sage, pp. 193–215.

Cheek, J. (2000) *Postmodern & Poststructural Approaches to Nursing Research*. Thousand Oaks, CA: Sage.

Chesney, M. (2000) Interaction and understanding 'me' in the research, *Nurse Researcher*, 7(3): 58–69.

Clegg, S. R., Hardy, C. and Nord W. R. (eds) (1999) *Managing Organisations: Current Issues*. London: Sage.

Coffey, A. (2002) Ethnography and self: reflections and representations, in T. May (ed.), *Qualitative Research in Action*. London: Sage, pp. 313–31.

Coffey, A. and Atkinson, P. (1996) *Making Sense of Qualitative Data: Complementary Research Strategies*. London: Sage.

Colwell Report (1974) *Report of the Committee of Inquiry into the Care and Supervision Provided in Relation to Maria Colwell*. London: HMSO.

Costley, C. and Gibbs, P. (2006) Researching others: care as an ethic for practitioner researchers, *Studies in Higher Education*, 31(1): 89–98.

Cotterill, S. (2005) *Critical Thinking Skills: Developing Effective Analysis and Argument*. Basingstoke: Palgrave Macmillan.

Cottingham, J. (ed.) (1996) *Western Philosophy an Anthology*, Part 1. Oxford: Blackwell Publishers.

Cramer, D. (2006) *Advanced Quantitative Data Analysis*. Maidenhead: Open University Press.

Crotty, M. (1998) *The Foundations of Social Research: Meaning and Perspective in the Research Process*. London: Sage.

Crowther, A. (ed.) (2004) *Nurse Managers: A Guide to Practice*. Melbourne: Ausmed, p. 38.

Cryer, P. (2000) *The Research Student's Guide to Success*. Buckingham: Open University Press, ch. 17.

Darlington, Y. and Scott, D. (2002) *Qualitative Research in Practice: Stories from the Field*. Buckingham: Open University Press.

Delamont, S., Atkinson, P. and Parry, O. (2000) *The Doctoral Experience: Success and Failure in Graduate School*. London: Falmer Press.

DEST (Department for Education, Science and Training) (2005) Research training in doctoral programs: what can be learned from professional doctorates? Available at: www.dest.gov.au/archive/highered/eippubs/eip02_8/default.htm (accessed July 2006).

Dietz, J. S. and Bozeman, B. (2005) Academic careers, patents, and productivity: industry experience as scientific and technical human capital, *Research Policy*, 34: 349–67.

Donaghy, B. (1996) Concern over 'US' style doctorates campus review: 24–30 April, in Maxwell, T. W. and Shanahan, P. J. (1997) Towards a reconceptualisation of the doctorate: issues arising from comparative data relating to the EdD degree in Australia, *Studies in Higher Education*, 22(2): 133–49.

Doncaster, K. and Thorne, L. (2001) Reflection and planning: essential elements of professional doctorates, *Reflective Practice*, 1(3): 391–99.

Drew, P. (1992) Contested evidence in courtroom cross-examination: the case of a trial for rape, in P. Drew and J. Heritage (eds), *Talk at Work: Interaction in Institutional Settings*. Cambridge: Cambridge University Press.

Drew, P., Chatwin, J. and Collins, S. (2001) Conversation analysis: a method for research into interactions between patients and health-care professionals, *Health Expectations*, 4(1): 58–70.

Eisner, E. (1997) The promise and perils of alternative forms of data representation, *Educational Researcher*, 26(6): 4–10.

Ellis, C. (2004) *The Ethnographic I: A Methodological Novel About Autoethnography*. Walnut Creek: AltaMira Press.

Ellis, L. (2006) The professional doctorate for nurses in Australia: findings of a scoping exercise, *Nurse Education Today*. Available at: www.sciencedirect.com/science (accessed June 2006).

Ellis, L.B. and Lee, N. (2005) The changing landscape of doctoral education: introducing the professional doctorate for nurses, *Nurse Education Today*, 25: 222–39.

Eraut, M. (1994) *Developing Professional Knowledge and Competence*. London: Routledge-Falmer.

Etzioni, A. (ed.) (1969) *The Semi Professions and Their Organisation*. New York: Free Press.

EUA (European Universities Association) (2005) Doctoral programmes for the European knowledge society, *Report on the EUA Doctoral Programmes Project 2004–2005*. Available at: www.eua.be (accessed May 2007).

Evans, T. (1997) Flexible doctoral research: emerging issues in professional doctorate programmes, *Studies in Continuing Education*, 19(2): 174–82.

Evans, T. (1998) Issues in supervising professional doctorates: an Australian view, *Staff and Development Association: Good Practice in Post Graduate Supervision*. Birmingham: SEDA.

Evans, K. and King, D. (2006) *Studying Society: The Essentials*. London: Routledge.

Evans, T., Macauley, P., Pearson, M. and Treganza, K. (2005) Why do a 'prof doc' when you can do a PhD? Available at: www.deakin.edu.au/education/rads/conferences/publications/prodoc/doc/3EvansMacauley&Pearson.pd (accessed July 2006).

Facione, P. A. and Facione, N. C. (1994) *Holistic Critical Thinking Scoring Rubric*. California: California Academic Press.

Fairburn, G. J. and Winch, C. (1991) *Reading, Writing and Reasoning: A Guide for Students*. Buckingham: The Society for Research into Higher Education/Open University Press.

Feletti, G. (1993) Inquiry based and problem based learning: how similar are these approaches to nursing and medical education? *Higher Education Research and Development*, 1292: 143–55.

Fiedler, F. (1967) *A Theory of Leadership Effectiveness*. New York: McGraw Hill.

Fox, N. (1999) *Beyond Health: Postmodernism and Embodiment*. London: Free Association Books.

Friedson, E. (1970) *Profession of Medicine: A Study in the Sociology of Applied Knowledge*. New York: Harper and Row.

Friedson, E. (1984) The changing nature of professional control, *Annual Review of Sociology*, 10: 1–20.

Galvin, K. and Carr, E. (2003) The emergence of professional doctorates in nursing in the UK: where are we now? *Nursing Times Research*, 8(4): 293–307.

Gemme, B. (2005) The changing career preferences of doctoral students. Available at: www.eric.ed.gov/ERICDocs/data/ericdocs2/content_storage_01/00000006/80/31/a6/30.pdf (accessed May 2007).

Gibbons, M., Limoges, C., Nowotny, H. et al. (1994) *The New Production of Knowledge: The Dynamics of Science and Research in Contemporary Societies*. London: Sage.

Giddens, A. (2006) *Sociology*, 5th edn. Oxford: Polity Press.

Glasby, J. and Beresford, P. (2006) Who knows best? Evidence-based practice & the service user contribution, *Critical Social Policy*, 26(1): 268–84.

Glaser, E. (1941) *An Experiment in the Development of Critical Thinking*. Columbia University: New York Teachers College, p. 5. (Reprinted in Thomson, A. (2002) *Critical Reasoning a Practical Introduction*. London: Routledge.)

Golde, C. M. and Dore, T. M. (2001) At cross purposes: what the experiences of doctoral students reveal about doctoral education. A report for the Pew Charitable Trusts Philadelphia PA. Available at: www.phd-survey.org (accessed Sept. 2007).

Gouldner, A. W. (1973) For *Sociology: Renewal and Critique in Sociology Today*. London: Allen Lane.

Gray, M. and Roy, C. (2005) Role of the supervisor/mentor, in S. Ketefian and S. P. McKenna (eds), *Doctoral Education in Nursing: International Perspectives*. London: Routledge, pp. 129–46.

Green, P. (2005) Coping and completing: the challenge of the professional doctorate in the knowledge economy. Available at: www.ecu.edu.au/conferences/herdsa/main/papers/nonref/pdf/Pam.Green.pdf (accessed Apr. 2005).

Green, H. and Powell, S. (2005) *Doctoral Study in Contemporary Education*. Maidenhead: Open University Press/McGraw Hill.

Greenhalgh, T. (2006) *How to Read a Paper: The Basics of Evidence-Based Medicine*, 3rd edn. Oxford: BMJ Books/Blackwell.

Gregory, M. (1995) Implications of the introduction of the doctor of education degree in British universities: can the EdD reach parts the PhD cannot? *The Vocational Aspect of Education*, 47(2): 177–88.

Gribbin, J. (2002) *Science: A History*. London: Penguin Books.

Gubrium, J. F. and Holstein, J. A. (1997) *The New Language of Qualitative Method*. New York: Oxford University Press.

Haigh, C. (2007) Peacocks and jellyfish: steps and strategies for successful conference chairing, *Nurse Education Today*.

Haith-Cooper, M. (2000) Problem based learning within health professional education: what is the role of the lecturer? A review of the literature, *Nurse Education Today*, 20: 267–72.

Haith-Cooper, M. (2002) An exploration of tutors' experiences of facilitating problem-based learning, part 2: implications for the facilitation of problem based learning, *Nurse Education Today*, 23: 65–75.

Haraway, D. (1988) Situated knowledges: the science question in feminism and the privilege of partial perspective, *Feminist Studies*, 14(3): 575–99.

Hart, C. (1998) *Doing a Literature Review: Realising the Social Science Research Imagination*. London: Sage.

Hart, C. (2001) *Doing a Literature Search: A Comprehensive Guide for the Social Sciences*. London: Sage.

Haskins, C. H. (1957) *The Rise of Universities*. New York: Cornell University Press.

Haug, M. R. (1973) Deprofessionalisaton: an alternative hypothesis for the future, *Sociology Review Monograph*, 20: 195–211. (Reprinted in E. Friedson (1984) The changing nature of professional control, *Annual Review of Sociology*, 10: 1–20.)

Heath, L. (2005) Supervision of professional doctorates: education doctorates in England. Unpublished PhD thesis, Brighton University.

Hersey, P. and Blanchard, K. H. (1969) Life-cycle theory of leadership, *Training and Development Journal*, 23: 26–34 (Reprinted in P. Northouse (2007) *Leadership Theory and Practice*, 4th edn. London: Sage.)

Hoddell, S. (2000) The professional doctorate and the PhD: converging or diverging lines? Paper presented to the Annual Conference of the Society for Research in Higher Education University of Leicester.

Hogg, P., Bentley, H. B., Parrott, J. et al. (2007) Reviewing articles of peer review journals: how to do it. Paper presented at the CPD in Focus Synergy Imaging and Therapy Practice, Aug.

Holloway, I. (ed.) (2005) *Qualitative Research in Health Care*. Maidenhead: Open University Press/McGraw Hill.

Horder, W. (2004) Reading and not reading in professional practice, *Qualitative Social Work*, 3(3): 297–311.

Horner, M. (1997) Leadership theory: past, present and future, *Team Performance Management*, 3(4): 270–87.

House, R. J., Hanges, P. J., Javidan, M., Dorfman, P. W. and Gupta, V. (2004) *Culture, Leadership and Organisations: The GLOBE Study of 62 Countries*. Thousand Oaks CA: Sage.

Howarth, M., Kneafsey, R. and Haigh, C. (2008) Centralisation and research governance: does it work? *Journal of Advanced Nursing*, 61(4): 363–72.

Hoyt, C. M. (2007) Women and leadership, in P. G. Northouse (ed.), *Leadership Theory and Practice*, 4th edn. London: Sage.

Hudson, L. (1973) *Originality*. Oxford: Oxford University Press.

Huff, A. S. (2000) Changes in organizational knowledge production, *Academy of Management Review*, 25(2): 288–93.

Hughes, W. (2000) *Critical Thinking: An Introduction to the Basic Skills*. Peterborough: Critical Broadview Press.

Hughes, J. A. and Sharrock, W. W. (1998) *The Philosophy of Social Research*, 3rd edn. London: Longman.

Hupp, J. R. (2006) Healthy scepticism: the essence of critical thinking, *Oral Surgery, Oral Medicine, Oral Pathology, Oral Radiology and Endodontology*, 102(3): 271–4.

Hyland, K. (2001) Humble servants of the discipline? Self mention in research articles, *English for Specific Purposes*, 20(3): 207–26.

Jewell, D. and Freeman, G. (1995) Approaching the literature, in R. Jones and A-L. Kinmonth (eds), *Critical Reading for Primary Care*. Oxford: Oxford University Press.

Katz, R. L. (1955) Skills of an effective administrator, *Harvard Business Review*, 33(1): 33–42. (Reprinted in P. G. Northouse (2007) *Leadership Theory and Practice*, 4th edn. London: Sage.

Keen, S. and Todres, L. (2007) Strategies for disseminating qualitative research findings: three exemplars, *Forum of Qualitative Social Research*, 8(3). Available at: www.qualitative-research.net/fqs/ (accessed Jan. 2008).

Kelloway, E. K. and Barling, J. (2000) What we have learned about developing transformational leaders? *Leadership and Organisation Development Journal*, 21(7): 355–62.

Kelly, M. (2004) Writing a research proposal, in C. Seale (ed.), *Researching Society & Culture*. London: Sage, pp. 111–22.

Kemp, S. (2004) Professional doctorates and doctoral education, *International Journal of Organisational Behaviour*, 7(4): 401–10.

Kiesinger, C. E. (1998a) From interview to story: writing Abbie's life, *Qualitative Inquiry*, 4(1): 71–95.

Kiesinger, C. E. (1998b) Portrait of an anorexic life, in A. Banks and S. P. Banks (eds), *Fiction and Social Research: By Ice or Fire*. Walnut Creek, CA: AltaMira Press, pp. 115–36.

Klein, J. T. (2004) Prospects for transdisciplinarity, *Futures*, 36(4): 515–26.

Kotter, J. P. (1990) What leaders really do, *Harvard Business Review*, 3: 103–11.

Kuhn, T. S. (1996) *The Structure of Scientific Revolutions*, 3rd edn. Chicago: University of Chicago Press.

Laming, H. (2003) The Victoria Climbié inquiry: report of an inquiry presented by the Secretary of State for Health and the Secretary of State for the Home Department by Command of Her Majesty, Cm 5730, TSO, Jan. Available at: www.victoria-climbie-inquiry.org.uk/finreport/report.pdf

Lave, J. and Wenger, E. (1991) *Situated Learning, Legitimate Peripheral Participation*. Cambridge: Cambridge University Press, p. 98.

Law, J. (2004) *After Method: Mess in Social Science Research*. London: Routledge.

Leathard, A. (ed.) (1994) *Going Inter-Professional: Working Together for Health and Welfare*. London: Routledge, p. 6.

Lee, N. J. (2002) International experiences and student nurses. Unpublished PhD thesis, University of Salford.

Lee, N. J. (2007) Enhancing the quality of research supervision to meet the needs of professional doctorate students, *Teaching and Learning Quality Improvement Scheme*. Salford: University of Salford.

Leicht, K. T. and Fennell, M. L. (1997) The changing organizational context of professional work, *Annual Review of Sociology*, 23: 215–31.

Leonard, D., Metcalfe, J., Becker, R. and Evans, J. (2006) *Review of Literature on the Impact of Working Context and Support on the Post Graduate Students Learning Experience*. York: Higher Education. Available at: www.heacademy.ac.uk

Letherby, G. (2003) *Feminist Research in Theory & Practice*. Buckingham: Open University Press.

Likert, R. (1967) *The Human Organisation*. New York: McGraw Hill

Lippitt, R. and White, R. (1960) *Autocracy and Democracy: An Experimental Inquiry*. Oxford: Harper.

Lloyd, M. (2007) Developing academic writing skills: the process framework, *Nursing Standard*, 21(40). Available at: www.galenet.galegroup.com (accessed Jan. 2008).

Lunt, I. (2006) Review of Professional Doctorates National Qualifications Authority (Ireland). Available at: www.nqai.ie/en/publications/File.1749 (accessed Apr. 2007).

Luthans, F. (1989) *Organizational Behavior*, 5th edn. London: McGraw Hill.

Lynch, M. (2000) Against reflexivity as an academic virtue and source of privileged knowledge, *Theory, Culture and Society*, 17(3): 27–56.

Macbeth, D. (2001) On 'reflexivity' in qualitative research: two readings and a third, *Qualitative Inquiry*, 7(1): 35–68.

Marion, L., Viens, D., O'Sullivan, A. L. et al. (2003) The practice based doctorate in nursing: future or fringe? *Topics in Advanced Practice Nursing eJournal*. Available at: www.medscape.com/viewarticle/453247_print (accessed Apr. 2007).

Marjosola, I. A. and Takala, T. (2000) Charismatic leadership, manipulation and the complexity of organisational life, *Journal of Workplace Learning*, 12(4): 146–58.

Martin, P. J. (2006) *Professional Doctorate Portfolios: Helping to Select and Present Best Practice*. London: Higher Education Academy.

Mason, J. (2002) *Qualitative Researching*, 2nd edn. London: Sage.

Maxwell, T. W. and Shanahan, P. J. (1997) Towards a reconceptualisation of the doctorate: issues arising from comparative data relating to the EdD degree in Australia, *Studies in Higher Education*, 22(2): 133–49.

May, T. (1999) Reflexivity and sociological practice, *Sociological Research Online*, 4(3). Available at: www.socresonline.org.uk/socresonline/4/3/may.html (accessed 29 Jan. 2007).

May, T. (2000) A future for critique? Positioning, belonging and reflexivity, *European Journal of Social Theory*, 3(2): 157–73.

Maynard, D. (2003) *Bad News, Good News: Conversational Order in Everyday Talk and Clinical Settings*. Chicago: Chicago University Press.

McCartney, W. W. and Campbell, C. R. (2006) Leadership, management, and derailment: a model of individual success and failure, *Leadership and Organisation Development Journal*, 27(3): 190–202.

McKenna, H. P. (1997) *Nursing Models and Theories*. London: Routledge.

McKenna, H. and Cutcliffe, J. (2001) Nursing doctoral education in the United Kingdom and Ireland, *Online Journal of Issues in Nursing*, 5(2). Available at: www.nursingworld. org/ojin/topic12/tpc12_9.htm (accessed Nov. 2003).

McVicar, A., Caan, W., Hillier, D. et al. (2006) A shared experience: an interdisciplinary professional doctorate in health and social care, *Innovations in Education and Teaching International*, 43(3): 211–22.

McWilliam, E. and Singh, P. (2002) Towards a research training curriculum: what, why, how, who? *Australian Education Researcher*, 29(3): 4–18.

Meads, G., Ashcroft, J., Barr, H., Scott, R. and Wild, A. (2005) *The Case for Interprofessional Collaboration*. Oxford: Blackwell.

Meindl, J. R., Ehrlich, S. B. and Dukerich, J. M. (1985) The romance of leadership, *Administrative Science Quarterly*, 30: 78–102.

Mellahi, K. (2000) The teaching of leadership on UK MBA programmes: a critical analysis from an international perspective, *The Journal of Management Development*, 19(4): 297–308.

Miles, M. B. and Huberman, A. M. (1994) *Qualitative Data Analysis: An Expanded Sourcebook*, 2nd edn. Thousand Oaks, CA: Sage.

Miller, T. and Boulton, M. (2007) Changing constructions of informed consent: qualitative research and complex worlds, *Social Science and Medicine*, 65(11): 2199–211.

Moon, J. (2004) *Learning Journals: A Handbook for Academics, Students and Professional Development*. Abingdon: Routledge & Falmer.

Morris, G. H. and Chenail, R. J. (eds) (1995) *The Talk of the Clinic: Explorations in the Analysis of Medical and Therapeutic Discourse*. Hillsdale, NJ: Lawrence Erlbaum Associates.

Murphy, R. and Dingwall, R. (2003) *Qualitative Methods and Health Policy Research*. New York: Aldine de Gruyter.

Murray, R. (2005) *Writing for Academic Journals*. Maidenhead: Open University Press/ McGraw Hill.

Nahavandi, A. (2006) *The Art and Science of Leadership*, 4th edn. New Jersey: Pearson Prentice Hall.

Neumann, R. (2005) Doctoral differences: professional doctorates and PhDs compared, *Journal of Higher Education Policy and Management*, 27(2): 173–88.

Newton, E. (2000) *Margaret Mead Made Me Gay: Personal Essays, Public Ideas*. Durham, NC: Duke University Press.

Nicolescu, B. (1999) The transdisciplinary evolution of the university: condition for sustainable development. Available at: http://nicol.club.fr/ciret/bulletin/b12/ b12c8.htm

Noble, K. A. (1994) *Changing Doctoral Degrees: An International Perspective*. Buckingham: Society for Research in Higher Education/Open University Press.

Northouse, P. G. (2007) *Leadership Theory and Practice*, 4th edn. London: Sage, p. 3.

Office of Public Sector Information (2005) Mental Capacity Act 2005 at http:// www.opsi.gov.uk/ accessed April 2008

O'Mullane, M. (2005) Demonstrating significance of contributions to professional knowledge and practice in Australian professional doctorate programs: impacts in the workplace and professions. Available at: www.deakin.edu.au/educations/rads/ conferences/publications/prodoc/doc2OMullanepdv.pdf (accessed July 2006).

Osborne, J. W. (ed.) (2007) *Best Practices in Quantitative Methods*. London: Sage.

Pahl, J. (2007) *Ethics Review in Social Care Research*. Kent: University of Kent.

Park, C. (2007) Redefining the doctorate. Discussion paper, Higher Education Academy, York.

Paul, R. and Elder, L. (2006) *The Miniature Guide to Critical Thinking, Concepts and Tools* p. 4 *The Foundation for Critical Thinking*. Available at: www.criticalthinking.org (accessed Feb. 2008).

Pawar, B. (2003) Central conceptual issues in transformational leadership research, *Leadership & Organization Development Journal*, 24(7): 397–406.

Peat, J., Elliott, E., Baur, L. and Keena, V. (2002) *Scientific Writing: Easy When You Know How*. London: BMJ Books.

Pels, D. (2000) Reflexivity one step up, *Theory, Culture and Society*, 17(3): 1–25.

Perkin, H. (2003) Crisis in the professions: ambiguities, origins and current problems. Available at: www.rsa.org.uk/professional_values.asp (accessed Mar. 2008).

Phillips, E. M. and Pugh, D. S. (2000) *How to get a PhD: A Handbook for Students and their Supervisors*. Buckingham: Open University Press.

Pierson, A., Field, J. and Jordan, Z. (2006) *Evidence-based Clinical Practice in Nursing and Healthcare: A Comprehensive Approach to Evidence-based Practice in Nursing and the Health Professions*. Oxford: Wiley Blackwell.

Plain English Campaign (2001) *How to Write Reports in Plain English*. Available at: www.plainenglish.co.uk/reportsguide.pdf (accessed Jan. 2008).

Plummer, K. (2001) *Documents of Life 2: An Invitation to a Critical Humanism*. London: Sage.

Polanyi, M. (1962) Tacit knowledge: its bearing on some problems of philosophy, *Reviews of Modern Physics*, 34(4): 601–16. Available at: www.missouriwestern.edu/orgs/polanyi/essays.htm (accessed Mar. 2008).

Polanyi, M. (1967) *The Tacit Dimension*. New York: Anchor Books.

Polanyi, M. (2003) *Personal Knowledge: Towards a Post Critical Philosophy*. London: Routledge.

Potter, J. (1996) *Representing Reality: Discourse, Rhetoric and Social Construction*. London: Sage.

Powell, S. and Long, E. (2005) *Professional Doctorates in the UK*. Dudley: United Kingdom Council for Graduate Education, p. 8.

Prior, L. (2003) *Using Documents in Social Research*. London: Sage.

QAA (Quality Assurance Agency) (2001) *The Framework for Higher Education Qualifications in England, Wales and Northern Ireland*. Gloucester: QAA.

QAA (Quality Assurance Agency) (2004) *Code of Practice for the Assurance of Academic Quality and Standards in Higher Education*, section 1: Post Graduate Research Programmes. Gloucester: QAA. Available at: www.qaa.ac.uk

Rafferty, A. M. (1996) *The Politics of Nursing Knowledge*. London: Routledge.

Reeder, L. G. (1972) Observations on the changing professional–client relationship, *Journal of Health and Social Behaviour*, 13(4).

Reitz, J, (1987) *Behavior in Organizations*, 3rd edn. Irwin: Homewood.

Reynolds, S. (2000) The anatomy of evidence-based practice: principles and methods, in L. Trinder with S. Reynolds (eds), *Evidence-Based Practice: A Critical Appraisal*. Oxford: Blackwell Science.

Richardson, L. (1990) *Writing Strategies: Reaching Diverse Audiences*. Newbury Park: Sage.

Richardson, L. (1998) Writing: a method of inquiry, in N. K. Denzin and Y. S. Lincoln (eds), *Collecting & Interpreting Qualitative Materials*, 2nd edn. Thousand Oaks, CA: Sage, pp. 345–71.

Roberts, B. (2002) *Biographical Research*. Buckingham: Open University Press.

Roberts, H. (ed.) (1981) *Doing Feminist Research*. London: Routledge & Kegan Paul.

Rudestam, K. and Newton, R. (2007) *Surviving Your Dissertation*, 3rd edn. London: Sage.

Sackett, D., Richardson, W. S., Rosenberg, W. and Haynes, R. B. (1997) *Evidence-Based Medicine: How to Practice and Teach EBM*. New York: Churchill Livingstone.

San Miguel, C. and Nelson, C. D. (2007) Key writing challenges of practice-based doctorates, *Journal of English for Academic Purposes*, 6(1): 71–86.

Schon, D. A. (1983) *The Reflective Practitioner: How Professionals Think in Action*. New York: Basic Books/Harper Collins.

Schon, D. (1987) *Educating the Reflective Practitioner: Towards a New Design for Teaching and Learning in the Professions*. San Fransisco: Jossey-Bass.

Scott, D., Brown, A., Lunt, I. and Thorne, L. (2004) *Professional Doctorates Integrating Professional and Academic Knowledge*. Buckingham: Society for Research in Higher Education/Open University Press.

Selinger, E. and Crease, R. P. (eds) (2006) *The Philosophy of Expertise*. New York: Columbia University Press.

Sellers, E. T. (2002) Images of a new sub-culture in the Australian university: perceptions of non-nurse academics of the discipline of nursing, *Higher Education*, 43: 157–72.

Shaffer, E. S. (1990) Romantic philosophy and the organization of the disciplines: the founding of the Humboldt University of Berlin, in A. Cunningham and N. Jardine (eds), *Romanticism and the Sciences*. Cambridge: Cambridge University Press.

Shaw, I. F. and Gould, N. (2001) *Qualtative Research in Social Work*. London: Sage.

Silverman, D. (1997) *Discourses of Counselling: HIV Counselling as Social Interaction*. London: Sage.

Silverman, D. (2000) *Doing Qualitative Research: A Practical Handbook*, London: Sage.

Silverman, D. (2004) *Doing Qualitative Research: A Practical Handbook*, 2nd edn. London: Sage.

Silverman, D. (2006) *Interpreting Qualitative Data: Methods for Analysing Talk, Text and Interaction*, 3rd edn. London: Sage.

Smith, M. K. (2003) Communities of practice, *The Encyclopaedia of Informal Education*. Available at: www.infed.org/biblio/communities_of_practice.htm (accessed June 2007).

Stanley, L. (ed.) (1990) *Feminist Praxis: Research, Theory and Epistemology in Feminist Sociology*. London: Routledge.

Stanley, L. (1992) *The Auto/Biographical I: The Theory and Practice of Feminist Auto/ Biography*. Manchester: Manchester University Press.

Stanley, L. (2004) A methodological toolkit for feminist research: analytical reflexivity, accountable knowledge, moral epistemology and being 'a child of our time', in H. Piper and I. Stronach (eds), *Educational Research: Difference and Diversity*. Aldershot: Ashgate, pp. 3–2.

Stanley, L. and Wise, S. (1990) Method, methodology and epistemology in feminist research processes, in L. Stanley (ed.), *Feminist Praxis: Research, Theory and Epistemology in Feminist Sociology*. London: Routledge, pp. 20–60.

Stanley, L. and Wise, S. (1993) *Breaking Out Again: Feminist Ontology and Epistemology*. London: Routledge.

Stanley, L. and Wise, S. (2006) Putting it into practice: using feminist fractured foundationalism in researching children in the concentration camps of the South African war, *Sociological Research Online*, 11: 1. Available at: www.socresonline.org.uk/11/1/stanley.html

Stanley, L. and Wise, S. (2008) Feminist methodology matters!, in D. Richardson and V. Robinson (eds), *Introducing Gender & Women's Studies*, 3rd edn. Basingstoke: Palgrave Macmillan, pp. 221–43.

Stogdill, R. M. (1948) Personal factors associated with leadership: a survey of the literature, *Journal of Psychology*, 25: 35–71.

Taylor, C. (2006a) Narrating significant experience: reflective accounts and the production of (self) knowledge, *British Journal of Social Work*, 36(2): 189–206.

Taylor, C. (2006b) Practising reflexivity: narrative, reflection and the moral order, in S. White, J. Fook and F. Gardner (eds), *Critical Reflection in Health and Social Care*. Maidenhead: Open University Press, pp. 73–88.

Taylor, C. and White, S. (2000) *Practising Reflexivity in Health and Welfare: Making Knowledge*. Buckingham: Open University Press.

Taylor, C. and White, S. (2002) What works about what works? Fashion, fad and EBP, *Social Work and Social Sciences Review*, 10(1): 36–54.

Tennant, M. (2004) Doctoring the knowledge worker, *Studies in Continuing Education*, 26(3): 431–41.

Teo-Dixon, G. and Monin, N. (2007) Guru of gurus: Peter Drucker, logology and the ultimate leader, *Journal of Management Inquiry*, 16(1): 6–17.

Thayer-Bacon, B. J. (2000) *Transforming Critical Thinking: Thinking Constructively*. New York: Teachers' College Press.

Thomond, C. (2007) Max Headroom, *Saturday Guardian*, 8 Dec., p.3.

Thompson, J., Pearson, M., Akerlind, G., Hooper, J. and Mazur, N. (2001) *Postdoctoral Training and Employment Outcomes*. Sydney: Department of Education, Training and Youth Affairs.

Thomson, A. (2002) *Critical Reasoning: A Practical Introduction*. London: Routledge.

Thorne, L. E. and Francis, J. C. (2001) PhD and professional doctorate experience: the problematics of the national qualifications framework, *Higher Education Review*, 33(3): 13–29.

Tillmann-Healy, L. M. (2001) *Between Gay & Straight: Understanding Friendship Across Sexual Orientation*. Walnut Creek: AltaMira Press.

Trinder, L. (2000) Introduction, in L. Trinder with S. Reynolds (eds), *Evidence-Based Practice: A Critical Appraisal*. Oxford: Blackwell Science.

Trocchia, P. J. and Berkowitz, D. (1999) Getting doctored: a proposed model of marketing doctoral student socialisation, *European Journal of Marketing*, 33(7/8): 746–60.

UKCGE (United Kingdom Council for Graduate Education) (2002) *Professional Doctorates*. Dudley: UKCGE.

University of Salford (2007) *Code of Practice for the Conduct of Post Graduate Research Degree Programmes*. Salford: University of Salford.

Van Maanen, J. (1988) *Tales of the Field: On Writing Ethnography*. Chicago: University of Chicago Press, p. 91.

Wallace, D. B. and Gruber, H. E. (1989) *Creative People at Work*. Oxford: Oxford University Press, p. 63.

Wallace, M. and Wray, A. (2006) *Critical Reading and Writing for Postgraduates*. London: Sage.

Wallas, G. (1926) *The Art of Thought*. New York: Harcourt Brace. (Reprinted in L. Hudson (1973) *Originality*. Oxford: Oxford University Press.)

Ward, A. (2002) The writing process, in S. Potter (ed.), *Doing Postgraduate Research*. London: Sage, pp. 71–116.

Ward, R. and Baume, D. (2002) Personal development planning: beyond the basics. Available at: www.heacademy.ac.uk/resources/detail/id470_pdp_beyond_the_basics

Wellington, J. and Sikes, P. (2006) A doctorate in a tight compartment: why do students choose a professional doctorate and what impact does it have on their personal and professional lives? *Studies in Higher Education*, 31(6): 723–34.

Wenger, E. (1998) *Communities of Practice, Learning, Meaning and Identity*. Cambridge: Cambridge University Press.

Wield, D. with Ashburner, L., Newholm, T., Oreszczyn, S. et al. (2002) Planning and organising a research project, in S. Potter (ed.), *Doing Postgraduate Research*. London: Sage, pp. 35–7.

Wikipedia (2007) Iteration. Available at: http://en.wikipedia.org/Iterative (accessed Dec. 2007).

Wikipedia (2007) Supervision. Available at: http://en.wikipedia.org/wiki/Supervision (accessed Oct. 2007).

Wilkinson, G. and Miers, M. (1999) *Power and Nursing Practice*. London: Macmillan Press.

Williams, M. and May, T. (1996) *Introduction to the Philosophy of Social Research*. London: University College London (UCL) Press.

Winfield, G. (1987) *The Social Science PhD: The ESRC Inquiry on Submission Rates*. London: ESRC.

Winter, R., Griffiths, M. and Green, K. (2000) The 'academic' qualities of practice: what are the criteria for a practice based PhD? *Studies in Higher Education*, 25(1): 25–37.

Wise, S. and Stanley, L. (2006) Having it all: feminist fractured foundationalism, in K. Davis, M. Evans and J. Lorber (eds), *Handbook of Gender & Women's Studies*. London: Sage, pp. 435–56.

Wisker, G. (2005) *The Good Supervisor: Supervising Post Graduate and Under Graduate Research for Doctoral Theses and Dissertations*. Basingstoke: Palgrave Macmillan, p. 1.

Wolcott, H. F. (1994) *Transforming Qualitative Data: Description, Analysis, and Interpretation*. Thousand Oaks, CA: Sage.

Wolcott, H. F. (2001) *Writing Up Qualitative Research*, 2nd edn. Thousand Oaks, CA: Sage.

Wolf, M. (1992) *A Thrice-Told Tale: Feminism, Postmodernism, and Ethnographic Responsibility*. Stanford: Stanford University Press.

Wood, M. (2002) Mind the gap? A processual reconsideration of organizational knowledge, *Organization*, 9(1): 151–71.

Wooffitt, R. (2005) *Conversation Analysis and Discourse Analysis: A Comparative and Critical Introduction*. London: Sage.

Yam, B. M. C. (2005) Professional doctorates and professional nursing practice, *Nurse Education Today*, 25(7): 564–572.

Yukl, G. (2006) *Leadership in Organisations*, 6th edn. New Jersey: Pearson Education, p. 8.

Index

transformational leadership, 109, 110,
    118–21
Trinder, L., 59
Trocchia, P.J., 92–3
type 1 knowledge, 141–3
type 2 knowledge, 142–3, 155–6

understanding, 122, 123
United Kingdom (UK), 5, 112, 192
    Graduate Programme, 31
United Kingdom Council for Graduate
    Education (UKCGE), 6, 7, 14
United States (US), 5–6, 10, 35
    presidential leadership, 110–11
universalist traits, 115
universities, 15, 17

Van Maanen, J., 63–4
verification, 33
    strategies, 36
virtual learning environment, 11, 28
vision, 118
viva voce, 161–3, 194
voice, 63–4, 82, 169–70
volume of work, 29–30

Wallace, M., 54–5, 56
Wallas, G., 33
Ward, R., 31
Warwick University, 14
Wellington, J., 17–18
Wenger, E., 38, 39, 40
White, R., 116
White, S., 61, 64
Wield, D., 65
Wilkinson, G., 135

Winch, C., 170
Winfield, G., 16
Winter, R., 7
Wise, S., 65–6, 67, 71, 73
Wisker, G., 85
Wolcott, H., 71, 80
Wolf, M., 81–2
women, and leadership, 111–12
Wood, M., 142
word limits, 158–9
workforce, skilled, 15
Workman, C., 60–1
workshops, 176
Wray, A., 54–5, 56
writer's block, 167–9
writing
    conference abstracts and
        presentations, 176–8
    developing, 81–3
    doctoral writing skills, 166–7
    for other audiences, 173
    portfolios, 163–5
    for publication, 178–81
    reflection, reflexivity and writing
        strategies, 42–3
    reflexivity and voice, 63–4
    reports, 174–6
    research proposal, 73–5
    style, 82, 165–73
    thesis, 158–61
    tips, 82–3

Yam, B.M.C., 172, 174
Yukl, G., 109

zones of choice, 122–6, 130–1

THE HANDBOOK OF ACADEMIC WRITING
A FRESH APPROACH
Rowena Murray and Sarah Moore

The Handbook of Academic Writing offers practical advice to busy academics who want, and are often required, to integrate writing into their working lives. It defines what academic writing is, and the process of getting started through to completion, covering topics such as:

- Gaining momentum
- Reviewing and revising
- Self-discipline
- Writing regularly
- Writers' groups and retreats

Academic writing is one of the most demanding tasks that all academics and researchers face. In some disciplines there is guidance on what is needed to be productive, successful writers; but in other disciplines there is no training, support or mentoring of any kind. This book helps those in both groups not only to improve their writing skills and strategies, but, equally importantly, to find satisfaction in engaging in regular and productive writing.

Underpinned by a diverse range of literature, this book addresses the different dimensions of writing. The fresh approach that Murray and Moore explore in this book includes developing rhetorical knowledge, focusing on writing behaviours and understanding writing contexts.

This book will help writers in academic contexts to develop a productive writing strategy, not only for research monitoring exercises, but also for the long term.

Contents
Acknowledgements – Preface – Part I – Defining and understanding academic writing – Advancing your writing: Starting, gaining momentum and engaging creatively in the academic writing process – Retreating: Reviewing, revising, crafting and enhancing your writing – Disciplinarity in academic writing – Part II – Retreating to advance: Planning, running and participating in writers' retreats for academics – A writing for publication programme – Writers' groups – Part III – Redefining academic writing practices – Integrating writing into your life – Using writing to reconcile teaching-research tensions – Advancing and retreating: The essential dynamic of academic writing – Bibliography – Index.

2006   216pp
978–0–335–21933–9 (Paperback)   978–0–335–21934–6 (Hardback)